Marilyn Grimes is a wife, a mother, a sister, and a daughter. Today, she's decided to make changes in her life, to do something different. Today, Marilyn Grimes has fina she has to find out w

The Interrup

"McMillan's books offer vindication to her most ardent fans: black women juggling work, family, friends, and the lingering effects of racism. Those readers, who have cheered her earlier heroines as they found themselves, drop-kicked bad-news boyfriends, and tumbled into love, will exult in Marilyn's nerve-racking journey to a new stage in her life."　　　　*—The Baltimore Sun*

"[McMillan's] stories are about everyday lives and her characters are memorable. . . . Along the way, a reader picks up helpful hints on resourcefulness, fortitude in the face of difficulty, and a calm sense of faith."
　　　　　　　　　　　　　　　　—Los Angeles Times

"With humor and heart and humanity, McMillan speaks to women on the verge and, as usual, does it with wit and wisdom."　　　　*—The Hartford Courant*

"Poignant, yet humorous."　　　　　　　*—Ebony*

"McMillan [has an] effervescent intelligence. Her sparkling repartee makes it easy to imagine her chuckling as she writes. Her portraits of people are equally evocative."　　　　　*—The Washington Post*

"Smart, spunky, and endearing . . . [an] entertaining and pointed novel."　　*—The New Orleans Times-Picayune*

"*The Interruption of Everything* has bestseller written all over it. . . . I found it hard to put down."
　　　　　　　　　　　　　　　　—Houston Chronicle

"McMillan writes this book with the same fast-paced, often witty, conversational tone that endears her to black women, who see themselves or people they know in her characters."　　　　*—Detroit Free Press*

continued . . .

"McMillan does what she does best. . . . With her trademark ability to write thought-provoking tales inspired by the lives and loves of contemporary African-American women, McMillan offers another novel sure to resonate with readers grappling with the questions Marilyn poses to herself."
— *Publishers Weekly*

"Won't disappoint fans who have come to expect the authentic voices [McMillan] crafts for her characters—and there are lots of them." — *The Cleveland Plain Dealer*

Praise for the Other Novels of Terry McMillan

Waiting to Exhale

"Terry McMillan is perhaps the world's finest chronicler of modern life among African-American men and women. Her characters' voices are honest and true as though she's wiretapped the deepest feeling of the heart." — *San Francisco Chronicle*

"Hilarious, irreverent . . . thoroughly entertaining."
— *The New York Times Book Review*

"Captures what life and love are all about today."
— *USA Today*

"McMillan puts someone you know, something you've felt or heard, on each page. . . . The characters are so real that you'll wonder if McMillan hasn't somehow overheard a private conversation." — *The Boston Globe*

"[A] paean to the sisterhood of all women."
— *Los Angeles Times Book Review*

"Terry McMillan has created a well-written, truthful, and funny story of four African-American women—four 'sistuhs' who are trying to make it in this world we all live in—and the sometimes volatile world of Black female–Black male relationships." — Spike Lee

"Terry McMillan has such a wonderful ear for story and dialogue. She gives us four women with raw, honest emotions that *breathe* off the page." — Amy Tan

"McMillan is not only a gifted writer but a social critic as clear-eyed as Mark Twain or Zora Neale Hurston or Edith Wharton."   —*Newsday*

A Day Late and a Dollar Short

"By the last pages you're weeping. You're laughing. You're hooked. It's oh so good."   —*Chicago Tribune*

"[McMillan] has a true comic gift. Funny, finely crafted, profound . . . contemporary African-American naturalism at its best."   —*The Village Voice*

Disappearing Acts

"A love story ready to explode."
                    —*The New York Times Book Review*

"Beautiful and easy to get lost in . . . a stunning achievement."   —*Cosmopolitan*

"If Ntozake Shange, Jane Austen, and Danielle Steel collaborated on a novel of manners, this . . . entertaining book might be the result."   —*The New Yorker*

"With *Disappearing Acts,* McMillan firmly places herself in the same league as . . . Alice Walker, Gloria Naylor, and . . . Zora Neale Hurston." —*Pittsburgh Post-Gazette*

How Stella Got Her Groove Back

"A cast of likable characters, funny lines, smart repartee, and a warm . . . ending. Irreverent, mischievous, diverting . . . will make you laugh out loud."
                    —*The New York Times Book Review*

"Terry McMillan is the only novelist I have ever read who makes me glad to be a woman."
                    —*The Washington Post Book World*

"A down-and-dirty, romantic, and brave story told to you by this smart, good-hearted woman as if she were your best friend."   —*Newsday*

THE
INTERRUPTION
OF
EVERYTHING

Terry McMillan

A SIGNET BOOK

SIGNET
Published by New American Library, a division of
Penguin Group (USA) Inc., 375 Hudson Street,
New York, New York 10014, USA
Penguin Group (Canada), 90 Eglinton Avenue East, Suite 700, Toronto
Ontario M4P 2Y3, Canada (a division of Pearson Penguin Canada Inc.)
Penguin Books Ltd., 80 Strand, London WC2R 0RL, England
Penguin Ireland, 25 St. Stephen's Green, Dublin 2,
Ireland (a division of Penguin Books Ltd.)
Penguin Group (Australia), 250 Camberwell Road, Camberwell, Victoria 3124,
Australia (a division of Pearson Australia Group Pty. Ltd.)
Penguin Books India Pvt. Ltd., 11 Community Centre, Panchsheel Park,
New Delhi - 110 017, India
Penguin Group (NZ), cnr Airborne and Rosedale Roads, Albany,
Auckland 1310, New Zealand (a division of Pearson New Zealand Ltd.)
Penguin Books (South Africa) (Pty.) Ltd., 24 Sturdee Avenue,
Rosebank, Johannesburg 2196, South Africa

Penguin Books Ltd., Registered Offices:
80 Strand, London WC2R 0RL, England

Published by Signet, an imprint of New American Library, a division of
Penguin Group (USA) Inc. Previously published in a Viking edition.

First Signet Printing, August 2006
10   9   8   7   6   5   4   3   2   1

To

LYNDA DRUMMER

For your friendship and those life jackets

and in loving memory of

MS. WILLIE LEE WILLIAMS

(1929–2003)

You are dearly missed

Acknowledgments

Throughout this long and arduous process, there were many folks who helped me swim and float and sometimes tread water, even when it felt like I was drowning. I appreciate each and every one of you for your friendship, time, listening ear, generosity, faith, patience, and tolerance, but mostly for caring about me. I am especially grateful to God for reminding me what happens when you try to swim against the current and live from the outside in. I finally made it to this shore, at least, and it was worth the journey. I am fortunate to have the following human beings in my life: my editor, Carole DeSanti, for understanding how this process works—that it is not like turning on the oven to 450°, bake for a year until it rises and browns and then pop that baby out until it cools. I wish. Which is why all of the *next-weeks* turned into *this-year*. Thank you for caring about me more than a book; Molly Friedrich, my agent, I can pretty much say the same holds true for you as it does Carole (they're probably in on this together). Your timing is pitch perfect because you know when to lighten up; Beena Kamlani, brilliant developmental editor for this and my last three books, who has a memory I covet, but also for being so picky picky picky and hallelujah for not sugarcoating it when something didn't work. I was told to make this short so I'm going to cut to the chase, but please don't feel slighted: Blanche Richardson (again and again), Cherysse Calhoun; Amy Tan, G. F. Grant, Molly Barton; Esther Jordan, Joan Diamond, Leila and Leroy Hannam, Pam Manool, Kristine Bell, Matt Shoupe, Samanda and Naomi Maloa, Valari Adams, Gilda Kihneman, Steve Sobel and Bonnie Ross, Elvira Chavez and staff; Dr. Calvin Lemon, Dr. Kulveen Sachdeva, John Burris, Esq., Deborah Sandler, Esq., Abigail Trillin; the Drummer Family; my sisters, Vicki, Crystal and Rosalyn; and last but not least, my one and only favorite Chocolate Chip, Solomon, for making me so very proud to be your mother and watching you turn into a fine young man, and for not being afraid to show me that you love me. Speak up! I can't understand you when you mumble. Do I have three dollars for the toll? The ATM machine is empty again? Maybe I have some quarters around here. But just remember: this is a loan and I want my three dollars back after you graduate from college and get your first paycheck. And I'm writing it down!

Author's Note

This is a work of fiction. All events and characters in this story are solely the product of the author's imagination; any similarities between any characters and situations presented in this book to any individuals living or dead or actual places and situations are purely coincidental.

Chapter 1

The only reason I'm sitting on a toilet seat in the handicapped stall of the ladies' room is because I'm hiding. My break is just fifteen minutes long and I'm trying to decide with the help of a book on the subject of "the change" if Paulette was really on to something when she suggested I get a blood test to see if my hormone levels were diminishing. And if it turns out to be true, I might want to get them replenished with something besides the Good & Plenty I've been eating by the handful for the last seven or eight months and I don't even like licorice. I'm also sitting here with an old issue of *Bead & Button* trying to figure out if I should've played it safe and used plastic instead of glass beads since I just had to make my very first jewelry attempt a gift, and because sometimes I do think that more is better, just had to add three strands more than the instructions called for and now I don't know how to close up the ends. I'm not used to asking for help.

Paulette claims I've been showing enough symptoms of a perimenopausal woman to warrant further examination, which initially irritated me. She merely closed her eyelids over those hazel contacts and sucked her tongue across those shiny white veneers and whipped over one shoulder all five hundred of those individual braids that are way too long for a forty-eight-year-old woman who is no Donna Summer and said, "I know what I'm talking about. You remind me of me four years ago."

Experiencing something once does not make you an expert on the subject.

The rampage I went on last week about Leon may have added more fuel to the flames. Perhaps my reaction to my husband's forgetting to set the empty water bottles out was a little strong, but it was totally symbolic of a lot of other things he neglects. Ten minutes into my rant, Paulette just said, "Girl, you need to hurry up and have that test so you can be restored back to full sanity. Assuming you once were! But seriously, you need to do something because your circuit breaker is not working. On a lighter note, don't forget: Pity Party next Friday at Bunny's. I can't wait to hear your latest bullshit, if there's anything left to tell. And as an FYI: Bunny's taking another online course, girl. This time it's psychology. So be prepared. She's probably going to be Freud's little sister. Just try to be nice, Marilyn."

"Nice" has been difficult for me lately. Paulette has also been kind enough to point out that all those who land in my path of wrath (as she calls my unconfirmed Pause Personality) deserve a break, especially Leon, and

Arthurine, his nosey mother who has eyes in the back of her head and lives with us along with her handicapped dog to whom I have the luxury of being a private nurse. I wish I could take all of them on a one-way cruise out to sea and then sail back to shore alone. This does sound mean, but some days I can't help it.

I have to admit that I have experienced quite a few of the symptoms Paulette was sweet enough to bring to my attention. But I didn't tell her. She loves being right and I hate being wrong. I snap the book shut. Should I break down and spend even more money on French wire and Bali silver cones to close up the ends of this damn necklace? Trying to achieve true beauty can be expensive. But *Bead & Button* seems to imply that using inferior (or cheap) materials will help deter that dreaded question: "Did you make that?"

I'm making this *damn* thing for Bunny, my other best friend, for her thirty-seventh, thirty-eighth, but most likely her fortieth birthday. I've got close to a month before she turns the big hand on the clock. But even with my 20 percent discount, we're still talking about explaining to The Husband Who Is Not at Sea why these sums are necessary when they appear on the Visa or Master-Card bill. And if I do mess up (or—just say it, Marilyn—if you fuck it up), since one never knows one has even made a mistake until after one has made it: at what price, friendship?

Not that Bunny would notice.

Class is something she doesn't respect, understand, or care about. "What can you do with it?" she's asked

Paulette and me over the years. Particularly when we've tried year after year to persuade her to trade in that Atlantic City–looking 1989 red Corvette she insists on driving; we dropped major hints that she might want to try going to a real furniture store to purchase real furniture one or two pieces at a time instead of decorating and designing her entire condo in a single trip to IKEA where they may as well have airbrushed the four showrooms directly into her crib; and we encouraged her to reconsider always having on display her recent purchase of a D cup. But Bunny has consistently ignored us. "It's all good," as one of my sons would say.

Tonight I'll be stretched out on her make-believe sofa with thirty minutes to pour out my suffering soul after we've eaten takeout at her little table for two and she and Paulette will say whatever it takes to lift my spirits to a level of clarity since I've obviously had difficulty doing it on my own.

The ladies' room door bangs. Shit! It's them. The crazy women I'm hiding from, the ones who always want me to take part in their thrice-weekly reality show. I have been ordained Craft Staff Supervisor here at Heavenly Creations, and these two are not only the store's very best customers, they also purportedly work here *and* provide live entertainment.

Now Maureen shouts: "I'm just so outdone! I'm going crazy, Trudy! I mean really frigging crazy! I can't believe he did this! To me! After fourteen years of what I thought was a good—no, great—marriage and out of the blue he just decides to tell me he's found a new torch that's been turning his low flame into a forest fire and that according to Dr. Phil he's been in denial for five years about how bored he's been with 'us' and the whole suburban lifestyle and he said he didn't want to hurt me and the kids by coming clean but there was no getting around it and by the way her name is oh who cares what her name is!? Trudy, I feel like such a fool! I mean, what am I supposed to do without a husband and three kids all under the age of twelve?"

"You really think you're extra special, don't you, Maureen? That's your whole problem. Well, welcome to the pool of pain millions of women have been swimming in for years, sweetheart."

"You're not making me feel any better, Trudy. I thought I could confide in you."

"You are. But let me finish my thought. It's a miracle to me just how well some of us have managed—those of us who are the unfortunate beneficiaries of out-of-control husbands. I truly believe that the women who were only given fifteen minutes to adjust to their newfound fame as Single Mothers and only used six or seven of them, have been touched by an angel of some kind because how else could any one human being adjust so quickly and handle so much responsibility without a quick stint in the Loony Bin? You and the kids are probably going to be better off, if you think of the odds."

"What odds?" Maureen asks.

"Let's face it. How much do husbands really do? I mean, what role do they really play around the house? Go ahead and say it, Maureen! Not much. I've managed to marry three cut from the same exact mold. Go figure. They think their paychecks and their penises equal making a physical contribution, which is why we're always too tired to fuck them. Am I on track here or what?"

She had a point, and I squirmed on the hard seat. Leon would certainly fit in if they were to take a group photo.

"I hadn't thought of it like that before, Trudy. But even still, I'll take his paycheck and his penis any day over nothing."

Maureen and Trudy are both what I call Craft Junkies because in the year and a half I've been working here, they've taken just about every three-hour and five-week class offered as long as it didn't involve fire, food, or fumes. They're also "repeaters" because they took my beginning pillow-making class so many times that once I realized theirs were actually better made than mine, I got the owner to hire them to help with the setups. HC (as I call it) is small enough that it feels intimate. Here, nothing is locked behind glass or steel cabinets except of course the spray paint, but that's only because of the teenagers. Other than this, nothing suffocates under plastic that we aren't happy to unwrap. You can touch anything we sell at HC and we carry the very best high-end arts and craft supplies available in the United States. And I should know, because I'm a junkie, too.

Trudy and Maureen often forget to pick up their paychecks, which they seem to think of as weekly gift certificates. I do not have the nerve to ask but I'd sure like to know where they put all those damn pillows. They think they're hot stuff because they can make up to twenty different kinds of knots that they learned in Stephania's—the spinster from Israel—Beauty of Knots class. Lord knows they've made enough floral arrangements to cover ten fake funerals; so many gingerbread houses that some of our Olympian ants stopped trying to penetrate them; and enough of those Little House on the Prairie year-round wreaths that ten years ago were like status symbols on front doors across America but now don't even generate a comment when a stranger rings their bell.

Trudy washes her hands then hits the dryer button. I'm starting to slide off this toilet seat. I lean forward and swirl these black denim hips around like they were thirty-six instead of forty-four inches as quietly as I possibly can while lowering my sneakers to the floor, but when my cell phone starts vibrating in the uniform pocket above my left breast, the magazine and book fall off my lap and hit the floor. Shit!

"If he thinks I'm leaving without putting up a fight, he's got another thing coming."

"I wouldn't jump so far ahead of myself," Trudy says. "Take a deep breath."

I hear Maureen inhaling and swallowing air.

"And another. One more."

"Trudy, I won't be able to breathe if I keep taking breaths! Now I'm standing in front of you with a busted heart so cut me some slack on the breathing, okay?"

"Okay, okay. Just trying to help you relax and not blow a gasket. We're at work, remember?"

"But we're not on the clock." Maureen blows her nose and then starts washing her hands. If I was really interested, I would wonder what they're doing here at this hour but it's anybody's guess. Sometimes they come in here to kill time between drop-offs and pickups at any number of sport venues for adolescents.

Trudy and Maureen would be the first to admit that making things that are unnecessary is not only fun, they're happy to have something to do that gets them out of the house. Something that has nothing to do with children or husbands. They aren't particularly fascinated by art or beauty, just grateful for the distraction: this is precisely why they had designers decorate their homes and gave them carte blanche. They wanted to avoid feeling overwhelmed by having to make too many conflicting decisions at once: from hardware to fabric, carpeting to faux finishes, to where the trampoline would be safest. They wanted to be surprised when they moved in.

"He cheated cheated cheated!" Maureen blurts out again as if she's trying to remind herself of it.

"But don't you worry one bit because he'll pay for it. Big time," Trudy says a little louder. I'm not sure if she's talking about karma, child support, or alimony.

"But I don't want a divorce!" Maureen slurs, which just means the Xanax she's "required" to take must have kicked in. Now she's crying. "I just want things to be back the way they used to be! Exactly, precisely like they were! Normal!"

I press the magazine against my chest like it has some kind of healing properties. Twenty-some-odd years ago,

I was drunken-in-love with Leon and life, and with all the possibilities my future held. I can't remember when the dreams stopped being real and reality wiped out the dreams. When everything that took up my time was always something tangible. How do you lose so much and not notice when it starts evaporating? Why does it feel like I missed something or that I forgot to do something? It feels like all I've been doing is shaking out wrinkles. Tears are rolling down my face because I realize how comfortable I've gotten with this numbness.

I just want things to be back the way they used to be. Exactly. Normal. I feel like yelling out to Maureen that nothing can ever be the way it was. We just long for whatever was once good. It's the longing that makes us slide into a nostalgic coma. It's a way of resisting what is happening right now. I loved raising my kids but I wouldn't want to go through it again. They're finally out of the house and off at college. If the truth be told, I crave the exact opposite of what Maureen wants: to go forward—not backward. I'm just not sure how to get there. Which is probably why I'm now bawling my eyes out.

Trudy knocks on the stall door. "Are you all right in there?"

"You wouldn't think so, Trudy," I say, gathering my composure and reading material before I open the door like I'm stepping into the light.

"Marilyn, what in Sam hell are you doing in the handicapped stall? I should give you a ticket! Are those tears in your eyes? What is this, the Tear Factory? I suppose you heard Miss Maureen's good news so we can pretty much label her tears, but what are yours for?"

"I honestly don't know. I think maybe it was hearing about your situation, Maureen. I suppose."

"It's a situation all right," she says, as if a thickness is coating her tongue.

"How many years have you been married now, Marilyn?" Trudy asks out of what seems like the blue.

"Twenty-three. Why?"

"That's entirely too long," Trudy says. "What I mean is, it's too long for you not to be just as miserable as the rest of us. So come on Miss Pillow Perfect, tell us you're on the one-Zoloft-a-day diet like the rest of us and we've got ourselves a club."

"Sorry, Trudy, but I don't think I qualify. I'm not exactly bursting with joy but I'm not miserable. You could say I've been living somewhere in the neighborhood of Mediocrity but have been waiting for a reserved parking space to open up in Happy Hills."

"Where? What are you talking about?" Trudy asks.

"It's not important. Anyway, I'm really sorry to hear about Roger, Maureen."

"It's fine. I'm fine. We'll all be fine. If he thinks he's going to just walk out of my and the kids' lives because he wants to live on Fantasy Island, I mean, hello? I didn't hear you flush, Marilyn. What were you doing in there?"

"I'd already flushed. But once Maureen got going, I didn't feel right opening the door."

"No worries!" Maureen says. "Look, we were here for the bread-making class, but I just can't handle it today."

To show that I understand, I nod. "Wait a minute! You did just say 'bread making,' correct?"

"Yes. We're evolving. Out of the fire and into the pan or something like that," Trudy says. "Come on, Mo, let me treat you to a mocha nonfat latte with no foam and one Equal?" She winks at me. "See ya next weekend for a little trim, Marilyn."

After they leave, I drop the book and magazine on the dry part of the sink and put my hands under the faucet. I look down at the silver stream that gushes out, but can still see a shadow of myself in the mirror above. If I look up, I'll see the truth in my eyes. What the hell am I doing? Here. Not in this store. But *here:* in this world, in northern California, in February 2004. Worrying about my hormone levels? Not only. I need to breathe. To stop pretending.

What I do know is that I'm forty-four years old. That I have been attached to my husband and kids for so long I need to find out what kind of person I'm capable of being as Marilyn Dupree and not just as Marilyn Grimes: mother and wife. But how do you make changes in your life without upsetting everything and everybody around you?

I'm scared. But I have to do something or the spirit I still have left is going to petrify. I just can't believe that I grew up and became one of those women who got married and had kids and forgot all about my personal dreams. At first I just tucked them away and then as the years passed, they got buried and I felt embarrassed or ashamed to have had them in the first place. I figured

after I finished raising my children I'd at least get the interesting man I married back (didn't happen) and reacquainted with my other self and pick up where I left off.

They call us housewives. But contrary to popular be-
lief, we're not all trophies like Maureen or as uneducated
as Trudy, no malice intended. In fact, I did more than go
to college. I got a degree, although I've almost forgotten what I majored in. Might as well have been Intro to
First Husbands 101 (Gordon) the soul mate I let get
away, and after two summer sessions of nothing close to
intimacy, was coerced into repeating the class and enrolled in Second Husbands 101A (enter Leon). But
then, after I'd barely flipped my tassel and was taking a
one-year sabbatical before heading back to grad school
because I thought being a social worker would help me
steer as many unfortunate folk—black folk in particular—
as far from self-destruction and poverty as they could get,
but then surprise, surprise, here comes what I thought
was only going to be a temporary interruption: Daughter
101 (Sabrina, a.k.a Isn't-She-Cute-and-Smart-Those-First-
Eleven-Years, and then The-Rebellious-I'm-Already-
Grown-and-Having-Sex-and-Getting-an-Occasional-
Buzz-I-Could-Strangle-Her-Teenager-Years), who is
now twenty-two and did a 360-degree turn. She became
a vegetarian, got spiritual, and may be her generation's
Iyanla. Next came Fraternal Twin Boys 202 (Spencer
and Simeon, nineteen): straight up and down computer
and math nerds like their dad, who makes sure buildings
are built properly so they won't buckle during earthquakes. Leon helped build our house a century ago. It's

big and boring. It's up in the Oakland Hills in what has been renamed The Fire Area since in 1990 almost all the homes up here were lost when some idiot set some eucalyptus trees on fire. Sometimes, I wished ours had burned to the ground so we could start all over. But it didn't. We only had minor smoke damage. Leon planned on doing the renovations himself, but fourteen years later, I stopped holding my breath.

Being a lifetime wife and mother has afforded me the luxury of having multiple and even simultaneous careers: I've been a chauffeur. A chef. An interior decorator. A landscape architect, as well as a gardener. I've been a painter. A furniture restorer. A personal shopper. A veterinarian's assistant and sometimes the veterinarian. I've been an accountant, a banker, and on occasion, a broker. I've been a beautician. A map. A psychic. Santa Claus. The Tooth Fairy. The T.V. Guide. A movie reviewer. An angel. God. A nurse and a nursemaid. A psychiatrist and psychologist. Evangelist. For a long time I have felt like I inadvertently got my master's in How to Take Care of Everybody Except Yourself and then a Ph.D. in How to Pretend Like You Don't Mind.

But I do mind.

"Marilyn? Are you still in here?" Trudy asks, sticking her head in the door. "Your fifteen minutes have come and gone, sister, now get your behind out here and sell some beads or something! And you've got a phone call."

"Did they say who it was?" I ask, pretending to fluff my flat hair. Leon's out doing seismic studies in a desert down in southern California where his cell never works and he won't be home until Monday afternoon, which also means he's golfing. He rarely calls me at work because I'm usually busy demonstrating, hunting for, or explaining something to someone. And . . .

"It's your favorite person."

Shit.

"Say it out loud. I don't mind."

"Shit!"

"Line three. Have a nice weekend, Marilyn. I'm outta here."

I walk behind the framing counter and press the blinking red light. "Hello, Arthurine. What's going on?"

"Well, you know I wouldn't bother you at work unless it was important . . ."

"Has something happened? It's not the kids or Leon, is it?"

"Hold your horses, chile. No. No. The Lord says . . ."

"Arthurine, I have a pretty good idea what the Lord had to say about being patient, but could you just get to the point, please? I've got customers waiting."

"Well, you didn't ask if something could've happened to me or Snuffy."

"Well, you're in good enough shape to call me so how bad off could you be? And if it was Snuffy I'd think you'd sound sadder."

"You've got a point, except what if I . . . Oh, never mind. Your doctor called and said you should call her."

"What?"

"You want me to say it louder?"

"Did she say why?"

"They don't usually say why unless it's a matter of life and death and we both know you aren't dying. So think about it for a minute and call her."

"Did she leave her number?"

"You want me to dial it for you and make this a three-way?"

"Never mind, I forgot I've got it stored in my cell. Thanks for letting me know."

"You're welcome. What time will you be getting home?"

"The same time I always get home, Arthurine. In plenty of time to pick you up from Bible study, but I'm going over to Bunny's tonight to play cards."

"Didn't you all just play cards last month over at Paulette's?"

"We did."

"Why don't you never want to play with me when I ask?"

"Because you only like to play solitaire, Arthurine, and it's hard to play with another player."

"Well guess what?"

"I can't . . ."

"Peggy's daughter is being a good Christian and has offered to bring me home after Bible study."

"Well, that's nice," I say, trying not to sound too relieved.

"I sure wish I could manage to cook something but my arthritis been acting up all week long and it's hard for me to open a can."

"Well, I wouldn't want you to strain yourself. I'll pick up something on my way home."

"Could it possibly be Mexican or Chinese?"

"Good-bye, Arthurine."

She's giggling when I hang up. She gets on the nerve that runs directly from the left and right sides of my brain. But God *don't* like ugly and I'm trying not to let ugly register anywhere near my heart or mind because Paulette probably has hidden cameras watching me. When I take my cell phone out of my jacket pocket I realize that it was my doctor who'd called while I was in the bathroom. I hang up and press "calls received" on my cell and get her office. "Yes, this is Marilyn Grimes and I'm returning Dr. Hilton's call. Is something wrong? Was my blood test abnormal or something?"

"No, no, no," the receptionist says, almost giggling, which makes me feel a little better. "The doctor just thought you might want to come in to talk about the results of your blood work, that's all."

"How soon?"

"How about Monday?"

"What time?"

"She could see you between two and four."

"I'll be there about two fifteen. And you're sure I'm not sick?"

"No, you are not sick, she just wants to explain what your test results mean and then let you weigh your options."

"Then it's pretty clear that I'm going through menopause? Are my hormones disappearing?"

"The doctor will explain all of that to you when she sees you, so don't worry, Mrs. Grimes. You have a nice weekend."

I hang up the phone. If I get in there on Monday and find out I'm dying, I'm going to strangle this bitch.

Chapter 2

I beeline it out of work early and pick up Chinese food for Arthurine and run in the house so fast Snuffy doesn't even have enough time to get up from his bed to greet me as I drop the plastic bag on the counter and sprint back out and get into my sputtering '98 Audi that's in dire need of a tune-up. If I run into Arthurine, she'll want to talk about a scripture they discussed in Bible study and she'll misquote it and get the interpretation all wrong—like she always does—and then I'll have to act like I don't notice and not correct her and try to keep the smirk off my face and present it to her as gratitude for enlightening me yet again. I don't want to be late for our Pity Party and I don't particularly need to hear how God doesn't have a Plan B. Or how part-time faith, like part-time jobs, can't fully support you. Not tonight. This morning as I was pulling out of the driveway, she yelled out: "Is God your steering wheel or your spare tire, Marilyn?"

"Both!" I fired back, which totally baffled her because she was still standing in the doorway when I pressed the garage door closed.

Arthurine came to live with us for a few months after she'd been in a fender bender that freaked her out but did not cause any immediate or residual harm. She had barely unpacked when she became plagued by one new ailment after another. She swore up and down she now suffered from night blindness whenever she drove, so her son made her stop. Enter Marilyn the Limo Driver. And during the day, she started losing her eyesight (except she had no difficulties whatsoever reading the price tags at every half-yearly and holiday sale at Macy's and Nordstrom's), but refused to go to an optometrist. Her self-diagnosis: it feels like its cataracts. Next, her hearing was going in and out except during the highlights of *American Idol*'s auditions when she had no problem memorizing and singing the lyrics to "She Bangs" right along with William Hung. And whoops! She was losing her balance but it turned out she just had bunions and needed to give up high heels.

This was a little more than a year ago and she's still here. In fact, she's everywhere. Sometimes I think there's more than one of her. On special occasions Arthurine is struck by the onset of what I refer to as "voluntary amnesia," since it mostly flares up on weekends when she claims she's too disoriented to help me do much of anything around the house. She never, ever, however, forgets to eat. And she is nosey as hell. I know she rambles in my closets and drawers because sometimes I deliberately put things in disarray only to find them neatly folded and in their proper place. I brought this to her attention but she just got defensive and looked so insulted I asked her to tell the ghost who was doing this to cease and desist and stay out of our bedroom. She took the hint. Poor thing. She's just lonesome. Her husband died six years ago, so I'm trying not to hold all the irritating things she does against her.

Even after she was given a clean bill of health, Leon still falls for her medical outbreaks. Arthurine has made it clear she doesn't want to move into one of those independent living complexes for seniors and what better way to guarantee it than by laying a guilt trip on her son, who believes everything she tells him?

As I'm heading down our street, I see a car I don't recognize, but in the front seat is Arthurine's famous black hat moving like it's attached to a marionette. She is running her mouth a mile a minute, which is why she doesn't see me. And for this, I thank the Lord.

"You know," I yell out, staring so hard at one of Bunny's mirrored walls that it feels like I can see right through to the plaster. "Sometimes I wish Leon would just go ahead and cheat on me so I'd finally have a good excuse to divorce him." Bunny and Paulette are in Bunny's miniature kitchen crushing ice as they try to make a blended drink called "Sex on the Beach" from a recipe book. Don't I wish.

"Oh shut up, Marilyn," Paulette says to my feet, which are propped up on the back of Bunny's beige corduroy sofa. "Did she not say this very same thing at my house four months ago, Bunny?"

"Yes, she did."

"And what term do they use to describe this behavior in your psych class?"

"We haven't covered this yet. I'll let you know when she says something that does. In fact, let me run and get my notes."

"No, don't!" Paulette says, but it's too late. Bunny's off to her bedroom. The thing I love most about Paulette and Bunny is that neither of them takes insults from the other personally nor do they give a shit what other people think about them. Take Bunny's party look. Just about everything she wears has sheen regardless of the time of day. Right now she's in silver satin pencil slacks. They're tight. And she's wearing three-inch silver mules. She's back before we know it. Her hands are empty.

"I thought I brought my backpack home from work. Anyway . . ."

"Wait a minute," I say, holding my hand up. "Are your cats incarcerated for the evening or what?"

"They are. Now shut up and let me finish. Your complaints about Leon are getting a little tiresome, if you don't mind my saying so. He's a good brother, so you ought to stop with the whining. And get your feet off the back of my couch."

I don't move them. "I think I might actually be starting to hate him. No. 'Hate' is too strong. I don't like him anymore."

"Okay, Cruella, take a chill pill for a minute. We'll be right out."

"You're welcome. I'll have my 'Sex on the Beach' now. I'm serious. I'm bored to death with Leon."

"What makes you think you landed on 'I'm So Interesting Avenue,' Miss Thang, huh?" Paulette asks. "Give us one good reason Leon couldn't say the same about you, even though we know you're not as dull as you can be on any given day . . ."

"Sugar, there's a whole lot of single women out there that would love to get next to a brother who's head honcho at an engineering firm, still looks somewhat presentable, can still get it up, his kids are grown and out of the house, which means no child support or alimony payments. Leon is a dream come true."

"Who said he could still get it up?"

"You did. Remember the engine and engineer jokes?" Paulette says.

"I lied. The engine needs to be at least eight cylinders and have four-wheel drive and cruise control and the engineer should know not to rev the engine and not get his rpm's so high that he burns up his engine just because he likes to accelerate to prove that his engine can go from zero to sixty in six seconds but if he were to look up or down at the passenger from time to time he might realize that he is not in a race so there's no need to slam on the brakes when he comes to an unexpected curve or when trying to get up a steep hill. After twenty-two years, he should know when to put it in low, when to downshift, when to put it in fourth gear, cruise control, or neutral, and how to steer smoothly. He should also know when it's time to pull over and put it in park . . . This isn't part of my time, is it?"

"No, but Marilyn I hope you *know* you've lost a few ounces of estrogen somewhere."

"Yeah, are you PMSing, too? Is that what made you bring this ugly attitude in here with you this evening?"

"No. For your information, I didn't have a period last month and am hoping I skip the next hundred."

"Did you go to the doctor and get that blood test like I suggested?" Paulette asks.

"I did. I see the doctor on Monday. However . . ."

"What?"

"There are a lot of things your blood can tell about you, but there are a lot of things it can't even begin to detect."

"We know you're going to explain what you mean by this, so just wait a minute while we get situated. I've gotta go to the bathroom first."

"And I need to call Aretha to make sure she fed the dogs," Paulette says. "Give us four minutes. And for the record: you still PMS after your periods stop."

I do not remember reading that in any of the books, but then again, I haven't gotten past "Symptoms."

We started this, what we ordained as our Private Pity Party four years ago. It's not a woe-is-me whining party, but because we never seemed to have an hour when we didn't feel like we should be doing something else, or had to be somewhere else, or were already thinking about what we had to do as soon as we cut out, we decided that one evening out of every month we would get together—even if it just meant venting, bitching, or lamenting—but mostly to help each other see ourselves more clearly. Where we can even 'fess up to our mistakes and misjudgments. Or admit stupid or embarrassing things we've done, should've done differently, or not at all.

You don't want to get labeled a "repeater": complaining about the same thing over and over and never making a genuine attempt to do anything to fix it, resolve it, or improve your situation, or playing the blame game in that whatever our problems are it's always someone else's fault. We want to rise above that, but sometimes it's just difficult to do and this is where friends come in: to call you on your b.s. We don't claim to be shrinks and we certainly don't think we have all the answers to each other's problems. But what we do have is empathy and we listen and try to be lighthearted when it seems appropriate and also recognize when our hearts are cold and lacking in compassion. Over the years, what has happened among the three of us is an amazing freedom that comes with being able to say out loud what you think and feel without having to apologize for it.

Because Bunny has never been married (not by choice) or had any children (this is by choice) we have come to believe that her taste in men is a lot like her taste in furniture. Temporary is long enough. She's unhappy pretending to be happy. When she's ready to face that fact, we'll be the first to applaud her. Paulette loves her second husband and it appears that the feeling is mutual.

She and Roscoe have been together for years and he is the reason she has her boutique. Paulette's biggest problems are her grown kids. The older one changes jobs every season. The younger one is a criminal. And her daughter Aretha tries to act like she's searching for the right career, while she jacks up half the neighborhood kids' hair with those tacky braids, charging $30 to $90, just enough to buy an outfit from Ross or Marshall's for the weekend and get herself a small bag of something to smoke. Everybody knows my biggest problem is my mother-in-law, my husband, and my daughter, Sabrina, who, as smart as she is, acts like she's a slave of love. She's been living with Nevil, a nice British Jamaican, for two years but I think she does everything except breathe for him.

Of the three of us, Bunny is the one in good physical shape but it's because she teaches two body-sculpting classes and an occasional spin class. Plus she jogs. She also oversees the exercise program at her spiffy health club where most of the men are either gay, high school athletes, or much older and obviously on steroids. Bunny says because they're in love with their own chiseled bodies, she rarely gets a date.

They finally both come back and sit down.

"Okay, the clock is ticking as of this very minute so make your feelings known, but keep them brief," Bunny says and looks at her watch which is really a heart-rate monitor.

"Okay. And no interruptions."

"Start!" Paulette yells.

"Okay. I've been thinking about this for weeks, so here goes: sometimes I can't remember what I ever saw in Leon. I mean when I try to think back to what attracted me to him, I honestly can't remember. I mean, he wasn't always dull and neither was I. But we never go anywhere or do anything except what we've always done, which is pretty much nothing aside from holidays, and those have always revolved around family members who are now either dead or living with us.

"We never have any fun. There's no excitement in our life. Unless I count taking Arthurine to the doctor or driving her back and forth to Bible study twice a week where I sit out in the car reading with a flashlight until she's through. Thrill thrill. Or maybe I should count standing in the long line at Blockbuster's on a Saturday night or praying there's a movie on satellite that I haven't seen. All this excitement is enough to give me a heart attack. Stop laughing!"

"We're not," Bunny says with her hand in front of her mouth.

"But it was sad-funny, Marilyn. I laughed. But now I'm not."

"Okay. Even on my birthday I wanted to do something fun, upbeat. I suggested we drive to Carmel and spend the night at a hotel by the ocean or go to the wine country and have dinner on the wine train around the vineyards, maybe take a mud bath or go to the one drive-in that's left or park at the beach or on a dark street and do it . . . whatever. You know what he wanted to do?

Take me to dinner. He thinks going to dinner is the only way to celebrate anything.

"Leon's turning forty-six in April and up to now he behaves more like a senior citizen. I'd swear he's getting Tourette's. He's just been blurting out what he's thinking and some of it is insulting or stupid or embarrassing and he doesn't seem to know he's saying it! He complains about so many things I feel like calling him a bitch! Stop laughing, Bunny! He can't hear worth anything, so he talks to me like I'm across the room or something. Oh. His glasses have suddenly disappeared and his eyes change colors from one week to the next. I'm about eighty percent sure that he's been dying his roots black. And on top of all this, he's grown quite fond of those velour leisure suits that zip and has been wearing them to work on casual Fridays."

Now we all crack up.

"Go, Leon," Bunny says.

"With his baaad self," Paulette chimes in.

"I still love him but there's just no passion. No fire. No rush. I can just about predict his next move, his next thought. I miss the suspense of where we're going from here, since the kids are pretty much grown. Nowhere, as it turns out. Because once we got 'here' I thought we'd be free to do all kinds of stuff. But nope. We've settled like our old-ass house. And I just don't buy all the testimonials by the experts who claim that mature love is more comforting than romantic and that as time passes it's childish to think you'll feel the thrills of romance like you felt in the beginning. A tremor every once in a while would be nice. And it should still be possible. It's one of the beauties of life. To feel the joy and thrill of love. Isn't it? If it wasn't, then why does everybody want it? On many a night I have rolled over and wished he was just half the Leon that he used to be: tender and attentive and sexy and a little wild.

"And sex? Don't even get me started. We've done it the same two, three, or four exciting ways in the same two exciting places—his side or my side of the bed for almost a quarter of a century and even though I've sort of gotten used to it, I'm really tired of being used to it. Of having empty orgasms—when I'm lucky enough to have one. I've told Leon that the clitoris has eight thousand nerve cells . . ."

"It does?" Bunny asks.

I just roll my eyes at her.

"Roscoe knows where they all are, baby. Sorry."

"Anyway, all I want is for him to find one. And remember where it was. He used to ask me what would make me feel good. He used to tell me I was pretty even though it wasn't true."

"But you are pretty," Paulette says.

"I agree," Bunny says.

"I am not. But hell, lie to me!"

"He might be trying to lower your self-esteem."

"Shut up, Bunny," I say.

"Please do," Paulette says. "And finish the whole textbook before you speak on a topic and embarrass yourself in public, would you?"

Bunny's eyes are scouring the room—she's looking for her notes.

"I'm almost finished. Anyway, it's insulting to me that he's assumed I'd always respond to the same stimuli when even mice don't. I'm a woman, not a damn mouse! But Leon doesn't seem to know it. They say ask for what you want. Well, what happens when you ask and you still don't get it? I don't mean to attack him." I take a sip of my drink and sink a little.

"Finished already?" Paulette says.

"Just one last thing," I say.

"May I interject?" Bunny asks, like she's in a courtroom.

"No," Paulette says. "Carry on, Marilyn."

"Try to make it snappy because I've gotta be up by six," Bunny says in what must be her personal-training voice.

"I just want a little passion."

"You already talked about that, Marilyn."

"Will you relax, Bunny," Paulette says, and pops her on the head. "You know how we do this and you know it takes as long as it takes. When we're listening to every detail of your health club dramedy and the emotional difficulties your damn cats are having or whatever . . . do we rush you?"

"No. Sorry, Marilyn. Go on."

"Thank you. But I need to say this. I'm not talking about the kind of passion missing in the Department of Love. There are so many other areas in my life where passion should exist. Like I wish I knew what I wanted to do with the rest of my life. But I don't. I don't count the twenty-four hours a week I spend at Heavenly Creations. I work there because it helps to support my hobbies, which I do for fun. Hell, I live for my employee discount and getting first dibs on all the merchandise. But it's just a job. I want to do something that I get a real charge out of. How do you find what really lifts your skirt or know if you have any talent or marketable skills?"

"I need to think about that one," Bunny says.

"I'll put it this way. I'll be fifty before I know it and then sixty and hopefully seventy. I watch elderly people and some of them are weary and some of them seem to have a look on their faces that says: 'I've lived. I've been through a lot. But I not only made it, I've come out ahead. It took some doing, but I did it. I paid attention to my heart and my brain once I stopped confusing the two. I finally got it right and here I am sitting on this park bench reading a good book, which I occasionally put down simply to watch all these young fools live as if life is some endless roller coaster when in fact it's a waltz.' "

"I think you're just lonely," Paulette says.

"How in the world could she be lonely with a husband and Arthurine and that dog in the house?" Bunny asks.

"Maybe you'll read about how that works in future chapters, ya think?" Paulette says to Bunny.

"I think that you and Leon have grown apart because you've been too busy being Mom and Dad when you both just need to get your freak on."

"All I was trying to say was I think I need to make

some changes, and I'm scared and it's not all Leon's fault and I don't blame him but I just don't want to end up old and be full of regrets. I don't want the list of all the things I meant to do or wanted to do to be longer than the things I did do. That's all."

"You need some courage," Paulette says. "And faith in yourself."

"And don't forget about God," Bunny says.

"I couldn't forget God if I wanted to."

"You miss those twins, don't you?" Bunny says.

"Of course I do. But this isn't about them."

"You should consider going back to school," Paulette says.

"I am."

"Where? And when? And in what?" Bunny says.

"I hope it's not online, is it?" Paulette asks.

"No. I applied to the California College of Arts and Crafts and the Academy of Arts in San Francisco for their MFA programs. Just for the hell of it."

"Right the fuck on!" Paulette says. "Why didn't you tell us?"

"Yeah, so what are you whining about?" Bunny says.

"I don't know what my chances are of getting in. And it may not have been the smartest thing to do."

"Well it's definitely not a *dumb* thing to do. What exactly is an MFA? I get my acronyms confused sometimes."

"We know you do," Paulette says. "Master of fine arts. Write it down. How does Leon feel about it?"

"I haven't told him. I want to wait and see what happens."

"What are you going to do with this degree if you get it?"

"I don't know. Color, Bunny."

"I'll pretend you didn't say that."

"You've seen some of the stuff the girl makes, Bunny. She'll be able to expand her repertoire and perhaps refine it even more."

"Thank you, Paulette. I could not have put it better."

"Okay, I want to hop back to the other topic before I forget what I wanted to say. I myself think you put too much emphasis on love and marriage," Bunny says.

"How would you know?"

"First of all, I don't buy the 'till death do us part' business. How can you guarantee that you'll love someone until you die? And how long is forever? How in the hell are you supposed to know how you're going to feel five, ten, or twenty years from now unless you're clairvoyant?"

"Good point," I say.

"I mean, should you feel bad because your feelings change? Hell, maybe we weren't meant to stay with one person forever. Maybe we weren't meant to get off on different exits at different times in our lives, I don't know."

"You certainly don't," Paulette says. "Marriage requires cooperation and compromise and patience. As soon as you're not willing to do that, you both lose."

"I'm getting sleepy," Bunny says.

"It still takes two to cooperate," I say.

"This we can all agree on. Now," Bunny says, standing up and finally kicking those high heels off. "I'm letting the cats out in two minutes. Oh shoot, there's my backpack!"

But it's not hers, it's mine. I bought her one just like it last year for Christmas. Before I can stop her, Bunny's already unzipped it and is pulling out the necklace.

"What in the world is this? It's gorgeous. I know you're not making this, are you, Marilyn?"

"Yes, I am."

"Don't be no fool, girl, you stay in school. Who's it for? And when did you start making jewelry, hussie?"

"It was supposed to be a surprise for your birthday but I don't know how to finish it . . ."

"Don't you worry about that. I can't believe you made this. Can you, Paulette?"

"As a matter of fact I can. Marilyn has completely underestimated her talent but overestimated her friend's taste. I think your neck is too short for that necklace, but mine is perfect. You can use my Nordstrom's card and get the girl a gift certificate. No. I'll give you twenty dollars and just go to Walgreen's."

"You go straight to you know where," Bunny says and walks over and gives me a kiss while handing it back to me.

"Don't kill yourself trying to finish it, Marilyn. But the people at your job should know how to do this, shouldn't they?"

"I guess so."

"It's the thought that counts. But anyway, this year, ladies, I'm afraid I'm off to Vegas with a friend for the celebration of my birth."

"And you'll be how old again?" I ask, not really wanting an answer.

"I'll be forty. You broads know that. Stop playing dumb. Now out!"

And we are gone. And somehow the inside of my chest feels lighter.

Chapter 3

I arrive at my doctor's office a few minutes late because the new but old receptionist neglected to tell me they had moved to a larger office two floors down. I didn't say a word, just smiled when I signed in. She looked up when she saw me and said, "Still alive, huh?"

I didn't think this was so funny but I winked at her and cracked a fake smile as I dropped my five-ton backpack on the floor and sat in one of eight uncomfortable lavender and gray curved chairs. "Is Dr. Hilton running pretty much on schedule, today?"

"As a matter of fact, she is, but there are two patients ahead of you. She should be able to see you in the next fifteen minutes. Give or take a few."

I didn't see anyone else in the waiting room, so maybe she was already playing musical doors. I looked down at the pile of women's magazines, searching for a headline that might speak directly to me: "Flip Your Fat-Burning Switch Instantly" *Like right now? There. It's flipped. Onto* the *"no" pile*. "Lose 10 Pounds in 48 Hours on the 7-Day Miracle Diet." *Worth a peek.* It goes on the "yes or maybe" pile to my right. "Buff Up Just by Thinking about Exercise." *Bunny, Miss Fitness Director herself, would have a stroke if I read this because I've been* thinking *about exercising for years.* "Go Dancing Now!" *Okay. But who would I go with? Leon the Dancing Machine?* "Surprising Medical Alert: Housework Can Make You Sick!" *I already know this.*

I continue my quest: "Your 10 Biggest Beauty Problems Vanish on Page 150." I say aloud: "But what if they don't and what if you have more than ten?" as I toss it on top of the "no" pile and slide all the rest of them over to form one big stack. Then I just stop.

Over the years, at the grocery store checkout, I've flipped through and read thousands of these articles, and by the time I reached the cash register, I'd already feel thinner, making it seem ludicrous to spend good money on the magazine. Last year I stopped buying them altogether when it finally hit me that in the years I'd been buying them, I'd never actually followed any of their diet or workout programs. I don't even want to add up the number of exercise videos I have that I've never even broken the cellophane wrappers on.

If I had done half the things these magazines and videos had suggested, I would have been or would still be an emotionally balanced, picture-perfect mother of three in excellent shape who was also a great cook and who not only fulfilled her husband's every sexual desire and fantasy but whose own would somehow have magically gotten met since she would have learned to ask for what she wanted, but this of course was assuming that I did in fact get it, which has turned out not to be the case.

I look at my watch. It's two forty-three. I clear my throat, get up, and get some water from the dispenser.

"Mrs. Grimes, did you bring the questionnaire Dr. Hilton asked that you bring with you?"

I knew it was something I was supposed to remember to bring! "I forgot it."

"Many do. Here's another one. Fill out as much as you can, as quickly as you can and I'll put it in your chart."

The form required that I check "yes" or "no" if I had been experiencing any of the symptoms noted below, and there was room for explanation, if I thought it necessary.

Memory Lapses? Yes. Mostly words. My once fertile vocabulary has shrunk to that of an eighth grader and I find myself using profanity to compensate. Sometimes it feels just like it did when I smoked an occasional joint in college: I can walk into a room and completely forget what the hell I went in there for; open the fridge and stand there for long minutes wondering what it was I wanted. Sometimes I actually feel like I'm going nuts, but I know I'm not because if I was, I wouldn't be thinking I was going nuts. Plus, I don't have enough good reasons to go nuts. At least none I can remember.

Hot Flashes? Yep. It's only been the past six or seven months, but it seems like they've evolved: it started out feeling like the inside of my body was being dabbed here and there with mild salsa and then a thick layer of very hot salsa. Now, I've had to switch from cappuccinos to decaf iced lattes because the combination of caffeine and hot liquid lingered inside me long after it passed through my body.

Mood Swings? Yes. For years I was just your average PMSer, but according to my mother-in-law: once a bitch, always a bitch.

Trouble Concentrating? Who doesn't? But I always have: on things I didn't want to spend too much time thinking about anyway.

Vaginal Dryness? Yes. Hah! Only when Leon didn't give me any advance notice that he had something in mind and before realizing he was already "inside the doorway to my love" so to speak. Dry was putting it mildly. It's probably closer to a big clam, like the ones you see in an aquarium: they're cracked wide open until you walk up and tap on the glass and then they snap shut. Except of course when I allow myself the freedom to fantasize and pretend that it's Rick Fox or the bow-legged guy from *CSI: Las Vegas* or the brother with the gray eyes from *CSI: Las Vegas* or the Latin brother on *CSI: Miami* or David Beckham or Sting or Seal or Ian Thorpe's father or Delroy Lindo or Omar Epps or the African brother from the movie *Amistad* who said "We want free," but then he also did a guest run on *ER*. On any given night any one of them might participate in the festivities by slowly sliding and slithering them-selves all over me so that I get moist all right, damn near liquid, and afterward, Leon once again thinks he's been magnificent when in fact he's had quite a bit of help.

Temper Changes? While driving I tend to scream at people, especially on the 680 South and it's probably a good thing I don't own a gun because if I did, over the past year, I probably would've used it. I am not a violent person and I'm afraid of guns so I know something's going on. Things that used to not even faze me now get on what's left of my nerves: waiting in any line for anything longer than thirty seconds; the blond woman on *Entertainment Tonight* who smiles incessantly; boring people who think they're interesting; sidewalks that end for no reason; cell phones ringing in public places and everybody reaching in their purse thinking it's theirs; children in cars with a parent smoking and those with no seat belts on but Mom is strapped in. And just because I know there are still more questions ahead, Arthurine's dingy-white toy poodle—Snuffy—(who should probably be dipping it), who's deaf, has arthritis, low thyroid and is too fat to walk up the stairs. Sometimes I have to carry him for her and he stinks because he has a hard time going not to mention giving him an arsenal of pills twice a day. Okay, STOP IT, Marilyn, RIGHT NOW! Move on!

Do you know at what age your mother went through menopause? No. And what difference does it make? As soon as I hear myself think this, I realize how stupid it sounds even in my head.

"Excuse me," I say to the receptionist. "I'm sorry, what's your name?"

"Nancy. All finished?"

"Almost. Nancy, I was wondering if I have five more minutes of waiting, and if so, I can call my mother to get the answer to this one question . . ."

"Dr. Hilton has had an unexpected emergency, but she'll be back in the office in about twenty minutes, Mrs. Grimes. So take your time."

I look at my watch. It's now 3:05. It's my day off. But I left clothes in the dryer that I could've folded and another load of whites soaking. I could've set the rhinestones on the lampshade I was making. I take my cell phone out into the hallway and then down the stairwell until I'm outside where I bump into a lemon tree but am able to get service. I dial Lovey's number—which is what she's always preferred to be called rather than Mama. When she answers, her voice is barely audible. "Lovey?"

"Yes, this is me. Who is this?"

At first I think she's kidding.

"Who does it sound like?"

"I ain't got time for games, so spit it out before I hang up this phone."

"It's me, Marilyn, Lovey."

"Then why didn't you say so? What can I do for you?"

"I'm at my doctor's office and she wants to know how old you were when you went through the Change."

"That's a very personal subject, Marilyn, and a very private matter and like I said, it's personal and private."

"Lovey, why are you whispering? Who's there?"

"Nobody but me and your daddy."

"What did you say?"

"I'm just feeling Herman deep in my heart today, that's all. What time is it there?"

"It's three o'clock in Oakland, Lovey. The same time it is right there in Fresno—two hundred whole miles from here. Lovey, is something wrong? Are you feeling depressed?"

"No no no. I just can't see the clock from where I'm sitting." Herman was my daddy. He's supposedly dead. I don't remember what he looks like. Lovey tore up all his pictures. Don't remember the sound of his voice. Just that I supposedly look like a female version of him. Word on the street was that he left Fresno city limits driving south on Highway 99 heading for Vegas on the Fourth of July, 1960, to find some woman named Petralee whom he'd met at—and apparently fell head over heels in love with while stumbling in and out of—an orchard bar. No one has ever seen or heard from him since.

My foster sister, Joy, whom I dearly love and hate as if we were born to the same parents, does not want to remember the people who abandoned her when she was six and turned her over to the state of California, county of Fresno, for love and caregiving. That person turned out to be my mother, whose real name is Louvelle Dupree and whose only other child would be me, Marilyn, who had two years earlier already left to attend college in the Bay Area causing "Lovey" to suffer a serious case of the empty nest. She said she felt useless and needed somebody other than needy parishioners and neighbors to talk to without having to pray with them or do their hair in her hot kitchen. So she fostered Joy and then adopted her. Lovey was so proud when Joy got stars on her report card for being thoughtful and helpful because she was the same at home. But as Joy became more high-spirited, her mannerisms were not as amusing to Lovey. Joy turned a corner and things went bad.

On several occasions, Joy did stints in juvenile hall for various youthful infractions. Lovey tried to give her back to the state, but waited too long. Joy had already turned eighteen and had one baby and then another and now she's done a grand job of convincing Lovey, who is all of sixty-seven, that she is needed around the house. It's most likely Joy and her undisciplined little brats who are probably Lovey's major source of stress.

"Is Joy there now?"

"I doubt it. She ain't never here. But those little Flintstones should be running around here somewhere."

"I'll call back later, Lovey. You sure you're okay?"

"I ain't answering no more questions. Good-bye." Click.

Something is wrong in Bedrock, since she brought it up. If I smoked, this would be a good time for a cigarette, but I just do what Trudy suggested Maureen do, and take a series of slow breaths as I walk back up the stairs and sit down inside the waiting room where two other women are now sitting. One, dressed in a conventional navy blue suit, is on her cell phone, which rings every fifteen seconds because she keeps saying her name and title and "hold" like this is her office without walls. The other woman is so thin she looks like a hard pretzel. She's in running clothes and looks to be in her early thirties. Her tiny muscles pop out like golf balls on arms. When she crosses her legs, I can hear them crack. I want her to eat something right now. I bet she doesn't get her period either.

Have You Noticed Any Unaccounted for Weight Gain? *Yes.* It's gotten to the point that I can't even stand to look at myself naked in the mirror anymore because it is not my body I see, it's the body of some middle-aged woman who's letting herself go.

I try to move my backpack with my right foot, which seems to have fallen asleep. It weighs a ton. Last night I took all the stuff out of both glove compartments and stuffed it in here so I could sort through it over a decaf latte, but *not* at Starbucks. I have started boycotting them since they've started appearing like dandelions on corners within urban, rural—and from what I've seen on MTV—even within international hotels and blocks of third-world countries, thus giving me a sense that they've come to Earth pretending to be philanthropic when in fact they are really an alien empire sent here to take over the world by sprinkling a little something extra into the drinks. We, their addicted slaves, don't even realize that we have learned a new language—their language. Many of us cannot even afford their stock since they went public, but have shown a different kind of loyalty by spending astronomical amounts of money once known mainly to drug addicts for coffee and tea, but somehow we don't seem to mind. Well, I mind.

Where was I? Oh, yeah: sorting through my backpack. I've damn near forgotten I was even in a doctor's office when the nurse or whatever she's called pokes her head through the door and says, "Marilyn, would you like to come with me?" I want to say: "No, I just came here to read magazines for an hour since I have nothing else to do," but I just follow her.

"Let's get your weight," she says.

"Let's not," I say.

"Oh, it's not that bad," she says.

I don't know what that perfume is she's wearing but it smells like gasoline. Why is it that people who wear cheap perfume always have to slather it on?

"So what brings you here today, Marilyn?"

Can't she read? I'm not repeating it. Not without screaming. So I say as calmly as I can, "Well, Dr. Hilton asked if I could come in today so she could explain the results of my blood test."

She opens a brown folder and flips it open. "That's indeed what I see here."

"Does it show my hormone levels?"

"Yes, it does."

"Am I in the early stages of menopause?"

"I'll let the doctor explain when she comes in. Let's get your blood pressure and temperature," she says, wrapping that padded thing tighter than usual around my arm and sticking the disposable thermometer under my tongue as if she's really trying to shut me up. "When was your last menstrual cycle?"

"I didn't have one in January, I'm happy to say, and I'm due again in two weeks, but good riddance," I say, holding on to the tip of the thermometer.

"And that date was?"

"Christmas."

"Your blood pressure is excellent: 121 over 70. Now let's get you to hop on the scale and then go right over there to the restroom and get me a clean urine sample, okay?"

"Sure. Be happy to."

I close my eyes when I get on the scale. I can feel it tipping too far to the right. In fact, I think that silver clip might just keep going straight through that shiny picture of a kitten and a puppy playing together on the wall. "Don't tell me what it says," I say. "I don't want to know."

I go into the bathroom. She's been in here quite a few times today. I try not to inhale any more of her toxic scent than I have to. After I come out, she guides me into Room #1 and gives me the take-everything-off spiel. I put the blue gown on backward and hop onto the table. When she tells me the doctor should be with me shortly, I feel like saying: "Sure sure sure! Heard this already. Save it for the next patient." I lie back on the stainless steel examination table. Decide to take advantage of this time by closing my eyes. The tissue paper on both sides of my hips crinkles and makes a crackling noise.

I bend over and pull my backpack up with both hands and start rummaging through it when I realize that this is not an appropriate place for me to clean this thing out, and since I'm trying not to always be "doing something" in every free moment, I decide to drop it back where it was, but a thick wad of notebook paper falls out. I forgot all about this! As I flip page after page, I wondered if I was having a "moment" because it's clear to see I was writing very fast:

January: Stop swearing. This is a lazy, cheap, and ignorant way to express myself. But I enjoy swearing sometimes, and don't always use it in a hostile or malicious way. In fact, I could probably come up with at least a hundred different ways just to use the word "fuck" in all its forms: Fuck you. I will fuck you up. Abso-fucking-lutely. My husband cannot fuck. You get on my fucking nerves. I can't fucking believe this. You fucker. This is fucking ridiculous. I'll try. *February: Improve my vocabulary.* Try to learn a new word every day and use it in a sentence. If I was around more intelligent people, I might be able to get some practice. This was a problem I had when my kids were little. I'd say something like "Go ahead and just gesticulate." And Spencer or Simeon would say, "Gest-who? Mom, come on. Give us the normal word, please!" I'd think: what the fuck? But I'd say: "Just try moving those little arms, then." *March: Eat smarter. April: Stop being so critical.* This is going to be tough because it's so much easier pointing out other people's shortcomings than it is recognizing and acknowledging your own. And so much more fun. But, sad to say, just about every negative thing I've said about someone eventually winds up becoming a problem I have to face. *May: Volunteer!* Stop being so selfish and shallow. This concept wasn't designed solely for rich white women with nothing else to do. *June: Go to church and Pray More Often! Let's be realistic: not neces-sarily every single Sunday but enough so that I feel re-deemed.* Remember not to waste God's time with chitchat and don't ask for any special favors because too many folks are asking for special treatment all day long. Don't *ask* for anything. But if I have to, ask for the ability to use common sense, be stronger, be more patient, compassionate, honest, and forgiving. The rest should fall into place. If not, it means I'm not paying at-tention. *July: Exercise!* Something. But break a sweat. (Hot flashes do not count! Ha!) *August: Cook something new at least once a week!* This is so last-year. I must've been out of my fucking mind. In fact, I'm thinking of taking a cooking hiatus. *September: Be more sociable.* I should do more things with my friends since I don't do much with my husband. Maybe make some new friends even though I love Bunny and Paulette. Try reconnect-ing with a few that I liked in college who found me on the Internet but whom I have yet to e-mail back. Try not to compare. *October: Write letters again!* Especially to people who think I've forgotten them because I have. Reminisce. *November: Change my hairstyle every three months.* (Why did I want to do that? Oh yeah, for vari-ety.) *December: Go somewhere I never thought I'd go.* Do something I never thought I'd do. (Like where? Like what?)

Did I really write all of this stuff? Was I on some kind of fucking medication around then? Nope. That's the reason why I'm here now. Does swearing in my thoughts count the same as actually swearing out loud? A knock on the door startles me and I throw my tablet on the floor like it's an illegal drug.

"Marilyn?"

"Yes?"

"May I come in?"

"Sure," I say, and sit up like a board is behind my back.

"How are you these days, Marilyn?"

"So-so," I say. "I like your new office."

"Thanks."

She looks good. Too good. Like she's had work done. But to that I say, right on.

"Well, let's see here." She sighs, flipping through my chart, and then she just closes it.

"How far into it am I?"

"Well, that depends."

"On what? I thought you said the blood test would show my hormone levels."

"It does, indeed."

"Are they high or low?"

"Well, Marilyn, I'm not sure how you're going to feel about the numbers."

"What does that mean?"

"Well, the levels indicate that you're probably pregnant."

I know I didn't hear her right. I couldn't possibly have heard her say the word "pregnant."

"What did you just say?"

"This is what the tests say."

"You can't really be serious?"

"Well, when you told the lab that you'd missed a period, they automatically did a pregnancy test when checking hormone levels, just in case."

"I don't fucking believe this!"

"So I take it this isn't good news for you then, Marilyn?"

"Preg-nant," I blurt out just to hear myself say it. "How pregnant am I?"

"I can't tell you that based on this test, but since your next cycle is due in"—she looks at my chart—"it says here, around the eighteenth of February—then it would be safe to put you at roughly six or seven weeks."

"Six or seven weeks?" I whisper and realize I've been tapping the base of this metal exam table with the heels of both feet, which I can't seem to stop until I place both palms on my kneecaps and press down. I take a few deep breaths and think of Trudy of all people. "Wait a minute. Okay. Wait. I thought I was supposed to be going through menopause! That's what I came in here for!"

"You probably were, Marilyn, but sometimes there's one last hurrah left."

"Hurrah?" I sigh, but I'm abso-fucking-lutely positive that she knows I'm not waiting for a fucking response.

Chapter 4

H i, honey. Two things: I've got a surprise to show you when I get home, and I'm going to be a little later than I thought." I look down at my cell as if I can see his voice coming out of it. I don't really like surprises because they usually disappoint. And in Leon's case it almost always means it's something more for his benefit than mine but he'll present it so it comes across like it was meant for both of us to enjoy. If it doesn't fall into this category, this is what will be an even bigger shock.

So he's going to be late. Good. Arthurine can eat frozen Stouffer's and be happy. I could whip up a low-fat dessert, but this, too, takes time and I feel like sewing or hot gluing something—anything—tonight.

"Marilyn? Are you there? Can you hear me?"

"Yes, but I can barely hear you. Hold on a minute, would you, I've got a call from Joy coming in, which must mean it's important because she never calls me on my cell. Be right back." I press TALK. "What's going on, Joy? Is Lovey all right? She didn't sound right at all when I talked to her the other day. Is her pressure up again?"

"And hello to you, too. No. Her pressure is fine."

"Is she taking her pills?"

"Yeah, she's taking all her pills. Her cholesterol is all right. And she still weighs a ton."

"Well, why was she talking crazy?"

"Because she's going crazy. Sometimes I wish to hell I *was* crazy and then I wouldn't have to worry about nothing. But I ain't. And I'm the one in bad shape. And I was . . ."

"I have to call you right back, Joy. Leon's on the other line and it's long distance." I hang up without waiting for her reply. Whatever she wants has got something to do with borrowing or needing some money or her world will end without my help and once again she's sorry to have to call me like this but she had no choice and after searching for and not being able to find any other avenues— like a job, for instance—she has come to me, her very last resort, which is supposed to make me feel grateful that she saved the "best" for last. I have no intention of calling her back anytime soon because when I don't, her world doesn't fall apart any more than it already has and she usually manages to find someone besides Lovey and me to squelch off of.

"Leon?"

"I'm still here, Marilyn."

"I've got a surprise for you, too," I say and then wish I hadn't.

"What kind?"

"Probably not as big a one as yours—so don't even think about it. Anyway, what time do you think you'll get home?"

"You're not at home, are you? No, because I can hear the other cars and the wind. Did you try out a class?"

"What class?"

"At the gym. You said you were going to try spinning or something."

I forgot all about that. Why didn't I just keep my big mouth shut until *after* I went? "I didn't make it because I forgot today was my annual Pap test and I couldn't miss that."

"I can understand that. Everything okay?"

"Appears to be, but they send the actual results by mail. Oh no!"

"What? You're not in an accident, are you?"

"No. I forgot that Sabrina and Nevil are going to some kind of metaphysical lecture tonight at Cal and I promised to keep Sage overnight. They're dropping her off around seven and it's almost six now."

"You couldn't be that far from home, are you?"

"No."

"Then what's the problem?"

"You wouldn't understand."

"What's to understand, Marilyn?"

"Nothing."

"Do we have any plans for the weekend?"

"Of course we do! We're flying to Vegas with six of our closest friends for two nights of nonstop partying and we're staying at the Bellagio and I've got tickets to Cirque du Soleil's *O* and Celine Dion, even though you don't like her, and while you guys are in the cigar lounge us girls will be sipping apple martinis and salivating over male strippers, but other than this little excursion, I think we're free."

"Very funny, Marilyn. What male strippers?"

"Why'd you ask?"

"I was just wondering. Some of the fellas wanted to get together and do eighteen holes on Saturday."

"What else is new?"

"But we could try and do something like this one day save for the strippers. They've got some great courses in Vegas. Do we *have* six close friends?"

"Forget it, Leon. I was just messing with you."

"Well, let me ask you something. Are there ever any men in those classes?"

"What classes?"

"The ones at the gym. Or are they just for women? I've been thinking. It's really time I start using my portion of that membership rather than let it go to waste."

"Am I hearing right, Leon? Did you just say you actually want to go to the gym?"

"That's right."

I'm trying not to laugh when I ask: "What part of your anatomy would you like to focus on first?"

"My whole body, actually. You haven't seen Frank in months and you know how huge he was? You probably wouldn't recognize him if you saw him. He's lost about thirty pounds and looks fantastic since he moved out."

"What do you mean 'moved out'?"

"He's getting a divorce."

"He? You mean Frank and Joyce?"

"Well, yes, technically, but Frank is the one who's filing."

"You can't be serious, Leon."

"Very. I thought I mentioned this to you a while ago."

"Mentioned? What happened?"

"I'll tell you more of the details later. But anyway, so many of the guys at work have turned to the gym to get rid of stress and they've reshaped themselves completely. I think I may be one of the last of the Mohicans."

I'm supposed to laugh but I can't. "What time did you say you'll be home?"

"I can't really say just now. We're finishing up the last-minute details on the Douglass project—you know the one in Riverside?"

I nod, knowing he's not really waiting for an answer. I listen to him ramble on but I don't hear a word he's saying. What I'm really thinking is that Leon's phone call—a cliché if ever there was one—most likely means he's on his way to an economy hotel (he's a miser, but wouldn't be caught dead in a motel) where in a couple of hours he will, if he hasn't already, order room service (at least a decent bottle of Moët), and his much-younger-than-me, slender and sexy girlfriend who probably works in a cubicle somewhere in his office, is spraying on some kind of popular perfume after having just come out of the shower so that after he arrives and imbibes a little he will have wiped me and Arthurine from his mind and loosened up enough to enjoy watching her suck his dick like he's in some porno movie and to be fair and make sure he can repeat this escapade, he'll also manage to go down on her the way he used to go down on me when there was more space between my thighs and they were ripple-free. And when he wakes up fifteen minutes later and looks at the clock, he'll drag himself out of bed and take a quick shower and drive home triumphant that he still "has it" and when he comes into the bedroom to see if I've been waiting up for him, which of course I will not have been because I'll either be sound asleep or pretending to be, he'll run back downstairs where he will take his dinner from the microwave and dump it down the garbage disposal where I happened to have left a spoon and the noise will give him a jolt and he will remove said spoon and place it in the sink and then take his second shower of the night and not think I'll notice that he's done either. However, in the morning while I'm putting dishes into the dishwasher—including the scratched spoon—he'll tell me how good dinner was and thank me for being so thoughtful.

"Anyway, you know how these guys can be," he's saying. "I might have to have a drink or two with them, but I'll call when I'm on my way if it's not too late. Promise."

"It's no problem, really."

"And how's Mom doing this morning?"

"What? I can't hear you. You're breaking up!"

"I said, *how's Mom?*"

I press END twice, which turns the phone off. I don't want to use up any of my minutes talking about Arthurine right now and Lord knows I don't want to think about going home and facing her. Sometimes she's telepathic and today she'll probably look right through my skin, directly into my belly and see that I'm pregnant. I wouldn't put it past her. Who knows, maybe I'll get lucky and she'll be in a six-hour coma or completely absorbed watching reruns of *Home Improvement* when I walk in.

My luck must have run out because Miss Holy Thang is sitting in the family room with the TV off. She's nodding like a junkie, those aviator-size glasses having slid to the tip of her nose, apparently from reading what looks like a real book. This is a first. The door chime must've had a delayed reaction because she just now snaps the paperback shut and slides it away from my view. "Hello there, Arthurine," I say.

"Evening to you," she says, trying to appear alert. She is dressed for church on a Monday but hasn't been anywhere today except for two trips to the mall. The first was about seven this morning when a bus picks up her and about thirty other senior citizens and takes them to the mall to walk before the stores open. She gets back about ten, leaving just enough time to shower and be ready for the shopping van that comes back around noon. They mostly have lunch, window-shop, buy lots of trinkets, or see a PG-13 movie.

"How're you feeling this evening?" This is a loaded question that I know I should not have asked.

"Fair to middlin, but this morning the voice of God said, 'The child is not dead but asleep. Little girl, I say to you get up!' Where've you been all day? You weren't at work."

I feel like saying, "None of your business, Miss Newly Resurrected. And since when did you start checking up on me?" But I don't, because it would be rude and disrespectful. "I had errands to do."

"I know that, Marilyn. But where exactly did you go?"

I want to say, "None of your damn business!" but of course I don't, for the same reasons. I grind my molars and say as softly as I can, "I also had my annual female checkup this afternoon."

"What'd the doctor say?"

"She didn't *say* anything, Arthurine. I just had a Pap smear, that's all."

"Yeah. And did she find anything up there?" She's being cute and I suppose she thinks what she just said was funny because she's laughing. I decide to humor her.

"Just a baby," I say.

"A what?"

"I'm just kidding, Arthurine."

She kicks off the navy blue pumps she is not supposed to be wearing and walks over here to the kitchen where she leans on the counter like an anchorwoman. "You ain't kidding with me, chile. I'll bet you 'bout two months and counting."

"What are you talking about, Arthurine? I'm serious. I was just joking."

"Well, the joke sure ain't on me. Remember, Jesus

wasn't planned either. And in case you didn't know it, I wasn't born yesterday. Anytime you can't stand to smell a little Clorox or unleaded gasoline, among other things—and don't think I haven't noticed—and all of a sudden you eating up all the starchy food in the house, especially the bananas that you know I like to put in my shredded wheat and the smoothie you keep promising to teach me how to make . . . you got something growing inside you all right, and I'll bet you ten smoothies it's a baby or my name ain't Arthurine Grimes."

"You don't know half as much as you think you know, Miss Grimes."

"Is that so? And I'm still *Mrs.* Grimes."

"Was that the doorbell?"

"I didn't hear any bells."

I don't dare comment but when I look over by the door, there's Snuffy, curled up and unconscious in his little nappy fur bed. "You think Snuffy heard it?"

She does not think this is at all funny. Snuffy's now on that deaf list Arthurine was pretending to be on. I'm pretty sure it's Sabrina. As always, she's late. "Would you mind seeing who it is while I start dinner?"

"I'm available to help, depending on how complicated this meal is you're fixing," she says, heading toward the front door.

"It's quite all right, Arthurine. I'm just tossing a salad and stir-frying some chicken for the pasta. And maybe have sorbet for dessert." I have decided to compromise since Sage will be here. She's Nevil's daughter from a previous relationship but Sabrina is the only mother she knows, which makes her my granddaughter. The pasta dish will come from the freezer, but I will spruce it up so it tastes homemade.

"You think this'll be enough?"

"Go, before I put some of Snuffy's medicine in yours!" She is giggling. I do care about Arthurine and would even go so far as to say I love her, but very often the people you really care about are the hardest to love. I hear Sage squealing and running at the same time. Boy can she move fast, like most two-and-a-half-year-olds. When Sabrina walks into the kitchen—with the exception of her long brown dreadlocks and the thin gold ring in her nose—she could be me twenty years ago. It's a weird feeling.

"Hi, Ma," she says, walking over to give me a kiss and a hug. She always smells like that oil or incense you buy from the vendors on Telegraph Avenue. "I wish I could stay longer and I'm rushing of course but I wanted to tell you my excellent news face-to-face."

"More news? Come here, Sage, and give Grandma some sugar-wooger!" I don't know if I can stand any more personal news right this very minute on this particular day. And here comes this little ladybug with a head full of braids, wearing yet another new-age outfit that turns into a parachute when she jumps into my arms and rubs her nose back and forth against mine the way we always do it. "Hello there, Miss Sagebrush!"

"Sage is going to have a little brother or sister in about seven and a half months! Isn't that just amazing, Ma!"

I lose my grip on Sage and she slips out of my arms

and I hear the rubber soles of those little purple and mustard boots land softly on the floor. "Well, congratulations, Sabrina. I didn't even know you guys were trying."

"Who tries?"

"Not me," I say.

"You're too old to have to worry about this kind of stuff anymore but when you're young and fertile and in love with the most brilliant man in the world, our first baby together is just what the doctor ordered."

"You think?"

"I think! I know! And gotta go! Love you!"

"Wait a minute, Miss Homeopath! Since Nevil got that fellowship, does this mean you'll be having the baby in England?"

"I hadn't thought of that yet. I just found out today! I suppose it does! But as they say in London, 'No worries, mate.' I've gotta go, Ma, or I'll be late, later than I am already and Nevil freaks when we have to rush! MaMo loves you, Sage! Bye Grandma Art! Hi to big-headed Daddy! And please don't forget to share our news with him and the twins! Speaking of which, how are they and have you heard from them lately? They've certainly forgotten my number. Anyway, don't answer right now. Tell me later. I'm outta here!" And she disappears.

Arthurine is now standing by the kitchen door like this is really not news. She has changed her clothes and is wearing yet another one of her favorite getups—those multicolored nylon jogging outfits with the jackets that zip and yet Arthurine, like most of the women who wear these suits, does not jog nor has she ever thought about jogging, especially in this number, which she thinks of as haute couture. I can't understand the color combinations these things come in, but when I find myself admiring them on the rack at Nordstrom's one day, I'll know that I've aged even further than I ever imagined. "Well, since you don't seem to be needing my help, I'm going in my room and read a little bit."

"What are you reading?"

"A book. You want me to take the baby so you can have a few minutes to move around without bumping into her?"

"No, she's fine. What kind of book?"

"A good one. Come on, go with Great Gram, baby," she says, holding her hand out to Sage, who seems to take to anybody who shows her some attention.

"What's the name of it?"

"I can't remember right off the top of my head."

"You left it on the couch over there. Go get it and tell me what the title is."

"Oh, shucks," she says, wobbling over and picking it up. Sage follows her. "Well, if you just have to know, it's called *The Widower's Folly.*"

"Hold it right there, Arthurine."

Both she and Sage seem to freeze.

"And what's it about? Where'd you get it and why are you reading a book about a brash widower?"

"You are one nosey daughter-in-law. Do I try to get all in your business? No, I do not. But if you're just dying to know, my friend Prezelle bought it for me at the mall today. It's a story about romance."

"Who is this Prezelle?"

"He rides on the van that takes us to the mall in the morning. We walk together. He lives in a very nice apartment complex for seniors right down the way on Skyline."

"Is he some kind of freak or something?"

"Watch your mouth in front of this baby. He ain't nobody's freak. He's a lonely old man and I'm a lonely old woman. He might be coming to visit me one afternoon in the very near future so don't act surprised when you see us sitting in the living room entertaining each other. Now go on and cook something so we can eat. I'm starving and this baby looks hungry, too. Did Leon say he'd be home in time for dinner?"

"Probably not," I say.

"These professional men just work work work. How much fun could they be?"

I'm not answering that. While cooking, I don't wipe the smirk off my face until after reaching for and sprinkling what should be paprika but turns out to be nutmeg all over the pasta! Today must have been Spice Day for Arthurine. One day I'm going to hurt this woman. However, after adding a little half-and-half and a tad more garlic, I discover that nutmeg provided a very nice flavor to an otherwise run-of-the-mill dish, which I will probably add even more of when I make it from scratch.

• • •

Little Sage's body is so warm we both fall asleep as soon as our heads hit the pillow. I'm holding her hands. Her fingers feel like feathers when they brush against mine. I could've put her in the guest room, but she likes cuddling with me and I like cuddling with her. I'm glad I saved most of my kids' books. Sage loves *Goodnight Moon*. I read it twice and she propped her feet on my thighs and listened with her eyes. I remembered when Sabrina used to do the same thing when I read her this story. In fact, I was having a hard time getting through it, so I decided to try *Liza Lou and the Yeller Belly Swamp*, which, thank God, Sage liked enough to laugh each time I scrunched up my nose and made a continuous sniffing noise.

The real smell of something rancid wakes me up. When I feel myself rocking, I realize it's Leon's hand on my shoulder, shaking me. "Honey," he whispers, "wake up for a second and come look out the window. I want to show you something."

"What?"

"I want to show you something."

"What's that horrible smell?"

"I hope it's not my new cologne," he says, as he folds back the corner of the duvet, slides his hand behind my shoulder and slowly leads me over to the window as if I'm handicapped.

"Look," he says, pointing to the driveway where I see what looks like a big fat yellow and black motorcycle. It looks exactly like those Harley-Davidsons I see in motorcades on the freeway, but I must be hallucinating because this is *our* driveway and I'm 90 percent sure that my forty-five-year-old husband, who is afraid of a mouse, would not be caught dead on one of these things nor does he or would he ever wear leather anything and he certainly has not come into our bedroom in the middle of the fucking night to wake me up and show me a motorcycle that he himself has purchased.

"Whose is it?" I ask, for the hell of it, while I wipe the sleep from my eyes.

"Ours," he says with what at first appears to be a wicked grin, but then I see it's sheer pride. There's something different about Leon. I can't put my finger on it. Like all of a sudden he wants to go to the gym? What's that about? And since when did he start wearing cologne? I walk back over to the bed in a somnambulant manner and slide under the covers. I hope he doesn't have anything more to say to me.

"Marilyn?"

"Yes," I groan. "Keep it down, please, Leon."

"Sorry," he whispers. "But what's your surprise?"

"I'll tell you about it in the morning."

"Come on, Marilyn. I showed you mine. Can't you show me yours?"

"No, I can't, Leon. It's not that kind of surprise."

Chapter 5

W hy didn't you call me back, Marilyn?"

"What time is it?"

"Early. Why didn't you call me back like you said you would? I waited and waited and waited until I just got tired of waiting."

"I forgot," I say, realizing that the sun should be out by now but it looks like it might rain. Leon's side of the bed is empty, I notice. I take the portable and walk out to the landing and look down. I don't see anybody but I do hear cartoons coming from the family room, which is right next to the kitchen. And then I hear the revving engine of the motorcycle that does not exist. What is he still doing here? He's usually at work by now.

"What if I was dying or something bad had happened to Lovey?" Joy is saying.

"You said Lovey was doing fine."

"I said she was losing her mind from one week to the

next and sometimes minute by minute, but other than that, she's healthy as a ox but that ain't why I . . ."

"What do you mean, 'losing her mind'?"

"Just what I said. She ain't putting two and two together like she used to."

"Hell, who can? Don't answer that."

"She keeps going back in time. Remembering stuff that makes her reminisce. It's about the only time you can get a smile outta her."

"Where is Lovey right now?"

"Probably asleep. She sleeps a lot."

"Well, you didn't sound like anything out of the ordinary was wrong. All you said was that you were in bad shape, which is pretty much the norm."

"Norm was my last boyfriend, Miss Smart-Ass, and I would appreciate it if you would not mention his name to me on this particular day, thank you very much."

"Get an education, would you Joy. And then try getting a job while you're at it!"

"You know what, Marilyn? Maybe if I'd married into money like you I probably wouldn't even be making this call."

"You kill me, Joy. You know good and well Leon was fresh out of college and broke as hell when we got married, so come up with a better one than this."

"How much money do you make?"

"How much money I make is none of your business. What's this got to do with anything?"

"Do you have a job, Marilyn?"

"Yes, I do."

"Doing what?"

"You know where I work and what I do."

"Refresh my memory. I'm drawing a blank screen."

"I work part-time at a craft store."

"Could you survive on your own if you had to, making the kind of chump change I know you make doing this kind of frilly shit?"

"I enjoy doing 'frilly' shit and if I downsized and increased my hours, yes, I could make ends meet, but what's this got to do with you?"

"You just a bored housewife, Marilyn, admit it."

"I'm not bored and I'm not a housewife anymore." I'm trying not to sound defensive because I'm lying through my teeth. Everything she's saying is true but I'll be damned if I let her know it. The surprising thing is that she's got more insight than I've given her credit for.

"If you ain't bored, then something is wrong with you. You got a college degree in some off-the-wall mess that you couldn't or didn't do shit with and for the next twenty years you act like a black Martha Stewart and then your kids grow up and make a mad dash for college and you act like they still at home. But ain't no more carpooling so what do you do with nobody to take care of except your mother-in-law? Run out and get some ridiculous little job to kill time that ain't got nothing to do with why you went to college."

"I didn't know you majored in psychology in the two and a half years you spent in high school, Joy, but you're missing the point here."

"I don't think so. You still just as wishy-washy as you always been."

"And what in the hell is that supposed to mean?"

"It means you always do what looks good on paper. And when you do shit and your heart ain't in it—like Stevie Wonder always said: 'you suffer'—but you did it anyway. Still doing it."

"Oh, really. Like what, for example?"

"Hell, how much time you got?"

"Very funny."

"Okay. If my memory serves me right you got accepted to that Fit School in New York, but Lovey wanted you to stay in California and go to a *good* college, and that's what you did. But where'd you end up?"

"It was F.I.T., and Cal turned out to be a good choice."

"Yeah, right. I thought you was supposed to find out what you liked in college."

"You do."

"What did you find out you like? Men? Kids?"

"You go to hell, Joy."

"No, you go first, Marilyn. You already knew before you got there what you liked to do. Anytime you can take an empty pork-'n'-bean can or a cheap-ass trash can or a rusty step ladder and turn it into something pretty, I don't think you was doing it for no grade. And who took our old dingy sheets and pillowcases, and some of our towels and clothes and dyed 'em a whole different color so they looked like new?"

"It was easy and it made sense, considering Lovey didn't have any money."

"You loved doing that kinda shit. You in denial like a motherfucker, Marilyn, and you know it."

"What do you know about denial?"

"I watch Dr. Phil. Damn near everybody's in it. Even Tiecey knows what it means."

I want to laugh. "I'm happy you're in tune with the lingo of our time."

"The what?"

"Never mind, Joy. To be honest, I'm working on making some changes in my life. But guess what? You still need a job."

"I've got a job."

"Since when?"

"Since I've been running this household and taking care of kids and our mother. I ain't jiving about Lovey either. She's acting loopy and I don't know if it's safe to leave my kids in here with her all by theyself."

"First of all, Joy, Lovey is sixty-seven years old and does not need to be babysitting for your bad-ass kids anyway."

"My kids ain't bad. They just high-strung."

"Don't even get me started."

LaTiece, who they call Tiecey, is seven. She is darker than bark and so pretty her face should be on a box of *something*. But she sucks her fingers. And she rocks. When she's sitting. Back and forth and back and forth. She doesn't even seem to realize she's doing it. And Little Lloyd, a.k.a. "LL," is five and has already experienced firsthand what violence feels like. Last year he beat up two little boys at preschool because he said he wanted to see if he could hit them hard enough to make at least one of them bleed. He didn't succeed. He cussed out his kindergarten teacher on the first day of school for making him sit outside of the circle after he pinched a little girl. These kids don't know who their fathers are. I don't know if Joy does either. But I'm not asking.

"Marilyn, you still there?"

"Yes, I'm here. What's she doing that's so peculiar?"

"You want some examples?"

"What did I just ask you?"

"Okay," she says, and I can hear her sucking on one of those nasty no-name-brand cigarettes. "You know all these plants in here she got?"

"What about them?"

"She's been watering 'em."

"What's wrong with that?"

"They ain't real, Marilyn! Every last one of 'em is plastic, except for one in the kitchen window and that's 'cause Tiecey grew it from a seed at school. For the past few weeks I been wondering where all this damn water been coming from that's running down the steps and why the carpet is all squishy in certain spots, and then the other day I caught her doing it."

"Maybe she was just confused."

"But these are *her* plants. Not mine."

"Did you ask her about it?"

"Ask her what? 'Lovey, are you losing your mind?' How do you ask your mama some shit like that?"

"I'll drive out there to see her by the end of the week."

"Don't tell her I told you this, please. Her temper is something else and she might just hit me."

"Get the hell outta here, Joy. Lovey wouldn't hurt a flea."

"Then that must make me a tick 'cause she's already done it!"

I suddenly feel like throwing up for three reasons: 1) The thought of Lovey doing any of these things and with Joy and her kids in the house is quite unsettling; 2) Leon is still gunning that damn motorcycle; and 3) Last night's meal is stuck in my esophagus. "I've gotta go, Joy. I'm feeling sick."

"Wait a minute! Can you lend me a couple of hundred bucks till I get on my feet, or not?"

"Are your kids hungry?"

"They will be."

"Go to Western Union in a few hours. If I get down there and it looks like those kids are being neglected on any level, Joy, I swear to God, first, I'm going to kick your ass myself, and then I'm calling Social Services on you. How's that sound?"

"Thanks M and M. But my kids ain't want for nothing. You been watching too many episodes of Special Victims' Unit of *Law & Order*. Three whole hours?"

I drop the phone on the floor and run into the bathroom and barf into the toilet until my ears are ringing and my head feels like it's expanding then shrinking. As soon as I stand up and walk over to the sink to get this awful taste out of my mouth, here it comes again. This time I don't make it to the toilet and as I'm crouched over, holding myself up with both elbows on the sink, I feel Leon hovering above me.

"What's wrong, Marilyn? Are you okay? What did you eat? This looks like it could be food poisoning."

"I'm okay, now. I hope." I stand upright.

"Can I get you something?" His fingers are spread out, grazing back and forth across my back like a slow windshield wiper. "What did you eat last night?"

"The shrimp pasta. Didn't you have some, too?"

"Just a few bites. I wasn't very hungry when I came in."

Lying son of a bitch. It was chicken, but I don't want to add to my nausea, which feels like it's subsiding. "That's not what's making me barf. I'm pregnant."

The weight of his hand now feels like he's pushing me away. He must realize it, because it falls off my back and now he's shoveling both hands inside the pockets of his dark green Dockers. He takes a few steps back and then looks at me like I'm some alien. "Did you just say you're pregnant, Marilyn?"

"Yes, I did."

"How in the world did this happen?"

"Well, let me think for a minute."

"When did you find out?"

"Yesterday."

"Is *this* your surprise?"

I just nod.

He looks disappointed. But who can blame him? I'm not exactly ecstatic about the idea of going through this again either. "A baby," he sighs, and sits down on the edge of the bathtub. The skylight is making his skin look olive green, putrid.

Here it comes again. I thought I was finished. What could possibly be left in there? This time, Leon stays put. By the time I start dry heaving, my thoughts get ugly, and I'm hoping that there's nothing left inside my belly for the seed that will grow into a baby to survive on.

Leon just sits there like he can't move. Like he wants to but can't. I understand. I rinse my mouth out with Listerine and then turn to face him. I feel light-headed but this I can handle. "I guess I'll have it," I hear myself say.

"Well, why wouldn't you?" he asks. It sounds more like a statement than a question.

"Can you handle this?" I ask.

"Can you?"

"You didn't answer my question."

"In all honesty, I'm stunned. Do we have any time to think if this is something we really want to do?"

"Leon, the thought of having an abortion at my age is too scary."

"I know. And I'm not suggesting it. But good Lord, Marilyn, have you thought about what this is going to mean for both of us?"

"It's spinning around in my head, but maybe you'd like to think about it on your motorcycle?"

He stands up. "Come on, cut me a little slack here, would you? It's not just *you* having a baby, Marilyn. I'm going to be forty-six in a few months. I've just recently started giving serious thought to making some changes in my professional life and . . ."

"What are you talking about, Leon?"

"I don't really know. All I know is that this is adding a variable that I hadn't considered, not to mention being unprepared for. But the thought of starting all over again . . . I mean we've already raised three beautiful children. I thought we were finished."

"I did, too, Leon."

"I mean we've spent most of our best years being parents, don't you think?"

"Our *best* years? I hadn't quite thought of it that way."

"It's just that I thought our household load was finally getting lighter. That we'd be able to try some new things. I always thought that this part of our lives would be filled with new experiences and excitement."

I do not believe my ears. These words are coming out of Mr. Predictable's mouth? "Such as?"

"Well, my mind is more on the present right this minute so it's hard to be specific about the future."

"Just name one new experience and one thing that might excite us both that a child might prevent."

He's wracking his brain trying to come up with something. He isn't good with quick responses when it's something he worries could be misinterpreted or makes him look bad. He's always been overly cautious, which is one of the reasons why spontaneity has been such a major issue. "What difference does it make, Marilyn?"

"I'm missing your point?"

"We have a situation here that we have to face. Yesterday I was excited about the idea of riding my Harley, and today I feel like I should've probably just stuck with the SUV."

"Ga'ma," Sage says, appearing in the doorway, "will you come pray with me?"

She means play. But praying sounds about right.

Chapter 6

"Girl, did you see Janet's boob during Super Bowl halftime?" Paulette asks, while she picks out all the pecans from the wild rice salad she's nibbling on. We're sitting outside at a café to keep an eye on her grandkids. They are asleep in the backseat of her truck, which is parked right in front of us. It's fifty-nine degrees out here.

"No I didn't. But I think Leon's seen it on the Internet at least a trillion times. I heard it was money well spent. Anyway, I didn't ask you to meet me here to make small talk. I'm seven weeks pregnant."

"You have got to be kidding!"

I roll my eyes at her.

"I guess not. Pregnant? Damn, Marilyn. How in the world did you get yourself knocked up, being a senior citizen and all?"

"My sentiments exactly. I go to the doctor knowing I've been off-kilter for a while and you can just close your mouth right now, Paulette, and here I am thinking she's probably going to give me a prescription for hormones so I can get my brain back in operation and what do I end up with? Fucking prenatal vitamins."

"I thought you said you were trying to quit swearing?"

"Go to hell, Paulette. I will. As soon I can have a whole week where no crazy or ridiculous or unbelievable shit happens and my mind is calm long enough to remember how to think. And don't you dare say anything about how wonderful this is when you and I both know how we make fun of all the over-forty mothers we see sitting in the parks on organized play dates marveling at their little miracles for hours and leaping up from the bench to convince the little farts to eat a spoonful of blueberry yogurt or an apple slice or carrot stick from the Ziploc bags—none of which they are remotely interested in and then they'll try to push that little straw from the juice carton into their closed mouth and finally accept that no means no and praise the Lord if they cough more than twice they must be choking or if the kid so much as sniffles or scrapes a knee—at the mere sight of blood it's off to the nearest emergency room they go where they will be asked if they are the child's grandmother, and now here I am in the same boat."

"So you're gonna have it, then?"

I roll my eyes at her.

"You mean you really want another kid?"

I roll my eyes at her again.

"What about Leon? Is he up for this?"

My eyes roll on their own.

"What about the kids?"

"I haven't told anybody. The twins'll be home for spring break in a couple of weeks and that's when I go back to hear the heartbeat so I figured I'd wait and tell them after. And ironically enough, Sabrina just told me she's pregnant, too."

"Get the hell out of here, Marilyn."

"Seriously. She probably would've freaked out if I'd told her. I can wait. I think I just saw movement in the backseat."

She and I peer into the tinted glass, but the slumping silhouettes strapped into their car seats are still. "Girl, I took them to Mickey D's and after turning a few corners, they were down for the count. But I don't have to tell you this, now do I?"

"No, you don't. I'm actually thrilled about replaying the entire miniseries of baby bottles and ballet or baseball and basketball and those boring soccer tournaments and begging for everything and thousands of birthday parties and sleepover after sleepover and bad plays and puberty and—Lord help me—not another period if it's a girl, and of course prescriptions for pimples, okay?"

"Okay," she says, as she leans back in the metal chair and starts twirling a group of braids. "A baby? Wow. Whoa. Damn. Okay, I'm shutting up right now."

"Thank you."

"Okay," she whispers and gets up, gives me a sympathetic kiss on my forehead and after rolling down the window, says to her two grandchildren who are now awake: "Grandma's getting in the truck and we are going home and have ice cream but only if you don't cry."

I see them both smiling. They are so cute! They are the products of her oldest son and his Asian wife. Of course now I'm suddenly ashamed for thinking of an innocent child as a burden. No child asks to come into this world and once it gets here, should be entitled to as much love and joy as it can get. In fact it is often we, the parents, who are ill-equipped to give it what it needs, so in effect, we are really the burden, the albatross around its little neck. I loved mothering my children and I love being their mother. I just thought I was finished giving birth. I wave as Paulette speeds off and try to finish this tuna melt.

My new daily ritual: I get up around eight and throw up from the smell of Leon's shaving cream or aftershave or shower gel or his new cologne. I brush my teeth with baking soda because toothpaste makes me cringe. I force myself to eat something and then throw up again. I eat crackers for lunch and once they settle, chase them with soup. I go into my hobby room and look around because there's not much I can do in here that doesn't involve chemicals, except sew, but I haven't been in the mood for it.

Leon's acting like I never told him. He hasn't mentioned it at all. It's almost as if he's pretending that it's not real or that I'm stewing it over, and any minute will change my mind and he'll drive me to a clinic and

I'll get it suctioned out. When I come out, he won't be in the waiting area. He'll be sitting in the car in the parking lot with the windows rolled down reading the latest issue of *Golfing* or *Black Enterprise* that he brought just in case he got bored. "All finished?" he'll ask.

But it's still in me. And Leon is lying next to me, much closer to the edge on his side of the bed. I slide over and try to pull him against me. He knows I need him. To cushion me. To be my shelter. To drown in his arms. He has always known when I need to sink. But he pretends he's asleep. I take my left hand and slip it inside his boxers, massaging him slowly, sliding my palm up and down, hoping to feel him rise, but he stays flaccid. This has always worked. "Leon," I finally whisper. "What's wrong?"

"Nothing. Just tired," he says, and rolls away from me. He curls up like a snail and locks his body and heart so my key doesn't work.

I am driving to Fresno because I got Trudy to cover for me, which she was more than happy to do. I was considering telling her what happened, but before I had a chance, she said, "I know this probably means you're having personal problems, Marilyn. We all do. So take as much time as you need. I'm here." And before I got a chance to ask how Maureen was doing, Trudy told me that she had pulled the kids out of school and had already moved back to Sacramento. "She is getting so divorced, it's not funny."

I also got my hair twisted so I wouldn't have to think about what to do with it for a while. And finally, after being tested for the third time, it has been confirmed that Arthurine does not have cataracts and will not have to have surgery of any kind. At first, she seemed disappointed to learn that all she needed was a new prescription. But then of course she knew why her eyesight had been spared: "So if your eye—even if it is your good eye—causes you to lust, gouge it out and throw it away. It is better for you to lose one part of your body than for your whole body to be thrown into hell." Matthew 5:29. Once again, I didn't bother to explain that this reference was about adultery. What she really was trying to say about healing one's sight was in Matthew 9:27–31. But at least she can see. The next step is to get her to at least try on some smaller glasses. This will probably be a battle since she as well as most of her aging compatriots seem to think that oversize glasses are a sign of sophistication or that they're able to see more at once. I don't know.

When I hit the Fresno city limits, I cross East California Avenue, passing alley after alley, where torn trash bags and garbage lie at the base of giant bins like dead animals. There are rainbows of graffiti sprayed in English and Spanish across the entire lengths of over- and underpass walls. When I was growing up this area wasn't called the Dog Pound. There were no SWAT teams or helicopters with infrared scopes prowling our neighborhoods. Dogs were pets. We had never seen or heard what an automatic assault rifle sounded like, except on TV.

Nobody got killed. People died of natural causes. It was safe here. It was pretty.

Before I turn down Lovey's street, it breaks my heart to see what used to be vibrant yellow, pink, and proud peach stucco bungalows now cracked and crumbling. Our house used to be mint green and white. The street is now lined with a small array of mesh fences in varying condition. Behind most of them are barking dogs: mostly pit bulls and rottweilers. Occasionally, there are the white wrought-iron gates that look like thick lace. I think these are meant to make a number of different statements, namely that they spent a little extra; they've got more class and pride than their neighbors, but mostly, they're saying, Keep Out. Behind each fence is a tiny patch of grass that is the front yard, many of which display an assortment of things that they feel requires protection: an old mattress that won't fit inside the blue recycle bin; a car parked directly on the grass or blocking the front door into the house itself; steel barbecue drums; and an awful lot of machinery.

When I pull into the driveway the garage door is up and Lovey's '89 Taurus isn't inside it. I called before I left home and told her the approximate time to expect me, but because my cell phone didn't work way out in farm country, I figured an hour wouldn't make much difference. But I suppose it does.

I honk and wait and realize that some of the flowers in the yard are real but some are also plastic. What has Lovey been out here doing? I honk again, but still nobody comes to the door or pulls back the gold drapes that are bunched up in spots where the hooks are probably missing. I used to have a key, but they've had the locks changed so many times I never know which one works. Burglars love this neighborhood even though most of these folks don't have much worth stealing.

The houses seem to shrink each time I visit. The living rooms are not much bigger than my walk-in closet and yet they're always full of the same furniture I have in mine: sofa, coffee table, two chairs, side tables. Lamps. The dining room is usually cramped with a table that's too big, and barely enough space for the chifforobe full of real or fake china, crystal goblets full of dust, and torn boxes of flatware posing as silver. The bedrooms have just enough room to walk around two sides of the bed before your foot will kick the dresser or chest of drawers. There could be a chair, but it will most likely be covered with clothes that need laundering or just never got put away. If you're lucky, the window has a giant air-conditioning unit taking up its bottom half, and sunlight may sneak into this room for hours at a time.

I get out of the car, open the aluminum screen, and knock on the front door. No answer. I try peeking in through a small opening in the drapes, but all I see is a cracked reflection of me in the wall of mirrored tiles with gold veins going through them. To the right is the fireplace, whose mantle is light pink tiles encased with one big wooden piece Lovey got at Home Depot a few years ago. It's also where she bought the self-adhesive wallpaper with brown and beige river rocks on it. The back of the green velour sofa is thinning in spots, thanks to the kids. This is where my mother lives.

I get my cell out and dial inside. I can hear the phone ring and then Joy's voice. "What is it?"

"Joy?"

"Yeah."

"Open the front door, would you. It's me. Marilyn."

"What are you doing here?"

"What do you think?"

"You didn't have to tell nobody you was coming. Damn. I got company and I need a shower."

"I don't care what kind of company you have. Where's Lovey?"

"I thought she was here."

"Are the kids in there?"

"I don't think so; it's too quiet. But let me go down and look."

"Open the damn door, would you. It's cold out here and I need to go to the bathroom."

"You have to use the one upstairs 'cause the one downstairs got a little problem."

The front door opens and Joy appears, looking like a crack head. Her hair is sticking out like four roosters. Her eyes are puffy and red. Her lips are chapped and her skin is ashy. She is downright waiflike. I can't even identify what it is she's wearing, except that it's a dark print and is hanging off her like it could be Lovey's housedress.

"Come on in, Sis. Good to see you."

She has no idea how bad she looks.

I don't want to hug her, but I do anyway because she's my sister. She smells like booze and tobacco. "Hi, Joy. I see you've got everything under control here," I say looking around at this pigpen. She knows damn well we were raised better than this.

"I'm trying," she says, and flops down on the twenty-year-old couch. "Forgive me, Sis. I had a rough night and was planning to get up early to clean, but as you can see, I ain't gotten around to it yet. I didn't even know you was coming."

"I told Lovey a few days ago."

"Lovey don't tell me nothin'."

"I wonder why?" I ask, not expecting an answer. I go upstairs to use the bathroom and I can hear movement in one of the bedrooms but I don't dare open the door. I come on back down and sit at the other end of the couch. I turn around to look at the photographs crammed on the wall behind us. The frames are old and cheap, many of them thin peeling gold, or the corners don't touch. The glass is cracked on some from falling to the floor when the front door was slammed too hard. Most of the pictures are yellowing from time and air. Quite a few are of my kids and me year after year after year. Leon's only in one, and that was at our wedding reception. We looked like nerds. The rest are snapshots of Joy's kids as babies and people I don't know. Some of the eight-by-ten frames had as many as twelve photos in them—from wallet-size school pictures to four-by-six, where sometimes an unwanted person has been ripped off to make room for somebody's baby.

"I just want to know where Lovey and the kids are," I finally blurt out.

"They usually don't go nowhere but to the store. And they ain't never gone too long 'cause it's just up the street a few blocks."

"I didn't know Lovey was still driving."

"Oh, yeah. She drive better than me."

I hear someone coming down the steps. It's a grungy-looking black guy in his mid- to late thirties. "What up?" he says to me, like I know him. He turns his Kangol cap around apparently so I can see his face.

His teeth are all the wrong color, at least the ones that are there. Joy doesn't seem to notice. He pulls her against his chest and squeezes her harder than necessary. His fingernails are filthy. He kisses her on the lips and says, "See you later, baby," and out the front door he goes.

I feel like throwing up for both of us. "And who in the world was that?"

"That's my friend, Ray Earl."

"Is he a neighbor?"

"No. What would make you ask that?"

"Because I didn't see a car out front."

"Ray Earl takes the bus," she says with a sick kind of pride.

"Do your kids see these guys coming and going?"

"It ain't like I have that many."

"You are making me mad, Joy. Really, really, mad. Are you using drugs?"

"Only when I can afford to. I'm just depressed. Can't you tell?"

"Everybody's depressed. Haven't you noticed? Where's the vacuum?"

"In the closet over there."

"Then why don't you get it and turn it on. I'll pick up these cups and let's get this place cleaned up."

I check Lovey's plastic plants for moisture, but, thank God, they're dry. When Joy fires up a cigarette, I snatch it out of her mouth. "Not in here you don't."

"I only do it when ain't nobody home."

"Well, I'm here and I'm allergic to smoke."

"Since when?"

I want to say since six weeks ago. But Lord knows what she would do with this information. I just give her a "look" and during the next hour she must make at least five trips out to the backyard. She seems to smoke more for pleasure than worry, but I'm getting worried. "Does Lovey usually stay gone for this long without calling?"

"What's the big deal, Marilyn? Damn. She lives in this town. She probably took the kids to the park or something. Chill out."

The kitchen is disgusting. One- and two-quart boilers are on the stove. One is half full of dried pork-'n'-beans. The other with remnants of oatmeal. There are two dead sausage links lying in state in a half inch of cold white grease. The sink is full of dishes, and what on earth could Lovey's hot comb and bumper curling iron be doing on that dish towel? The table has a stack of mail that's higher than the empty cereal bowl it's next to. I flip through the envelopes and notice that at least nine or ten of them are from the bank. They haven't been opened. Which is strange. Even stranger is the fact that they're all addressed to Mr. and Mrs. Herman Dupree. If my daddy has come back to life in Fresno, I guess this should clear it up. I open one envelope.

Inside is a returned check, made payable to Farmer's Insurance Company for $52.31, and stamped across the face of it are the words: ACCOUNT CLOSED. The remaining envelopes all appear to have been written against this same account and in Lovey's handwriting. Looks like she was paying bills, but why would she do this? Something's not right around here, and I don't want to ask Joy.

I'm eating Top Ramen and trying to find a channel on the TV that works without cable when a car finally pulls up. The kids come running in through the front door before it sounds like Lovey has turned off the engine.

"Hi, Aunt Marilyn. Guess what? Lovey got us lost!" LaTiece shouts.

And then right behind her, five-year-old LL. "Her did, her did!"

"Stop yelling," Joy yells. "Where have y'all been?"

"All over," LaTiece says, waving her arms to show the range they covered. She sounds seventeen instead of seven. "It took us forever to get to the store."

"What store?" Joy asks.

Here comes Lovey sashaying through the door like she just learned a new dance step. I don't know how she walked out of this house in that getup. She's wearing a black sequined after-five dress that's too tight, over which she has a gray zip-up sweatshirt. To finish this look, she's got on knee-high stockings that are a shade too light. Her sneakers look brand new. This is hard to swallow, but I just take the plastic bag she's handing me, realizing that she still looks a bit confused, despite that smirk on her face. "Well, hello there, Daughter! What in God's name are you doing sneaking up on us like this?"

Maybe she's kidding. But by the look in her eyes, I can tell that she's not. I walk over and give her a kiss on her cheek. Her skin is still smooth and the color of an old copper penny. It is the one thing on her that is not aging as fast as the rest of her. "Lovey, don't you remember me calling the other day and telling you I was coming down?"

"Nope."

"Seriously?"

"If I did, I'd tell you, now wouldn't I? Here, take this bag for me, would you? My feet feel like they're swelling up."

"What store did you guys go to?" I ask.

"Seven-Eleven," LaTiece says. She is eating a bag of nachos and has a bag of some kind of candy clutched tightly in her other hand.

"What did y'all eat for lunch?" Joy asks her.

LaTiece holds her bags up. LL has disappeared.

"That ain't enough. Where else did y'all go?"

"Nowhere. I told you Lovey got lost and I had to show her how to get us home."

"Hold up," Joy says. "You mean the Seven-Eleven five blocks from here that we always go to?"

LaTiece is shaking her head up and down.

"Well, where the hell did you go, Lovey?"

"If I knew that I would tell you. I thought I just made a wrong turn is all."

"We was on the freeway, Mama!"

"The freeway!"

This feels like a bad sitcom, one that's so bizarre it's not funny. Something is wrong with my mother.

"Can I fix you something to eat, Marilyn? You hungry?" she asks, heading for the kitchen.

"No thanks, Lovey."

"I'm glad to hear you say no 'cause you look like you need to say it more often. You bigger than when I saw you last time."

"Don't remind me. Why don't you go sit down and take it easy."

"I'm fine. Joy, did you water the plants like I asked you to, girl?"

"Yes I did, Lovey."

I walk in the kitchen after my mother and LaTiece follows us. "Wait out there until we come back out," I say to her.

"Why?"

"Because I said so, that's why."

"But you ain't my mama."

I was one second away from snatching that bag out of her hand but all I said was, "I know I'm not your mama, but I'm your auntie which is almost the same thing. Now

I'm only going to say this one more time. Go on back in there and leave me and your grandmother alone for a few minutes."

"You spending the night?"

"Yes!"

"Where you gon' sleep?"

"I don't know, now go!"

She strolls down the short hallway and disappears. Lovey is standing at the stove, turning on all of the eyes.

"Lovey, how are you feeling these days?"

"I feel fine. Sometimes I admit I have a little trouble remembering things, but other than that, I feel just dandy."

I hold up the envelopes. "Do you remember writing these checks?"

She looks at them like she doesn't.

"When was the last time you had a physical, Lovey?"

"I don't know."

"Joy?!"

"What?!"

"Come in here for a minute, would you?"

LaTiece beats her here. "Did I call you?"

She shakes her little head, as if to say, "Too bad, I'm here anyway."

"Joy, when was the last time Lovey had a physical?"

"Whew, let me think."

"Well, when was the last time she went to the doctor?"

Lovey is looking at us both, waiting for the answer.

"Has it been over a year?"

"Probably," Joy says.

"She needs to go," I say. "Because something's not right. And I want her to get checked out."

"You can take her then, since you here."

"But I've gotta go home tomorrow."

"Well, ain't that just too bad. You the one who opened your big mouth."

"You know what I want to do?" Lovey says.

"No, what do you want to do?" I ask.

"I would like to move out of this dump and someplace where somebody can help me do things that's getting hard for me to do. I don't want to cook another meal or mop another floor. I want to live where I can make some friends my own age who might have health problems but can still walk and talk, anything to get me away from these brats and this trifling daughter who got the wrong name—Joy, my foot—as soon as humanly possible."

It is hard for me to believe that this is my mother talking. In fact, she used to say she should charge extra to all the women who sat in her kitchen chair while she pressed and curled their hair just complaining away about their husbands and gossiping to no end about this person and the next, and Lovey would just say the same thing over and over: "I know what you mean, sugar," and for some reason they always felt consoled. She never repeated a word they said because she said then she would be part of the mess and "if you don't start no *mess*, won't be no *mess*." This was one reason why she never lost a customer. "Do you realize what you just said here, Lovey?"

"Oh, she knows, all right," Joy says. "I told you she can be herself and then turn on you like a pit bull. You didn't believe me, but here's the proof," she says, and storms on up the stairs.

"You need to shut up, girl! I know exactly what I'm saying and it don't matter if I forget this, because I got it all wrote down," Lovey says.

"What do you have written down?" I ask Lovey.

"What to do if I ever get too sick and can't think for myself."

"And where is this written down?"

"On that piece of paper with little lines on it. I filled it out a long time ago when Joy took me to the hospital."

"When did Joy take you to the hospital?"

"A long time ago."

"For what? What was wrong with you?"

"I don't remember but I didn't die in the ambulance so it couldn'ta been all that bad."

"Ambulance? Why didn't . . . oh, never mind. Do you remember where you put that piece of paper, Lovey?"

"It's somewhere safe. That's all I know. Go find it."

"I will," I say, without knowing whether she's telling the truth or not.

I sleep in a twin bed with LaTiece. She apparently rocks in her sleep, too. I slide my arms around her waist and she snuggles even closer to me, as if no one ever hugs her like this.

When I hear somebody walking around I get up. It's coming from Joy's room. I hope it's not a man. I walk down there. Her door is cracked. I tap it open and there's Lovey standing next to Joy's bed. I hear her snoring. I open the door and go in. "Lovey," I whisper, "what are you doing in here?"

She doesn't answer me but is staring down at Joy. "We should just take a pillow and hold it over her face," she says.

I tap her on her shoulder. "Come on, Lovey, let's go back to sleep."

She turns to leave without being ushered. I walk her back downstairs to her room. She gets in bed and I pull the covers under her chin. "Good night," she says, and closes her eyes. I wipe the perspiration mixed with tears from mine.

In the morning I'm shocked when I don't throw up. Even after I smell LaTiece's bubblegum toothpaste and bacon coming up the stairs. I must be over the hump. And although Lovey's been going to the same doctor for the past four or five years, she doesn't remember his name. It takes me almost an hour to find it. I'm put on hold for what feels like another hour but when the doctor finally gets on the line, I explain who I am and the reason why I'm calling instead of Lovey. He suggests that she have a complete blood workup before coming in for her physical. I tell him how far I have to drive. He says she can have it done on the same day but the results won't be back for a few days. He'll call me to discuss what he finds. He gives me back to the receptionist to schedule them both.

At breakfast, I tell Lovey that I'll be back down to take

her. She seems happy. "Joy, why did you have to take Lovey to the emergency room?"

"What in the world are you talking about, Marilyn? I ain't never had to take Lovey to no hospital and definitely not in no ambulance."

"But that's what she said last night, didn't you, Lovey?"

"I don't know, girl."

"I told you, didn't I?" Joy says like she's pleased.

"Regardless if it's true or not, please, do not under any circumstances let her get behind the wheel of that car. Promise me that?"

"Yeah. Well . . ."

"I don't want that huzzie driving my car! She's too reckless and she drinks too much!"

"Lovey, why don't you shut the hell up!" Joy says.

"Who in the hell do you think you're talking to?"

LL walks over and hits Lovey on her butt and I grab him by his SpongeBob pajama top. "Have you lost your mind, boy?"

"Her being mean to my mama again and I don't like it!"

"I don't care what you don't LIKE, that's your grand-mother and you do not for any reason EVER put your hands on her like that, do you understand me?"

He crosses his bony arms like he's got nothing to say.

"Do you understand me?"

Not a word.

"Joy, you better get this boy. And tell him something before I snatch a knot in his little behind, I'm not playing."

"LL don't hit your grandma."

He cuts his eyes at me and uncrosses his arms.

"I ain't never hit Lovey," LaTiece says. "Even when she's mean to me."

"I ain't never mean to you and you know it."

"Okay, let's just stop this children's version of the *Jerry Springer Show*," I say.

"What she talking about?" LL asks.

"Jerry Springer, LL. You know, when they throw chairs at each other and fight on TV?" LaTiece says with entirely too much authority.

He just nods.

"Joy."

"What now?"

"If you have an ounce of sense, just promise me that you will not drive that car under the influence of anything stronger than Coca-Cola."

"Give me some credit. Do you really think I'd put my kids' lives in danger? Or mine or your mother's?"

"Yes, you would," Lovey says. "But I'm not getting in the car with you behind the wheel. No way."

"First of all, let me set the record straight here. I ain't nobody's alcoholic. I just like to get a buzz, and personally I like herb a lot better, okay?"

"What herbs?" Lovey asks.

"Joy, how do the kids get to school?"

"We ride the bus," LaTiece answers for her.

Hearing this brings me some relief.

"Look, I promise I won't drive if I'm too stoked," Joy says. "Now tell me this, who turned on all the eyes on the stove and left 'em on all night?"

Lovey slowly looks around the kitchen at the kids and then me, waiting for one of us to confess.

Chapter 7

Arthurine is sitting in the living room with a man who looks like a mortician. "Hello," I say.

"Why hello there, sugar. You must be Marilyn," he says, getting up from the sofa. What a little shrimp of a man he is. I can see how he used to be handsome. Arthurine jumps up to stand near him, as if she's protecting him from me.

"Marilyn, this is my very good friend, Prezelle Goodenough. I told you about him, remember?"

"Yes, I do. Very nice to meet you, Mr. Goodenough."

"Please call me Prezelle. I've been admiring your lovely home. Arthurine gave me a tour and showed me some of those very unusual whatnots you made. This lampshade, for instance," he says, pointing to an old lamp I repainted the base of and covered the shade with about a trillion tiny beads. It was always ugly. I was bored. And after I finished, I felt like I'd resurrected it.

But some of the stuff I make does not work for every-body, including me, sometimes.

"Anyway," he says, leaning forward, "I don't rightly understand some of their appeal, but different strokes for different folks. Now, I do like this here pillow," he says, pointing to a black-and-purple suede thing.

"Why, thank you, sir," is the only response I can think of.

Arthurine is actually blushing. She is also wearing her favorite tinted glasses that have slid down her nose until they look like they're pinching it. There are two empty cups on the coffee table in front of the sofa and a saucer with a few Girl Scout cookies on it that have been in the pantry since last year.

"You two go right ahead with what you were doing. I didn't mean to interrupt."

"We're just getting to know each other better," Arthurine says as Prezelle nods his head up and down in agreement. His hair is almost white and his cheekbones are so big they look like golf balls. "Oh, by the way, Mar-ilyn, I think you may have quite a few messages because that phone's been ringing off the hook."

"Thank you, Arthurine."

"You're quite welcome. And how's Lovey doing these days?"

"She's fine. Everybody's fine."

"Praise God," she says.

"Will you be staying for dinner, Prezelle?" I ask. I'm praying he says no because I do not feel like cooking.

"I wish I could," Prezelle says. "But tonight's bingo night where I live."

"Sounds like big fun," I say. "Maybe some other time."

Arthurine looks at him like she's bursting with good news. "I've been invited to play, too," she says.

"But isn't tonight Bible study?"

"I know the Bible baby—backward and forward—I just like to go as a kind of refresher. It won't hurt to miss a class every now and then. Besides, I haven't played bingo in years and something tells me I might get lucky tonight," she says, giving Prezelle what I presume is her sexy look.

"Well, that's just great," I say, even more pleased that I don't have to drive her.

"But it would be nice if you could give us a lift and pick me up about what time, Prezelle?"

"Well, that depends on how long you want to play, Reeney. It's usually over about ten or ten-thirty."

Reeney? I'm smiling at this Sudden Senior Sex Goddess in her purple and pink paisley jogging suit. Arthurine's cheeks seem extra rosy today. "Well, maybe Leon can pick you up. Just let me know when you two want to leave."

"About six if that's all right with you," Prezelle says. "I'm right up the hill. Not even ten minutes away."

I look at my watch. It's only a quarter to two. "No problem. About what time does bingo start?"

"Seven sharp. In order to get a good seat."

"Well, what are you going to do for fifty whole minutes, Arthurine?"

"She can either sit downstairs in the lobby where she might get bored or bothered by nosey folks wondering who she is, or she can come up to my apartment and wait until I get cleaned up," Prezelle says matter-of-factly.

My first thoughts are: is it safe for an old lady to be in an apartment with an old man? But what on earth could they possibly do that wouldn't be kosher? I can think of absolutely nothing. "I'll be ready at six then," I say, and head into the kitchen, past the laundry room. I smell bleach, but it's not making me nauseous. I'm relieved to be getting over morning sickness and able to tolerate certain smells again. While I deliberate whether to eat an apple or a bear claw, I hit PLAY on the message machine:

"Marilyn, this is Paulette! And Bunny! And we've got an extra ticket to see Jill Scott tonight at the Paramount and we want you to get your dead behind out of the house and come with us. Your husband can't come. We know you're preggers so take a nap. We won't take no for an answer. Fifth-row seats, girl. Don't bother calling back, just be standing outside the box office at seven sharp."

Shit. Arthurine has a date. Lord only knows what time Leon's coming home. Too bad, I'm going. I bite into the bear claw. I'm not on a diet which is why it probably tastes better than ever.

"Hello, Mom, this is Spencer. How are you? Fine I'm sure. Look. I wanted to ask you something and you can run it past Dad or not. I wanted to bring a friend home with me for spring break. She's never been to California and I wanted to show her around. But I need to know by today in order to get the cheapest fares online. So call me back as soon as you get this message, okay? Thanks. Love you. Hi to Dad and Grandma. Oh, Simeon's got some really cool news to share with you, but I won't spoil it. Would you mind if we went up to the cabin to ski for a couple of days—no parents—if you don't mind? You've got my cell number. Love you."

She?

I call Spencer first. "Yo, Mom. What up? You got my message?"

"Yo? When did you start saying that word?"

"It's just a cool way of saying hello, that's all."

"When did you get so hip?"

"If you don't like it, I won't say it."

"I'll think about it. It just sounds so out of character. Now who is this girl you want to bring home?"

"Her name is Brianna. She's sweet. You'll love her, Mom. She's smart, she's in the premed program. She's from Georgia and she is truly a peach."

"Is she your girlfriend, then?"

"Well, let's just say we've been getting to know each other better week by week."

"Is she your girlfriend or not? Don't play games with me, Spencer."

"Will it make a difference in whether or not she can come?"

"Of course it does."

"Then, yes. She's my girlfriend."

"I've got to run this by your father, but as far as I can tell, it doesn't seem like it should pose much of a problem. She can sleep in the guest room."

"You don't think Dad'll trip, do you, Mom?"

"Why should he? He brought me home for Thanksgiving to meet his parents. I would like to talk to her parents, just to make sure this is okay with them."

"Mom, she's almost twenty-one years old!"

"So what! You're only nineteen!"

"What if I told you she was adopted and doesn't know who her parents are?"

"I'm ignoring you now. What's the deal with Simeon?" I ask. Spencer always was the bolder, quicker one of the two. But Simeon was also more poised and reserved, held his cards face down on the table until he had to turn them over. I liked both qualities about them.

"Sim's doing great. He hasn't called you guys?"

"I don't have a message from him. What's he up to?"

"He should tell you, not me. But you'll be proud."

"You're driving me crazy, Spencer. At least give me some clue as to what's going on."

"Call him!"

"Why hasn't he called me?"

"Because he's been busy rehearsing. Oh, shit!"

"What did you just say?"

"My bad. I meant, oh, shoot."

"Rehearsing for what?"

"Well, let me just say that all those piano and saxophone and guitar lessons are paying off. And I'll leave it at that. I gotta run, Mom. Love you. Later."

I dial Simeon's number. When he answers I can barely hear him because of the music blasting in the background. "HELLO!"

"MA, GIVE ME FIFTEEN MINUTES AND I'LL CALL YOU RIGHT BACK!"

"OKAY," I scream and hang up.

I go upstairs to hunt for something interesting to wear that might actually fit. I feel like I may have already gained five or six pounds just since I found out I'm pregnant. As I walk along Leon's side of the closet to get a better view of my own, my leg bumps into a bag. As I go to push it back, I realize there are quite a few of them stacked on the shelf under his suits and sport coats. It's obvious they were being concealed. But why? I take them into the bedroom. Bags from Macy's, Nordstrom's, Foot Locker, Mr. Rags. I peek inside each bag before taking the items out because I can't believe my eyes. Leon's been doing some major shopping. But these clothes look too hip and sporty for his conservative taste: jerseys like the twins wear, Sean Jean and Enyce shirts, an assortment of Rocawear T-shirts and baggy blue jeans that look too small, a pair of Air Force Ones like we got LL last year for Christmas and even a pair of those suede ankle boots all the rappers wear. And Kangol hats just like the ones Samuel Jackson sports. Is he tripping? Maybe these are going to be a surprise for the twins when they come home for spring break. But upon closer inspection, I realize they're all Leon's size.

I want to laugh, but there's a part of me that's pissed. Have I missed something? I don't want to embarrass him, so maybe I'll just wait for him to make an appearance in one of these getups before saying anything.

The phone is ringing as I head out of the closet. "Simeon?"

"No, it's me, Leon. What's going on?"

I turn toward the closet with a smirk on my face. "Nothing, Snoop Dogg! You tell me."

"What the hell is that supposed to mean, Marilyn?"

"Did you just swear at me?"

"No, I didn't swear *at* you. And please, don't you start. I've got these assholes breathing down my back here, and I'm ready to get on a rocket and head straight for the moon and just say, fuck it all!"

"Leon, are you okay?" He just said the f-word. I've never heard him say the f-word before. Ever.

"I'm just tired of playing this game."

"What game?" This is all news to me.

"The try-to-stay-on-top game. It just doesn't add up," he says.

"What are you talking about?"

"Never mind. Look, I have to meet a potential client at seven and probably won't even be home until ten or eleven."

"Then we have a problem."

"What kind of problem?"

"Your mother has a date and needs a ride home."

"Mother has a what?"

"You heard me. A date."

"With whom?"

"Her friend Prezelle."

"Pre-who?"

"He walks the mall with her and rides on the bus that takes them. He's downstairs right now. They're playing bingo at his complex and I promised to drop her off but I can't pick her up."

"Why not?"

"Because I'm going to a concert."

"You're going to a what?"

"You heard me. What? Are you going deaf? A concert."

"What concert?"

"Jill Scott."

"Who is Jill Scott?"

"She's a down-to-earth jazzy bluesy hip-hop-ish, R&B, sexy sister who writes and sings the kind of songs that tell the truth and speak to us but it wouldn't hurt for you to listen to her CD since we don't have an extra ticket and plus you're not invited."

"Who are you going with? Wait, let me guess. The Queens of Oakland: Paulette and Bunny."

"Good guess."

"But it's a weekday, Marilyn."

"Yeah, and the world turns three hundred and sixty-five days, Leon, not just Friday through Sunday. I'm going because I need to get out of this house and be sociable and you need to figure out how to get your mother home from B-I-N-G-O because I can't do it."

"Then she'll just have to stay home."

"Then you'll just have to tell her."

"I can't. I'm almost late for my meeting as it is."

"Well, that's just too bad, isn't it? I'm also tired, Leon. Tired of being the mule that carries the burden for everything and everybody in this house."

"But who pays for everything?"

"You may pay in dollars but I pay in sense. And by the way, Spencer's bringing his girlfriend home for spring break. Got a problem with that?"

"No, I don't. What about Simeon?"

"I don't know yet. All I know is I think he's in a band."

"A what?"

"Oh, stop it, would you, Leon! Call me back when you can hear better." Click. I hang up. But, I'm certainly not going to leave her out there stranded.

The phone rings again immediately. "What is it now?"

"Mom, it's me. Simeon."

"Hi, Sim. Sorry for yelling. What are you doing? What's with the loud music? And are you and Spencer and Brianna all on the same flight?"

"Whoa. Slow down, Mom. First of all, I can't come home for spring break."

"Why not?"

"Because I'm in a band and we've got a gig at this really cool jazz club here in Atlanta and it's a great opportunity and I don't want to blow it."

"When did you become part of a band?"

"Not long after we got here. Some dudes who could play were trying to hook up this sound and we worked it out."

"What do you mean by 'this sound'?"

"It's called jazz fusion. It's a combination of jazz, rock, the blues, a little country. It's sweet."

"That's nice. But you haven't quit school or anything stupid like that, have you?"

"No no no no. I'm not crazy, Mom. But I am changing my major."

"To what?"

"Computer music and its applications."

"To *what*?" Now I'm sounding like Leon.

"It's basically a new form of music production."

"Your father's going to have a stroke."

"I don't see why, it's my life."

"I couldn't agree more."

"So, it's all right with you?"

"It's fine with me, Simeon. Just as long as you know what you're doing."

"I think I do. And when I don't, I'll call. Isn't that what you always told us to do?"

"Yep."

"Well, look, Mom, we're rehearsing like mad hours and we're videotaping our best session and I'll send it to you on the computer to check out."

"Wow, technology is something. You do that," I say.

"Oh, and I haven't met Brianna. Just Morgan, Faith, Dasia, Nadine, and Chanelle. Your other son is quite the

Casanova down here in Atlanta, you know, but you didn't hear it from me. Love you. Peace out."

Peace out?

Prezelle's senior citizen facility is really a very nice apartment complex. They have a better view of the bay and San Francisco than we do from our house. I tell Arthurine that I'll try to be here between ten and ten-thirty to pick her up. Jill may have sung enough of my favorites by then to hold me for a while. I do not, however, bother to tell Mr. Spitfire.

I look through the buzzing crowd for someone tall that's sparkling and has lots of cleavage, and I spot Bunny. She's waving to get my attention, or to get attention, which she gets, as she gulps the rest of her drink down. "I can't believe you actually bailed yourself out of Housewife Prison to join the party people, Marilyn. Two stars for you!"

"Baby and all!" Paulette says from behind, pinching me on my butt. Thank God she has finally taken those dreadful braids out of her hair. Now it looks like a short curly wig, but when I turn around to hug her, I can see her scalp. It's her own hair! Her eyes, however, are now green. Dare I say anything?

"I'm here to enjoy myself, not to be ridiculed, so shut up and let's go sit down."

Jill is sold out. People are standing outside, begging to buy unused tickets. Luckily our seats are good. Bunny has all kinds of connections. A pleasant group warms up the crowd, but we're waiting to be wooed by the woman herself. I tilt my head back to look up at the paintings on the domed ceiling of this magnificent theater, which has been painstakingly restored to what appears to be its original state. My head swirls to follow the floating women whose eyes look both sad and happy. I'm feeling drunk from the vastness of the ceiling, the flowers, and the sudden appearance of angels.

A tap-tap-tap on my shoulder brings me back down to earth. A baritone voice from close behind me says, "Don't tell me you still haven't found what you're looking for, Marilyn?"

The weight of Gordon's words enter my eardrum like heat. I don't believe this. But when I turn around, there he is, my first husband, the man I knew for sure was my soul mate, the man who was so smart and courageous that he scared me. I divorced him because he wanted me to know who I was before I was ready. His love was impatient. Mine, too young. He had too much faith in me. More than I had in myself. He was the first person to tell me that if I used my eyes and hands together, one day I would be an artist. I didn't believe him. I hadn't created anything. He had all kinds of gifts. He taught others how to accept magic. I resisted. His heart was like a sponge. He cared fiercely about our condition as black people. He was not afraid of the world or his role in it. I wasn't sure what mine was. It was his clarity and vision that first appealed to me, but then I found it intimidating. Because he expected more of me than I even knew I had to give. And when you're scared, you back away.

"Well, how in the world are you after all these years, Gordon?"

"I'm fine. Older." He leans back in his seat. Smiles at me out of the corner of his eye. His moustache is mixed with gray. His dreadlocks are, too. He might not even be handsome but he looks like he stands for something. Before I can utter a word, he says, "You look good. I saw you come in but didn't want to say anything."

"Why not?"

"I don't know. You just looked majestic in that purple. Like nobody should have too much to say to you tonight."

"That's what I'm doing here. Jill will say it."

"I'm here for the same reasons."

"Hi, I'm Bunny, Marilyn's best friend."

"And I'm Paulette, her less-nosey friend."

"Hello, Bunny and Paulette. I'm Gor—"

"We know who you are, sweetheart," Bunny says.

"Nice to meet you, Gordon. Enjoy the show." Paulette must have pinched Bunny or something because she jerks away from her, then snatches the mint from her hand that Paulette was about to put in her mouth.

"Same here, ladies." He leans forward. I can feel his breath on my neck. I am uncomfortable. "Good seeing you," he says, and squeezes my shoulder to show that he means it.

I hear Jill's smooth voice coming from behind the black curtain and Gordon whispers, "Just tell me one thing, Marilyn. Are you happy?"

Jill walks out on stage. She is wearing orange and she

is big and beautiful and sexy and proud. Before I join Bunny and Paulette as Jill's backup singers, I turn and whisper back to Gordon, "Do I look happy?"

"You ho!" Paulette says, squeezing me by my elbow.

"I'm telling your husband you cheated on him on your first night out of the house! You're worse than a preacher's daughter!"

"What exactly have I done? Nothing. Except run into my ex-husband and said hello. That's it!"

"He gave you his business card. Where is it?"

I reach inside my purse. "Right here. What's the big deal."

Bunny snatches it out of my hand. "He's a high school principal?"

"That's nice," Paulette says.

"He doesn't look like any principal I've ever come across."

"You weren't married to him but a hot minute if I remember correctly, right?" Paulette asks.

"Three months. And don't ask."

"He wasn't wearing a wedding ring. I looked," Bunny said.

"You guys are making too much out of this. I've gotta go pick up my mother-in-law. Thanks for inviting me and I'll see you two scuzz-buckets later."

We kiss each other on the cheek and by the time I hit Skyline Boulevard and look out and see the lights of San Francisco I feel a sense of delight.

Arthurine is sitting out on the bench with Prezelle

when I pull up. He walks her to the car and opens the door. I think I hear a smooch. She gets in and he bends down to wave as we drive off. "I told you I felt lucky tonight," she says, holding up two fake twenty-dollar bills. "God is sure good. He gives you just what you need just when you need it. Wouldn't you agree?"

I'm almost ashamed when I feel myself grinning and nodding in total agreement.

Chapter 8

"hanks for picking up Mother," Leon shouts from the bathroom.

"You're welcome," I say dryly. I'm in bed, trying to finish a novel I started two months ago. "But what if I hadn't?"

"I thought she was going to stay home."

"I told you she had a date."

"She's too old to date. And this will be her first and last."

"Just who do you think you are?"

"I'm her son, that's who!" and he slams the bathroom door. I hear him in the shower. I hear him brush his teeth. And then the door opens. I haven't flipped a page yet.

"Arthurine is a sixty-eight-year-old widow. If she wants to spend time with a seventy-one-year-old man, it's her prerogative and her business! Not yours!" I realize I like yelling, too.

"What can they possibly do at their age to entertain each other?"

"All kinds of things. Tonight they played bingo."

"Well that should raise her blood pressure. Surely they can't have sex."

"You don't know that, now do you?"

"The thought itself is disgusting. And how in God's name . . ."

"The same way you do. He probably has help." I'd love to say *and you might want to look into getting some aid yourself.*

He looks repulsed. "What do you feel like watching tonight?"

"Nothing."

"Now what's wrong?"

"I'm waiting."

"Waiting for what?" he asks, and I can tell he's looking for the remote, which of course is under his pillow but I'm not budging. He's now also wrapped in a plaid flannel bathrobe that just barely ties.

"For my apology."

"Apology for what?"

I snap my book shut and look at him like he's crazy. "Think hard, Leon."

He pretends to be thinking hard, but of course he's drawing a blank because his mind is on that fucking remote.

"Yesterday? You not only yelled but you also swore at me."

"I did not!" he says, yelling again. Maybe he really is going deaf. Just like his mother claims she is.

"You did, too."

"I simply stated that I was just feeling the pressure of bidding on yet another job and how draining it's becoming."

"So that's how you see it?"

"I did not swear at you and I certainly didn't raise my voice."

"Fine. No harm done," I say. He knows I don't mean it. I know I don't mean it.

"Would you like to go to dinner tomorrow night?"

I feel like jumping out of the bed and drop-kicking him in his big fat stomach. But I stay put. "No."

"Why not?" he asks, looking in the drawer of his night table, then under the bed, then has the nerve to walk over to the TV and looks around it. Of course it's not there, but would it occur to him to turn the fucking thing on manually? He totters back and stands at the foot of his side of the bed, looking stumped.

"Because I just don't feel like it."

"How do you know how you're going to be feeling tomorrow?"

"I don't. But I know right now that I don't want to go out to dinner."

"Why not?"

"I just told you, Leon!"

"You haven't told me anything."

"Because it's boring."

"I've got reservations at Chez Panisse."

"Yahoo."

"Look, what's really bothering you?"

"Nothing."

"Is it the baby issue?"

"The baby 'issue'? Oh, so it's an issue, is it? No, that's not it, and so what if it was? I've got eight more months to deal with the *issue*."

"I didn't mean it that way. What I meant was it's both our problem."

"You know what, Leon. Just be quiet, would you? I'm not going to hold the baby hostage because I'm pissed at its father."

"Look, can we just stop talking and go to sleep?"

"Wait a minute. Let's be honest with each other for a moment, shall we?"

I cross my arms. I'm ready for this.

"Can you look me in the eye and tell me that you really want to have a baby after nineteen years?"

"No, I don't."

"Finally, an honest answer. How do the kids feel about this?"

"I haven't told them yet."

"Why haven't you?"

"Because at my age, Leon, I'm going to have to take a test to make sure it's going to be healthy."

"Understood. When will the boys be home?"

"Spencer's getting in next Friday and he's bringing a girl and Simeon's not coming."

"What? Who? Why not?"

"He's in a band and they're playing at some club."

"For crying out loud. A band? What kind of band could he possibly have time to be in with the course load he's carrying?"

"Apparently enough. He's in a jazz band. And just so you won't be the last to know: he's also changing his major from computer engineering to some kind of music producing or something. Good night."

"Has he gone and lost his fucking mind?"

"Not like you have."

He takes off his robe and then starts pacing the floor. His plaid boxers are so tight they should be briefs.

"And by the *fucking* way. I need you to pick Spencer and his girlfriend up at the airport because I have a doctor's appointment."

"What time next Friday?"

"Four-thirty."

"I absolutely can't."

"And why not?"

"I just started working out with a personal trainer and he's giving me my nutritional assessment, my meal plan, and all these supplements to help me burn fat and build muscle, and I can't miss it."

"Sorry for the inconvenience, Mr. La Lanne," I say, trying not to laugh even though I'm really pissed just listening to this bullshit. "You're serious, too, aren't you?"

"I told you I was going to start working out and I meant it. Can't they take a cab? Or can't you change the time of your doctor's appointment?"

"No, I can't. Because that's the day I hear the heartbeat."

"Really."

"Don't get so excited," I say, as I reach under his pillow and toss him the remote. He catches it, looking quite relieved. "I'll just get his real father to meet them at the airport because he won't mind," I say, as I pull the covers over my head to drown him out.

"Mom, I need your help," Sabrina is saying. She has once again stopped by unannounced, but I don't really mind. "I feel horrible! Why didn't you tell me being pregnant makes you feel so miserable in the mornings?"

"You never asked," I say. "It doesn't last. Just a few more weeks is all."

"Can you remember if you got nauseous in the mornings?"

"I did."

"And what did you do?"

"I ate saltines and drank club soda."

"Well, I'm going to the acupuncturist tomorrow. They say it can do wonders and it's safe, don't worry."

"I'm not. I've got too many other things on my mind and I know you're no dummy."

"What's pressing down on your mind?"

"Lovey, for one."

"What's wrong?"

"I think she's getting or has Alzheimer's."

"For real? How do you know? What makes you say that?"

"Quite a few things, really. Sometimes she says things on the phone that don't make a lot of sense. She doesn't call me like she used to. And when I call her, sometimes I don't even think she really knows it's me. She whispers. She's been watering fake plants and last week she got lost driving to the Seven-Eleven which is five blocks from her house."

"Wow. What are you going to do to help her?"

"I can't really help her, but I'm going back out there in a few weeks to take her to the doctor to get a complete physical and be tested."

"I thought they couldn't test for that?"

"Well, they can rule out things, that's what I've seen on the Internet and some TV specials about it."

"Lovey with Alzheimer's? That's a hard one for me to even fathom."

"It's what I'm thinking. Maybe I'm wrong. I'm hoping I am."

"Let me know if there's anything I can do to help. How's Aunt Joy?"

"The same."

"Is she working?"

"What do you think?"

"Well, how's LL and LaTiece?"

"They're about two years away from being candidates for juvenile hall, thanks to their loving, caring mother."

"How old are they now?"

"LL is five and Tiecey is seven."

"Kids grow up so fast. Seems like they were just born!"

"They were."

"Oh, wait. I see the mailman. I'll go get it for you."

I stand here in the kitchen and watch my daughter. She has her whole life ahead of her. I know it's terrible of me to even be thinking this, but I can't help it. I wish she wasn't pregnant. I wish she had waited. She's only twenty-two. I had hoped she'd go to graduate school like she planned and not do what I did: take a quarter of a century detour. Men don't usually give up their plans for us and I'll be glad when we stop being so accommodating. I want to tell her again that being in love is a good thing but it shouldn't mean you have to forfeit your dreams. Babies are not romantic. They require attention and care and almost all of your time. They don't disappear. They grow up right in front of your eyes. But you won't see it happening. You'll wonder how the years went by so fast. Which is why this is the time in her life she should be exploring the world, and her role in it. But now is not the time to repeat this.

I was just about to make a peach smoothie right before Sabrina walked in, since I don't have to be at Heavenly Creations until noon. Arthurine's been gone since early this morning, and Snuffy must still be asleep at the foot of her bed. Hallelujah. Sometimes it's hard for me to swallow when he's in the same room. I drop about eight frozen peaches into the blender along with half a banana and a splash of orange juice. I'm reaching to get the vanilla soy when Sabrina comes back with a huge pile of mail.

"Wow, I didn't know you guys get so much junk, Mom!"

"We normally don't get this much."

She's curious and flips past the bills. "What do we have here?" Her eyes get big. "Mom, why are you getting catalogs from the Academy of Art and California College of Arts and Crafts?"

"I just wanted to look through them."

"Are you thinking of going back to school?"

"Maybe in the future."

"These look like *soon* to me. There are apps in here and everything. Do it, Mom. Please!?"

"I'm just curious, is all. I have no idea if I can even get in." I don't want her to know I've already applied—just in case.

"You can get in. I've seen all of the things you've made. And they're amazing. Dazzling if you don't mind that word. Believe me, you're in. Can I get a smoothie, too, please?"

"Sure," I say, turning on the blender.

"These schools sure aren't cheap, but Dad's loaded and the least he should be willing to do for the woman who raised his children, ran this household, spoon-fed him, and babysat his Loaner Mother (God forgive me for I know not what I say), I think twenty grand a year for tuition is a very small price to compensate you for years of sacrifice. It's time for him to ante up!"

I'm laughing so hard I almost choke on my first sip.

"I'm serious. He owes you. And you owe it to yourself to do whatever you are so moved to do. Hey, Mom. You're forty-four, right?"

"Yes, I am."

"Have you started going through menopause yet? Any signs? I've been seeing stuff about it everywhere."

"I could be."

"Well, when you're certain of it, promise me you won't ever take any of those synthetic laboratory-made things?"

"I promise."

"There's a test you can take to measure your hormone levels. Did you know that?"

"Yep, I'm having it done soon."

"Good. Let me know what you find out. But check this out, Mom. Did you know that forty million of you boomers will all be going through the big 'M' at the same time?"

"Surprise, surprise."

"I think it's so cool. Don't you, Mom?"

"I'm ecstatic," I say, wanting to put an end to this conversation. "Now drink up. I've got to get to work."

Chapter 9

On Friday I leave HC early. I'm nervous, which is why I'm sitting out in this parking lot watching the clock so that I walk in at four-thirty on the dot. I pray I don't have to wait forever. I pray that this is quick. I want to get home in time to make Spencer his favorite: a peach schnapps cake. Plus, I can't wait to meet this Brianna. I hope she's "all that" as the kids say, but then again, if she is *all that* maybe he'll fall too hard too soon. If he hasn't already. Spencer's always been a little fickle when it came to girls. I think he must've fallen in love at least four or five times in his junior year alone. He's too mushy for my taste and so sentimental it's almost embarrassing to watch. Obviously some girls love it. But then again, maybe they don't. He hasn't had one make it through two holidays yet. When they were home for Thanksgiving, Simeon told me that Spencer is almost like a stalker when he falls for a girl because he calls her five and six times a day, and wants to be with her every waking minute. She suffocates. And then flees. Apparently his childish behavior cancels out his good looks and brains. We'll see how this Brianna holds up.

I get out of the car and walk up the steps instead of taking the elevator to the third floor. It's a tiny little office, but lo and behold, an entire wall is full of hundreds of baby pictures. I sign in. The receptionist, who is black and looks like she can't be more than eighteen or nineteen, hands me the clipboard with the standard forms to be filled out. "The doctor will be with you shortly," she says. "Can I get you anything?"

"No, thanks, I'm fine." I say hello to three very pregnant women all reading parenting magazines. It's easy to see that they're in their early thirties. To my surprise, there are only two very generic forms, which take me less than a couple of minutes to complete. I'm now prepared to wait. *Forever.* I lean my head back and close my eyes for a second. *I'm in the delivery room. My husband is not my husband anymore so he's not here. Gordon is holding my hand. Paulette is rubbing my left foot. Bunny looks like she's about to faint. For some reason I am not having any contractions and don't even have to push. A baby girl pops out! Everybody claps. Whoops! Not quite finished. Here comes another one! Twins again! Aren't you lucky, the doctor says?*

"Marilyn Grimes?"

Is that my name I just heard?

"Marilyn?" the young girl says.

I open my eyes and sit up straight. "Yes. Sorry."

"It happens a lot here."

I look at my watch. Only five minutes have passed.

A door opens and a striking Middle Eastern woman with long black hair holds her hand out. She looks young enough to be my daughter. "Hello, Marilyn. I'm Doctor Rageh. Very nice to meet you. Is your husband here with you today?"

"No. He had another commitment."

"That's fine. Won't you follow me, please?"

We go into a room smaller than my pantry. There's a tiny TV, and a large silver machine next to where I've been asked to lie down after I undress. The doctor leaves. I remove my lavender sweatshirt and sweatpants. It feels spooky in here. I'm scared. Freezing. I don't know what I'm doing in this room. And I should not have come alone. I don't care that I've done this twice before. This time feels different. Like I should be me twenty years ago and not the *me* I am now.

I open my gown and look at my soft brown belly. Is it beginning to swell already? I wish I could see inside. The longer I stare, it dawns on me that this whole process, this amazing experience, is really a blessing, which makes this baby a gift. Why didn't I see this before? When I hear a tap-tap on the door, I say, "Come on in."

"So, Marilyn. How're you feeling these days?"

"Tired. Hungry. Fat. But I haven't thrown up in almost two weeks, so I'm not complaining."

"Good," she says looking over my chart. "Dr. Hilton sent over your medical history and pregnancy test results, so it looks like you should be about ten weeks which would make your due date about September twenty-first. I'm sure you've been taking the prenatal vitamins she prescribed, right?"

"I have."

"And I see here she's discussed with you the risks involved with a pregnancy for a woman at your age, right?"

"She did, but I pretty much know what they are. I've done a lot of research on this and I can tell you right now that I want to take the CVS test instead of the amnio."

"It's your choice. You can actually have that done from this stage on, preferably in the next few weeks."

"Good."

"I also see that you've got three children."

"I do. Nineteen-year-old twin boys who're away at college and a twenty-two-year-old daughter."

"Are the twins identical or fraternal? Just curious."

"Fraternal. In fact, they actually have different birthdays: Spencer was born at eleven fifty-seven p.m. and Simeon popped out six minutes after the clock struck midnight."

"Wow, that's amazing! So, tell me, Marilyn, how do you feel about this pregnancy?"

"Well, to be honest, at first I was just in shock, because I thought I was going through menopause."

"You probably are."

"And then I resented this happening because I felt like the next eighteen years of my life were being taken away from me."

"That's understandable."

"It is?"

"Of course. You've been a caregiver and nurturer for

a long time, and now you feel like it's time to nurture yourself."

"This is so true. I mean, I was even thinking of going back to school to get my master's."

"What's to stop you? Babies don't rob you of anything. If possible, you get help and learn to manage your time more wisely."

"I know. That's pretty much how I'm feeling now."

"Good. So today, let's see if we can hear your baby's heartbeat."

"Okay." I lie down on the flat table like a corpse.

"Now, just relax and try to breathe normally. I'm going to rub some gel all over your belly. It's going to feel very cold at first but it acts as a conductor so I can hear better. You know all this, right?"

"I think I remember."

I forgot that this stuff feels like icy hot! She places the stethoscope in her ears, then leans forward and starts rubbing the metal wand at the base of it all over my belly. After five or six minutes of this, she pulls her stethoscope from her ears and lets it fall on her shoulders.

"Is something wrong?" I ask.

"Well, I'm having a heck of a time finding this little creature, it's so tiny. It's probably hiding. Tell you what. Let's look for it another way. Watch that little screen over there."

I say nothing but watch the little black monitor as she rubs another instrument all over my stomach, while looking back and forth at the screen. I don't see anything except what looks like a neon green graph. She rubs on more gel and continues the search, even more carefully, as if she missed a spot. Then she stands straight up.

"What's wrong?"

"I didn't see a heartbeat."

"What's that mean?"

"It means that the baby has no heartbeat."

"Are you sure?"

"I could see the fetus but no heartbeat and there should be one at this stage."

"So, are you saying that my baby is dead?"

She looks at me, eye-to-eye, woman-to-woman, not doctor-to-patient, and I can see she's trying to keep a neutral face when she says, "I'm afraid it is. I'm so sorry."

For a split second, I don't know who this woman is. And why are my clothes off? When she touches my arm and then squeezes my hand, I realize that a lot has just happened. I can't believe that fifteen minutes ago I was pregnant. And now I'm not. I suppose she was waiting for me to scream or burst into tears but I don't. "Could I have caused this?"

"I don't think so. Marilyn, I'm sure you're aware of how much harder it is to get a healthy egg after forty, and that the odds of carrying a pregnancy to term decrease even further."

"Yeah, but . . ."

"Tell me something. Have you been exercising heavily?"

"I wish I knew how."

"Taking any medications you didn't disclose?"

"No."

"Okay, then. So. You've experienced what we refer to as a missed abortion."

"A what?"

"I know it sounds terrible, but it just means that the fetus has miscarried, or died, and hasn't been expelled."

"But I haven't been bleeding. Haven't had any cramping. Nothing."

"Miscarriages can occur in a variety of different ways."

I say the word "miscarriage" in my head. I even spell it: m-i-s-c-a-r-r-i-a-g-e. "A miscarriage of justice," I say aloud.

"Are you okay?" the doctor asks.

"I'm not okay but I'm okay. How old are you?"

"Thirty-five."

"Do you have children?"

"A six-month-old and a three-year-old. Both boys."

"That's nice. Very nice."

"Do you need a few minutes alone?"

"No, don't leave yet. Please."

"Okay. Now. I know you're saddened by this news, but we need to shift our focus a little to your health. Since the fetus and placenta tissue are still inside you, in order to avoid the risk of your getting infected, instead of waiting for you to expel it, it would be wise for you to have a D and C as soon as possible."

"How soon?"

"Soon. Have you ever had an abortion before?"

"Unfortunately, yes."

"This is pretty much the same kind of procedure. I think the earliest opening at the hospital is Tuesday or Wednesday, if that works for you."

"Hospital?"

"It's strictly on an outpatient basis."

"Tuesday."

I just sit there while she tells me that I'll need to stop in late Monday to get some seaweed sticks inserted into my cervix to help make the surgery go smoother. It'll only take a few minutes. That I might feel mild cramps but it's nothing to be concerned about. That I'll only be at the hospital about four or five hours. That someone should drive me and pick me up. She apologizes again for something she didn't cause.

"There are ways you can still conceive with little risk if you'd like to try again," I hear her say as if she truly believed that I tried this time.

"Try again?"

"With donor eggs. Didn't I read that you have a sister?"

"Yes, I do."

"And how old is she?"

"Twenty-six."

"Terrific. Do you think she'd be willing to give you some of her eggs if you wanted to try again?"

"I wouldn't want any of her eggs. If anybody's eggs are chromosomally deficient, it'd be hers."

The doctor seems confused by my response. She

doesn't know how relieved I feel, as if I've been cramming for a big test and the professor has just canceled class and even though I was prepared, I now have plenty of extra time to study.

Chapter 10

can't remember where I parked the car. Or did I drive the truck? I walk around the side of the building to see if I spot a black Tahoe. I see one, but it's not mine. I circle the building until I'm almost back where I started and that's when I see them: Paulette and Bunny leaning on the trunk of my Audi. I feel like I've been rescued.

"Took you long enough," Paulette says. She's got a red bandanna tied tight around her head and those braids are back. She looks like a thin football player because she's wearing layers of denim and fleece since it's not quite spring.

"You just had to see the doctor during rush hour, didn't you? It took us a southern hour to . . . Marilyn, are you crying?" Bunny asks.

I didn't know I was until she asked. I wipe my eyes on my lavender sleeves. Bunny pulls and pops the waistband of her hot pink leggings then shakes out her legs like Marion Jones does right before she runs the hundred.

Paulette bends down to look at me. "Yeah, what's going on? Are those happy tears or sad ones? Talk to us, girl. We're here for you."

"Both," I say.

Then they start hugging and squeezing me so hard my breasts hurt. "Tell us something, okay? We tried you on your cell but you didn't pick up so we got a little worried since we didn't know where your appointment was and we tried calling Leon at work but his assistant said he left early to pick up his son at the airport and against our better judgment we tried your house and Hail Mary Full of Grace answered and after she deposed us, I asked if she knew your doctor's number and she said she had to think for a few minutes and while she was thinking I started thinking who else we could call and that's when I remembered your GYN's name was a hotel: Hilton! So we called her and Bunny did some explaining—you know she's good when it comes to exaggerating the truth—but to make a long story short, she gave us the information we needed but it took us forever to get here but here we are."

"Thank you, guys. I mean it. For real."

"So, did you hear the heartbeat or not?" Paulette asks. Her arms are folded in anticipation.

"No, I didn't."

Her arms drop to her side like a rag doll's.

"Why not?" Bunny asks.

"Because there wasn't one."

"What's that supposed to mean?" Bunny asks again.

She not only does not have children, she has never been pregnant.

"The baby is dead."

"Oh, no," Paulette says, crossing her arms again, only tighter. "I'm sorry."

"Good," Bunny just blurts out.

"I know I didn't hear you right," Paulette says, getting right in her face.

"I don't mean it's *good* that it's dead, but it's good she doesn't have to go through that whole ordeal of raising another kid all over again. It's a whole lot of other things she can do with her time besides changing Pampers and breast-feeding. Let me shut up. You know I'm not glad that it happened this way, Mar."

"It's all right. Everything happens for a reason."

"See, that's all I'm saying," Bunny says.

"And you're feeling okay about this?" Paulette asks, staring me down. "I mean, this is some devastating stuff, any way you look at it."

"It's okay. I mean it's almost surreal. One minute you're pregnant and the next, you're not. I didn't expect anything like this, but I don't feel devastated."

"So does this mean it's still inside you?" Bunny asks.

"Shut up, would you, Bunny?"

"I have to have a D and C on Tuesday."

"I'll come with you," Paulette says.

"I wish I could, but I can't get out of a training seminar for this new equipment we're getting. It's in the city."

"Right now, I just want to go home, see my son, bake him a cake, and make a fattening dinner," I say.

"How can you even *think* about cooking today?" Paulette asks.

"Because I want to. Spencer's home for spring break for ten days, and brought a girl."

"Mac Daddy," Bunny says. "Isn't SimSim coming?"

"Nope. He's in a jazz band. They're playing at a real club. I thought I told you. Anyway, Sabrina, Nevil, and Sage are coming over, too."

"Dang, you've got all *this* going on today of all days?" Bunny says.

"You do what you gotta do," I say, and finally get in the car. I roll the window down because it's obvious they've got plenty more to say.

"Is Mother Teresa not going to be there?" Bunny asks. "I didn't hear you say her name."

"Arthurine is a given. And she's got a boyfriend who she's probably invited because she wants to show him off, but that's a whole 'nother story. I gotta go."

"And you're okay to drive home?" Paulette says.

"I'm fine," I say, starting the car.

"And now you have to go home and tell your husband and mother-in-law and son this bad news when he's just coming home from college on a short vacation with some strange girl you don't know from Adam that you might not even be able to stand and wait a minute! I forgot. Sabrina's pregnant, too. Lord have mercy, this is too much for me to handle. How in the world are you gonna deal with all this psychological and emotional activity at one time, Marilyn?" Bunny asks, looking at me out of the corner of her eye. She's just waiting for me to set up Act II, but since she's already cast it, and as the producer, I throw my hands up and back out. I'm not in the mood for a rehearsal when tonight is opening night.

I have five messages. The first two are from Leon. I don't feel like talking to him yet. And I forgot. I have no peach schnapps for the cake and I feel like grilling some rib eyes, which means I'm driving ten miles out of my way to go to my favorite market where I buy most of our meat, fish, and produce. Before I turn onto the street that leads to the freeway, an elderly couple is pushing a baby carriage through the intersection. Perfect timing. Until I see the fuzzy white head, and floppy ears and realize it's a dog.

I stop laughing when I get on the freeway because traffic is bumper-to-bumper. But I'm in it and it'll probably take me just as long to get off as it will to stay on it. I feel like I need to talk to somebody. Somebody who cares about me. I speed-dial Lovey's number and she answers on the first ring. "Hi, Lovey!" I say, trying to sound perkier than I am because I don't want to bother her with any of this. I just want to hear her voice. See if she's doing okay since we still have a week before her appointment.

"Hi! And how are you doing today?" she asks. Boy, does she sound cheerful. This makes me feel better already.

"I'm doing fine, Lovey. And you?"

"No complaints."

"That's good. I called to tell you that Spencer's gonna be home from college for a week and he told me he wants to drive out to see you and Joy and the kids before he goes back."

"That sounds like a winner."

"Simeon couldn't make it."

"Oh, I'm sorry to hear that."

"He's in a band."

"Is that so?"

"Yep. But, Lovey, tell me something. Why don't you call me much anymore?"

"I don't know. Who *is* this?"

I have to hit the brakes to stop from rear-ending a Volvo. I know my mother knows *my* voice. What is going on here? I get off at the next exit and decide to take the streets. "Lovey?" I say as I swerve into the parking lot of what is apparently a brand-new market I didn't know about.

"I'm still here," she says.

"This is Marilyn." I turn off the engine and jump out of the car and head toward the entrance doors that pop open before she finally answers.

"Marilyn who?"

"Your *daughter*, Marilyn." I grab a cart even though I should get a basket but I always buy more than I need.

"Oh, hi there, baby!"

"Lovey, are you fooling around or did you not know it was me on the phone for real?"

"What difference does it make, I know who I'm talking to now."

I open my mouth to say something but nothing comes out. I drop my head so that other shoppers won't see my tears as I push the cart down the spirits aisle. I'm trying not to make that crying sound. My mother is going through something, and I pray it's not what I think it is. Just as I'm about to grab a bottle of peach schnapps, I hear her singing a Nina Simone song, as if she doesn't have a care in the world. "Lovey?"

"Yeeeesss," she says, like she's straining to hit a high note.

"Who's there with you?"

"Those kids are always here."

"What about Joy?"

"That bitch is gone."

This makes me want to laugh. But I don't. "Hold on a minute, Lovey." I'm at the meat counter staring at the thick red beef with hardly any trace of fat.

"I ain't got nothing but time," she sings to a new melody.

"I'll take four of the rib eyes and four of those fillets," I say pointing. "Gone where, Lovey?"

"Who?"

"Joy."

"How in the world am I supposed to know?"

"How long has she been gone?"

Now there's silence on the other end. I take the two shiny white packages and drop them in my cart and head for the produce section. "Lovey, have you seen Joy today?"

"I don't believe I have."

"What about yesterday?"

"Maybe."

"Just think about it for a minute, okay? Take your time." I grab a bunch of bananas, more salad stuff, and for some reason, a fresh pineapple—which I'm allergic to—and drop it in my cart. I head for the express checkout.

Now she's humming "When the Saints Go Marching In."

She is scaring me. *"Lovey?"* I shout out, not caring who hears me.

"Yes, sweetness."

"Would you give the phone to LaTiece for me, please?"

"Yes, I can do that." I hear the phone drop on what sounds like the parquet floor she got from Home Depot that one of her friends installed wrong so the lines don't line up and there are places where they don't even touch the baseboard.

I'm in my car now and for some reason I'm starting to hear static. Hurry up, little girl.

"Who is this?"

"This is Aunt Marilyn. And that is not how to answer the phone. You say hello first, and then ask who it is. Where's your mother, LaTiece?"

"I don't know."

"When was the last time you saw her?"

"What day is it?"

"It's Friday. Didn't you and your brother go to school today?"

"Nope."

"Why not?"

" 'Cause ain't nobody made us nothing to eat for dinner since Wednesday when we was watching *The Simpsons.*"

"Wednesday! Are you telling Aunt Marilyn that your mama's been gone since Wednesday?"

"Nope. She went somewhere on Tuesday but Grandma Lovey tried to cook dinner for us on Wednesday but it wasn't good so me and LL had some microwave popcorn and macaroni and cheese."

I have to make myself slow down when I realize I'm doing eighty-five. I feel like I'm going to explode. I don't believe this shit. My mother is out in the middle of nowhere-ville with two little kids and her mind is slipping and my foster sister is probably in a crack house somewhere. I get off at my exit, pull over and put on my hazard lights. I'm thinking. Trying to figure out what to do, before something terrible happens to any one or all of them. "LaTiece, are you still there?"

"Yeah."

"And it's yes—not yeah. I want you to listen to me very carefully. Can you do that?"

When she says, "Yeah," I realize this is not a good time to have speech class.

"I need you to do *exactly* what Aunt Marilyn tells you to do, okay?"

"Okay."

"Do you know your mama's cell number?"

"It don't work no more."

Why am I not surprised? "Okay, you know where Grandma Lovey writes down all those telephone numbers in the kitchen?"

"Yeah. But she scribbled all over it."

"Okay, but there's some pages underneath the top one that she scribbled on."

"Want me to go look?"

"Can you?"

"Hold on a minute."

She drops the phone on the floor just like Lovey did. This has got to be a nightmare because I could not have picked a better day to go through any of this. I start the car and head on up the hill toward my house. When I see that Joy, I might just strangle her. How can you just go off and leave your young kids with their grandmother, knowing her mind is not what it used to be? And Joy had to have known that Lovey's condition was a lot more serious than she's let on. I wouldn't put it past her if the reason she's been keeping this from me is because she's probably worried that if something were to happen to Lovey, or if she required medical attention or worse, supervised care, where would that leave her and the kids? Bitch.

"It's still there, Aunt Marilyn."

"Go GET it, LaTiece, and bring it back to wherever you are right now."

"Can't LL brang it to me? I already just went in there once already?"

"I asked YOU to go get it! Now DO it and be quick about it!"

I think I just heard her say "Shit!" because this time it sounds like she tripped over the phone.

Lord, what I wouldn't pay to have these kids for about a year. They can't fucking speak correct English. They have no damn manners because they haven't been taught any. I feel sorry for them. To be stuck with a mother like my sister.

She has been out of control since junior high school. Lovey used to call me late at night in my dorm, at first, worried when she discovered Joy was already smoking cigarettes, and then for advice on how to handle her once marijuana, drinking and hanging out with a bad crowd entered the picture. Lovey couldn't say enough to stop her. And by the time Joy dropped out in her junior year, Lovey couldn't persuade her to go back.

Joy doesn't seem to know how to love her kids. They live on sugar and grease. Watch whatever they want to on television and go to bed when they get tired. When LaTiece was in kindergarten, her teacher asked what her real name was and she said, "Tiecey." The teacher said, "No, I mean your *real* name," and LaTiece said, "Tiecey!" She didn't know that wasn't her real name and Joy was cracking up telling me this story.

Last Christmas, she "forgot" to send Santa his check so the kids didn't have anything under that stingy little fake tree except what me and Leon had sent them: a black Barbie with a change of clothes for a week, a jewelry-making kit, PlayStation 2 with four games, a Jerry Rice #80 jersey that LL begged and pleaded for and a pair of Air Force One sneakers he said that everybody at his school was wearing. Plus, we put substantial gift certificates to JCPenney and Target inside Christmas cards addressed to them, which I later learned that Joy sold. This is why Lovey started hiding her checks, but my sister figured out how to intercept them.

At this rate, these kids don't stand a chance. They don't understand grace or tenderness or pride. I do not believe they even know what it feels like to be loved. Except what Lovey may have shown them before they started getting on her nerves. Last summer they spent a week with us, but then didn't want to go home, so we stretched it into two. I was caught completely off guard when LaTiece just blurted out that she wished I were her mama because she didn't like hers. LL concurred. I was in shock. But the real blow was when they said their mama doesn't like them either. I asked what would make them think that and LaTiece said because she tells them. "Sometimes she say: 'I can't stand yo' little grown ass,' or 'You make me sick,' or 'I wish I could give y'all to somebody.' "

Somebody gave her away. Maybe you can't forget that fact no matter what happens. But now, her kids are being forced to fend for themselves. "Okay. I got it," she says.

"What took you so long?"

" 'Cause I had to pee."

I am grateful to her for sharing that. "Can you read, LaTiece?"

"Not cursive."

"Where is Lovey?"

"Sitting on the couch over there."

"What is she doing?"

"Nothing."

"Where's LL?"

"Upstairs playing video games."

"Ask Lovey if she would come to the phone, please."

"Gran'ma Lovey, Aunt Marilyn said come get on the phone."

That is not what I said.

"Here her come."

"It's here *she* comes," I say, because I have to.

"Hello there, Marilyn. How are you?"

I cover my mouth with my hand. But that's not going to help the situation. I'm only five or six minutes from my house but I slow down to a crawl and let other cars pass. It's almost dark and through the rearview mirror I see San Francisco all lit up. It doesn't move me tonight. I take a deep breath and say very slowly, "Lovey, can you look on that paper pad and tell me when you see your friend Miss Saundra's phone number? And before you ask me whom I'm talking about, it's not important right now. Just look for the name: S-a-u-n-d-r-a-N-o-r-m-a-n, and tell me when you see it."

"I'm looking. I used to do somebody's hair by that name. I see it."

"Would you read it to me, please?"

"Why you want her number?"

"Because I would like to talk to her."

"About what?"

"Lovey, just read me off the number, please!"

"You just wait a minute, sister! Joy just walked in. She

can read it to you. Joy, take this phone before I pop you upside the head with it. Did you bring us something from McDonald's like you said you would?"

"Shit, I just walked in the house and my head is killing me. Who is it?"

"I don't know but she wants a phone number. Here," she says, and that damn phone hits the floor for what I hope is the last time.

"Marilyn, hey, Sis, what's going on? I was in a car accident a couple of days ago and was laid up at a friend's house trying to get back on my feet and they put me on some kinda medication that knocked me out and that's why I just got myself together in time to come home to feed the kids and get Lovey her Big Mac but I'm all right except my head is hurting like a motherfucker—what number was it you wanted?"

"Never mind. Just tell me something, Joy. Are you staying home tonight?"

"I can't go nowhere like this. Yeah."

"Then I'll call you back tomorrow. Do you have any money?"

"I might have ten dollars."

"Go look in the kitchen drawer under Lovey's straightening comb and bumper curlers and get that twenty-dollar bill I left just for this occasion and order those kids a pizza or something."

"You love telling people what to do, don't you?"

"Can you just do it?"

"Tiecey," she yells. "Go look in Lovey's hair drawer and find me a twenty-dollar bill and when I hang up this phone I want you to call Domino's like I showed you and order a pizza and tell 'em to deliver it to this address and don't act like you can't remember where you live."

"I know where I *live*," I hear her say to her mama like she's thirty. "But I don't remember the address."

"It's done," Joy says. "Anything else?"

"Yes. Were you driving Lovey's car?"

"I wasn't, but somebody else was. It wasn't his fault and that car is all right."

"Where is the car now?"

"I'm trying to thank," she says, slurring so bad now I can hear the drool.

"Come on, Joy," I moan.

"My bad! It's getting fixed at the wrecked-car place. Ma'bad. But don't worry it's gon' be all right. Can we finish this conversation tomorrow?" She doesn't wait for my response and I hear her struggling to put the phone back in the cradle, but of course she misses and it hits the floor.

Chapter 11

Every single light in the house is on like it used to be when Spencer and Simeon were little and they were having a sleepover. I wish the people who lived here were having a party and that I was an invited guest. I want to ring the doorbell. I want to make small talk with people I don't know. I want to eat food prepared by someone else. I want my real feelings to be so well disguised that even I'm fooled into thinking I'm having a great time. I also want to offer to help clean up so that the hosts can say, "Don't be ridiculous," and push me out the door with a plate of food to take home.

But I am home. And there are enough cars in the driveway and parked out front so that it looks like a party could be going on. Not telling them I was pregnant was a smart move: no explanations are now necessary.

As soon as the garage door goes up, that Harley is the first thing that catches my eye. It looks like a shiny steel bumblebee. I have yet to see Leon ride it. I pull in between his boring beige Volvo and Arthurine's 1990 white Coupe de Ville. It's been parked in this exact spot since she got here and her night blindness set in, but then she also doesn't have a license anymore because she's afraid to take the test. Our Tahoe lives outside and its black body has dulled some, but what can you do?

Even with my windows up I can hear that hip-hop music thumping through the door and then when I get out of the car, the infectious laughter of what sounds like an entire basketball team trampling through the kitchen toward the stairs. There's a house full of happy people inside. I'm praying no one will detect anything remotely close to grief on my face. I don't want to ruin the mood.

Later, when I'm marinating the steaks and Leon's turning on the grill, I don't want to pretend to be looking for my special renegade sauce or the seasoned rice-wine vinegar even though I know precisely where they are but it'll be because I need to turn away from all this insulated joy just for a second, to get centered and grounded, enough to make myself feel their presence so they won't notice my absence. And as the mixer is swirling through the yellow cake batter I'll let little Sage pour in the peach juice and I'll add the peach schnapps myself. I'm going to try my hardest to feel the pleasure of the moment.

When I pull into the garage, Spencer is standing there. "Mom!" he yells, like he's been waiting all day to say it. He grabs the bags out of my hands and drops them on the concrete floor without even thinking if there's anything breakable inside and in one continuous motion he kisses me on my cheek and forehead and squeezes me so tight that my body rises and my shoes fall off. "What took you so long, woman? We've been waiting for you to make your grand entrance for the past couple of hours!"

"I had to stop by the store. Plus, it was rush hour."

"Why don't you leave your cell on? Did you not get our messages?"

"No. I haven't checked them all day. Is that food I smell? I know Arthurine didn't cook, did she?"

"No, we stopped by Le Cheval on the way home from the airport and Dad picked up a ton of Vietnamese food, so don't even think about cooking. I've missed you, Mom."

"I miss you, too, Spencer. And your missing-in-action twin brother. But 'it's all good,' " I say, mimicking him.

"Mom, what's going on with Dad?"

"What do you mean?"

"That Harley over there for starters. What's up with that?"

"I don't know. I think he's going through something. He might be a little depressed."

"About what?"

"He said work has been stressing him out a lot lately."

"He's been saying that for years. That's one of the things I thought he got off on."

"Maybe, but short of being a schizoid, I don't know what else it could be."

"Well, he's tripping hard, whatever it is. You'll see. Anyway, it's good to be home," he says, ushering me into the house and down the hallway into what suddenly

feels like a stage in an auditorium and the curtains are
about to go up any minute. But this is my kitchen. And
this is my nineteen-year-old son Spencer standing right
here in front of me. He looks like a leaner, taller,
younger, and much better-looking version of his father.

"Hey, Dad, Mom finally made it home!" he says,
when we turn that corner and it's curtains up.

At first, I don't believe my eyes when I see Leon coming toward me in baggy jeans and a gigantic blue jersey
on top of a white T-shirt. On his feet are light blue suede
boots, just like Spencer and Simeon wear. After all this,
he still has the nerve to have on his head a light blue
Kangol cap turned backward. He is clearly confused
about his identity today. Even his face looks extra clean
and shiny, like there's more of it or something. And
that's when I realize it's because this idiot has gone and
shaved off his moustache and goatee! I'm staring at him,
trying to remember what it was about him that ever appealed to me, but I'm drawing a blank. Just what is he
trying to prove?

"Hello, Marilyn," he says. "You finally made it. Did
everything go okay?"

"Everything went just fine. What happened to you?"

"You like it?" he says, twirling around in slow motion.

"This is what I'm talking out, Mom. I didn't even recognize Dad at the airport. I told him that we might have
to start calling him P. Diddy Senior if this is the track he's
on. But it's all good."

Leon is grinning his butt off. Like his son has finally
accepted him into his club. He can't be this stupid all of

a sudden, can he? In fact, he's actually blushing. He doesn't seem to realize that he hasn't impressed anybody but himself, that if he had only spent a few more minutes in the mirror he might have seen the truth staring back at him: a middle-aged conservative businessman dressed up for Halloween as a chubby old hip-hopper twenty years later.

Leon's demeanor is much looser than I've ever seen, almost as if he's under the influence of something besides a couple of chardonnays. But he never has more than two glasses because the thought of being out of control scares him. Which is why I've never seen him drunk. Maybe he's just gotten what he apparently needed: an audience. No doubt people will notice him in this getup. I just hate that Spencer's girlfriend had to see his dad like this—and I certainly hope she doesn't think Leon is *representing* us. I wouldn't dream of leaving this house with him looking like a complete fool. And where is the girl, by the way?

"Oh, before I forget," Leon says. "You'll never guess in a million years who I ran into at the airport."

"I'm not in the mood for guessing, Leon, it could be anybody."

"No, not just anybody. Who'd you marry by mistake and then come to your senses about when you met me?"

I feel a lump forming in my throat. I swallow hard because my lips want to say, "Gordon wasn't a mistake. It was just bad timing," but instead I say, "That's nice. How's he doing?"

"Fine. He looks great! I can tell *he* works out. He said

he saw you and your girlfriends at that Gill Scott concert but you didn't mention it."

"I wasn't sure if that was him or not, it's been so long. And it's *Jill* Scott, Leon."

"Anyway, he was picking up what looked like his new girlfriend the way he greeted her, and man oh man, I must give the man credit for having good taste because she was absolutely breathtaking. I kid you not. I think she might be from Africa. She just looked exotic and unbelievably graceful. Anyway, I told Gordon that they should stop by sometime, and he said he'd love to."

"That's nice," I say. What breathtaking girlfriend? Why wasn't she at the concert with him? What part of Africa? And what was she doing to appear to be so graceful? And why do I even care? This is ridiculous to be this curious. I'm privately embarrassed by it. "It'd be good to see him," I say, and leave it at that.

"I gave him my card and put our home number on the back. He said he'd give us a call real soon. Hey, Spence," he says, turning away from me, "don't you want to introduce your mom to Brianna?" Before Spencer has a chance to answer, Leon's already heading toward the doorway. "Tell you what, I'll go check on her. We wouldn't want anything to happen to her, now would we? She's something," he says with a look in his eye that's downright scary. "Would you mind pouring your dad another glass of chardonnay? I'll be right back. Catch up with Mom," he says, and not only sashays down the hall but if I'm not mistaken, I do believe he runs up the stairs.

I look at Spencer, and he hunches his shoulders up like he doesn't get it either. "Where are those young men whose cars are blocking half the driveway? Go upstairs and tell Omar, Milton, Tavis, and Conrad that they better get their butts down here to say hello and give me my hug or no edibles like steak or cake."

"I'll go get them right now. They're watching the Lakers. And my sister who has just advised me that she's with child crashed about ten minutes ago. I believe Sage is in your room with her. Nevil's somewhere in a corner with a book."

"Where's Arthurine hiding?" I ask, walking over to the kitchen island that's completely covered with open Styrofoam containers. I can smell the dry-fried crab and the curry, but I walk around peeking inside every container until I see the grilled quail, which of course no one has touched. This is one of my favorites.

"I'm right over here!" she says, trying to speak over the music. I don't see her until Spencer, who's at the bar, goes over and turns it down to adult level. She and Prezelle are sitting side by side inside the curve of the leather sofa that's hidden by the bar. The television is on mute, but it looks like that hasn't stopped them from watching it.

"Hello, Arthurine. And how are you, Prezelle?" I ask. They both look as if they've come to the wrong party by mistake but decided that since they were here, what the hell, they might as well stay.

"Was Leon nice enough to give Prezelle a lift, Arthurine?"

"No, he did not."

"Then how'd you get over here, Prezelle?"

"Arthurine picked me up."

I know I didn't hear him correctly, so I say, "Repeat that for me again, please."

"I went and got him myself," she says.

"In what?"

"In my car."

"Arthurine," I sigh. "First of all, this isn't exactly the right time for us to have this conversation, and I apologize in advance if I embarrass you, however, I have to ask: what on earth would possess you to drive that car when neither of you have driven in over a year and you know your driver's license is expired, not to mention your night blindness?"

"Slow down, Marilyn. My Lord. First of all, nobody was here to go get Prezelle and since Spencer had all his friends coming to the homecoming, I wanted my friend here, too. And yes, I know my license is expired but I only went up the hill a few miles. I was willing to suffer the consequences if I got caught but the Lord was in the front seat with me, guiding me the whole way so I wasn't really worried about darkness. And for your information I'm going down to take the test again next week 'cause I'm tired of depending on everybody to take me places, especially since I'm starting to get a whole new social life."

"I'm happy you're becoming a social butterfly. But what do you mean by 'again'?"

"I took that test last month but they've made it much harder than it used to be and I had a few problems with

some of those questions which made no sense whatsoever the way they worded them so they told me to study
a little harder, then come back and try again. But that's
neither here nor there. And just so you'll know, when I
first moved in here, Leon told me to start my car up at
least once a week and let it run for twenty minutes or so,
which I've done. I have also driven it back and forth in
the driveway to rotate the tires," she sighs, and then
takes a deep breath. "Now what do you have in those
bags?" She pushes the palm of her hand into the back of
the sofa to get to a standing position, and Prezelle gives
her a little help. Of course she's headed over here to see
for herself.

"I've been truly enjoying myself," Prezelle says. Now
he's trying to get up, but the sofa is too low and he
loses his balance, drops back into a sitting position, and
decides to stay. He's wearing tweed trousers that probably once belonged to a suit, and they're being held up
by red-and-gray striped suspenders that are wrinkling
his used-to-be-white-and-he-ironed-it-himself shirt.
Prezelle sinks deeply into the soft cushions of the sofa
and crosses his legs like Superfly. He seems to know
he's sharp.

"I'm glad you're having a good time, Prezelle. You
look quite dapper today."

"Why, thank you, Mrs. Grimes."

"Call me Marilyn."

"Why, thank you, Marilyn." Now he's blushing.

I better watch it, before his girlfriend gets jealous.
"What have you guys been doing?"

"Just sitting here. Watching. And listening."

"Watching and listening to who?"

"Who's supposed to eat all this meat? Waste not, want not," Arthurine says after opening both packages of steaks. But I don't bother answering her.

"Don't worry, Grandma, my boys and I will devour those things tomorrow if nobody else does," Spencer says.

"So, how's Brianna?"

"Sweet, Mom. You'll like her. I sure do."

"And how long did you say you've been seeing her?"

"I don't know—almost two months, give or take a week. Long enough to know."

"Long enough to know what?"

"That I've got it bad."

Oh Lord, here we go again. What is it with this boy? I'm beginning to wonder if he falls in love with every pretty girl that makes him come. But I don't want to go there, so I ask something generic: "Where's she from?"

"Actually, she grew up on what sounds like it might have been a farm, but she doesn't call it a 'farm.' I mean they had cows and pigs and chickens and everything. It's a little town. They still have dirt roads! I can tell you this much, driving between there and Atlanta, you wouldn't want to have car trouble at night. Mom, is that peach schnapps I see?"

"It is."

He runs over and gives me another hug. "Were you planning to make this today?"

"I was, but you said not to bother cooking."

"We didn't mean *cake*. Unless you're too tired." But now he's giving me that please-baby-baby-please look.

"Then turn the oven on," I say. "And go check to see what's going on with your girlfriend. It feels like I've been here an hour and I still haven't met her."

"Bet," he says, turning the dial to 350 degrees. "Thanks, Mom. Be right back." He takes a bottle of water from the refrigerator and pours his dad a glass of wine, spilling half of it on the hardwood floor. Some things just don't change. I hand him a paper towel and he cleans up the mess.

"I'm sorry, Prezelle, you were saying?" I'm hoping and praying he remembers so I won't have to embarrass him, too.

"I said I've been enjoying watching and listening to the youngsters."

"What were they talking about?"

"Well, seems to me that they started in on the most recent events of the day: this war over there in Iraq and the whole 9/11 tragedy and then they started in on that Jackson Five boy and his sister exposing herself at the Super Bowl—which they all seemed to enjoy, and from there it was that Kobe Bryant basketball star I believe was accused of raping some Colorado girl that they all agreed was nothing but extortion. And things quieted down there for a minute until Leon decided to flip the calendar in the other direction and asked how they felt about that Million Man March. That's when things got heated, I'll tell you. It was pure entertainment."

"That it was," Arthurine chimes in.

"Really? How so?" I ask.

"I'll tell you why, Mom. Because your husband felt that it was a senseless expression of black manhood and even though most of us were kind of young when it went down, we all agreed that it was an incredible display of solidarity and how often have we seen it since then?"

"Well, Prezelle, did you express how you felt about it?"

"I didn't think nothing about it, one way or the other. But if I had felt like talking I probably would'a said that I don't think getting on no bus proved all that much. All a man needs to do to prove he's a man is work hard. Take care his family. Pay his bills on time. And try to be a good father. A good husband. That's all there is to it. You don't have to go nowhere if you already doing right where you are. But I'll tell you, Marilyn, it was really nice just listening to these young men talk about so many different issues, using big words and sounding so intelligent I couldn't say anything for smiling. And to think that they are all in college just made me feel good."

"We're all very proud of them," I say.

"I had hoped they'd bring up the snipers. I can't believe they were black. We didn't used to behave like other people."

I don't dare ask who he's referring to. But it feels like we need to lighten up a bit in here. "Did you have any of this delicious Vietnamese food, Prezelle?"

"No, baby. I can't eat none of that."

"Why not?"

"I don't know what they eat in Vietnam. But we're in Oakland and I don't know what all that's supposed to be. There's not one thang on that counter I could rightly say I recognize except the rice, and even that had speckles of something orange in it."

"I'm sorry. Arthurine, why didn't you describe what was in each container to Prezelle, or at least offer him something else to eat?"

"Because he didn't ask. And I just told you. Waste not want not. He said he was just waiting to get used to the smell because I told him that I'm not afraid to try new things, even at my age, and if he is, I don't know how this relationship is going to work."

"Oh, all right," he says, this time giving himself a big push and he's upright. He is sharp as a tack. All he needs are some dark sunglasses and he could be mistaken for a short Ray Charles. I think she's taller than he is. But so what? If she likes him.

"Arthurine, would you mind helping Prezelle sample some of the food?"

"I don't mind at all," she says.

"Hello, Mrs. Grimes," I hear a southern voice coming from behind me. When I turn around, I see a young woman who probably could've been a black Breck girl. Everything about her looks sweet and tender. Her eyes are big and bright, as if she's always interested in what people have to say. And what a tiny little waist! I bet she's the size they just recently invented: a zero.

"Hi there, Brianna. It's very nice to meet you, honey. Make yourself comfortable and have a seat," I say, pointing to the table in the nook, which seems to be the only clean surface in this kitchen.

"Yes, ma'am. It's very nice to meet you, too. And I want to thank you for inviting me to your home," she says, looking up.

"You're quite welcome."

"Well, this has to be the most interesting candelabra I've ever seen. Where did you find something like this?"

"Oh, I made that thing. Or, I should say, refurbished it."

"No kidding? How? What made you think to use all these different things on a light fixture? I mean, I see seashells and pearls and isn't that dried fruit?"

"Sure is. It was an old boring wrought-iron fixture that I got tired of looking at, so I just painted it blue and then just scrounged around the room and started gluing on anything I saw that I felt might bring it back to life."

"Well, it worked. Do you make this kind of stuff a lot?"

"I always have something lying around that's waiting to be finished. But it's just a hobby."

"Well, before I go, I'd love to see some of the other things you've made if you don't mind."

"Sure," I say.

"Is there anything I can do to help you?"

"I don't know. I was just about to make Spencer his favorite cake," I say. "But after looking at all these boys, I better make that cake."

"I'd like to help, if you don't mind."

"No, come on over here. Look in the pantry and get an apron that's hanging next to the pots."

As she walks past me toward the pantry, I realize she's tiny from the front, but as the kids say, "Baby got back" and I see what Spencer's weakness might be. Now I hear what sounds like a stampede coming down the stairs, but Leon saunters in before Spencer and his friends almost trample him over.

"Hi, Aunt Marilyn," one says, followed by three more, then hugs and kisses. These boys are almost men. In one short year they have major facial hair and their voices have dropped quite a few octaves. I can remember when they looked and sounded like girls!

"It's nice to see you guys back in the 'hood."

They all laugh.

"So, Mom, I see you've met Brianna," Spencer says.

"I have indeed and she's going to help me make the cake."

"Cool."

"Aunt Marilyn," one of the boys says. "Would you mind if we run back up to finish watching the game and we'll come back afterward to chat with you? Would that be all right?"

"That's fine. You're on spring break. Go."

When Brianna comes out of the pantry, because her hair is long, she's having a hard time tying the apron string behind her neck. "Spencer, would you mind helping me tie this, please?"

But before Spencer can go to her aid, Leon beelines it over there and is standing behind the girl so close I can see his stomach touching her back. "I'll help you, young lady," he says, lifting the strings over her shoulders but so close that his palms appear to brush the top of her breasts. "Anything my son can do, I can do better," Leon says.

"What did you just say?" I ask.

"Yeah, Dad, chill out, man. And back away from her, if you don't mind. You are tripping too hard, dude."

Leon drops the strings and looks at us like we're the ones tripping. "What did I say? I was just kidding."

The poor girl looks like she's afraid to move.

"Your joke wasn't funny, Dad," Spencer says.

"I agree," Arthurine says, once she gets Prezelle settled in at the table in the nook. "You were way out of line, Son."

"But I didn't do anything. Look, if I offended you, Brianna, I apologize. I was just trying to say that my son takes after his dad, and that you're just getting a younger version of me. Didn't you get it?"

She nods her head as if she knows she should, not because she wants to.

"It's not just what you did but also how you did it, Leon," I say.

"I was just trying to be helpful!"

"Who needs help?" Sabrina asks, as she comes into the kitchen holding Sage's hand but she quickly lets go of it when she sees the open containers. "I'm starving."

"Hi there, Sage. Want to help Grandma and Brianna make a cake?"

She just nods. I can tell she just woke up.

Now here comes Nevil. The oddly handsome Jamaican. "Hello there, Mum," he says, kissing me on the head. His dreadlocks are almost to his shoulders. They scratch.

"Mom," Spencer says. "A bunch of us want to go up

to Tahoe for a couple of days to do some boarding and I was wondering if we could drive down to see Grandma Lovey on Tuesday?"

"No," I say, too fast.

"Why not?"

"Because I can't get off work."

"Well, if you can't go, Brianna and I can drive down."

"But I don't want you to go without me."

"Why not?"

"What I meant was, I have to take her to the doctor next Friday, so if you could wait until then, that would be better."

"No problem. But we have to bail on Sunday. She's not sick or anything, is she?"

"She's having a little trouble remembering some things."

"Like what kinds of things?" Sabrina asks.

"I don't feel like talking about this right now."

"But we should know if something's not right, Mom," Spencer says.

"Okay. She gets lost driving a few blocks from home. She forgets things she does or says not too long afterward and sometimes hasn't recognized my voice. That's enough."

"Both of my grandmamas and my grandaddy on my mama's side had that. It's awful," Brianna says. "How many eggs, Mrs. Grimes?"

"Eight," I say.

"Had what?" Spencer asks her.

"Alzheimer's."

"We don't know yet if that's what she has."

"It probably is," Brianna says. "Everybody tried to pretend like that wasn't what was happening to them, and they prayed real hard for it not to be, but even God can't stop this disease."

"God can stop anything," Arthurine butts in.

"Not when He didn't start it," the young girl says, like she knows exactly what she's talking about. "I don't mean to be disrespectful, but I'm just saying that I've watched three of my elders go through this and they all started out the same way: forgetting a little bit and then more and more until they don't even remember you when they see you. It's terrible."

"I wish I could go see Grandma Lovey," Sabrina says. "But I have an appointment with my adviser that I absolutely cannot miss."

"Why not?" I ask.

"Well, because I have to postpone my admittance to grad school now that we're going to England in the fall."

I don't dare say what I'm thinking now. I would love to tell her that I made that same mistake. Postponed my plans and dreams so your father could pursue his. Would Nevil do the same for you?

"So," Leon says, obviously feeling left out of the loop now. "Since I'm the bad guy here, maybe I should say something nice that might get everybody's approval."

"Like what?" I ask, hoping he's not going to say what I think he's going to say.

"Yeah, Dad, like what?" Sabrina asks.

Everybody's looking at Leon. Waiting to hear what he has to say. He likes this attention. And then he takes a deep breath and blurts out: "Marilyn's pregnant!"

At first there is utter silence all over the room.

"I thought you were going through menopause!" Sabrina says.

"My mama was forty-four when she had my little brother and he turned out just fine," Brianna says.

"You ain't telling me nothing I didn't already know," Arthurine says in a self-congratulatory way.

"This is deep," Spencer says. "A real baby?"

"I think it's wonderful," Nevil says. "Mum and daughter carrying a baby at the same time. This is divine."

Leon's grin is wide. He isn't even thinking about me standing here center stage, surrounded by a crowd of onlookers who are probably waiting to hear what melody will come out of my mouth. Lovey would probably sing it for them. But I can't sing. "I'm not pregnant anymore. I had a miscarriage. It happens," I say and dump the contents of the first box of yellow cake mix into the stainless-steel bowl.

Chapter 12

I wait all night for Leon to get in bed. It's close to three in the morning when he does and he smells like booze. He must be regressing by the hour because he never stays up this late. Either he's completely deluding himself into thinking he's one of the boys, or he wanted to avoid being alone with me. Right after I explained my reasons for not telling anybody about my condition and what I'd just learned earlier that day, the look of relief on Leon's face was almost embarrassing.

Spencer wasn't quite sure how to take both aspects of the news but seemed to get a great deal of comfort putting his head in Brianna's lap while she stroked his back. On her way out, Sabrina expressed how disappointed she was that I hadn't confided in her, especially when she thought I could talk to her about anything. Arthurine—as my greatest source of comfort—said that I shouldn't forget that Sarah was ninety years old when she conceived and said that "God has given me cause to laugh." She couldn't remember where in Genesis this was.

"Ha ha ha," I said, and excused myself.

I get up about six-thirty and leave Leon snoring. I'm thinking about checking Spencer's room just to see if he's alone, but decide against it. As I walk past the game room, it looks like the floor is covered with humpbacked whales that have been washed ashore. The boys are still in their clothes. I get four blankets from the linen closet and cover them one by one. A few of them stir and snuggle, wrapping the blankets around themselves tightly, as if they've been waiting for their mothers to do just this.

When I get downstairs, the kitchen is spotless. I'm sure Spencer is responsible. He's worse than me when it comes to cleanliness. Of course both cakes are gone and every soda can has been crushed and flattened into bulging blue recycle bags. I make a fresh pot of coffee, pour myself a cup, and go get the paper. Now that it's safe, I go into my workshop. It is my sanctuary; the only place in this whole house where I can dream with my hands. I begged Leon to add this room a few years back because I used to sew in a corner of the family room but there was no place to store my supplies and I had to clean up the mess I made each and every time. Then when I started experimenting with other materials, I couldn't exactly spray paint or sand while catching the evening news.

You'd never know just by looking around how many different kinds of materials are in here. Even I don't remember half the time. I keep most of my "hard" supplies in a huge metal cabinet I found at Home Depot. It has about thirty clear drawers in various sizes where I store metal and wire and beads from all over the world; broken, cracked, clear, and colored glass; tubes and jars of fabric; glass and acrylic paint; pebbles and rocks; seashells; and hundreds of unidentified objects I haven't found a use for yet. Of course there's my sewing machine and serger, which are in a typical Formica cabinet, and a six-foot-long cutting table that doubles as a serving table at Thanksgiving and Christmas.

I sit down in an old wooden rocker I had started stripping a couple of months ago but when I couldn't tolerate the odor, was forced to stop. Of course I know why now. I take a sip of my coffee and look out the back windows. I can see hundreds of acres of a green valley, the tops of which look like broccoli. It is beautiful to say the least. As I rock back and forth, the wooden joints creak. I like this sound. I look over and spot Bunny's necklace. I forgot all about it. I'm sure she understands. I'll take it to work and see if anyone there might be able to help me finish it once and for all.

I place it inside my backpack and start reading the paper. Sometimes I skip over all the horror happening in the world and read the stupid, funny, gossipy, inconsequential stuff first. And right now I'm not in the mood for more war when it feels like there's one going on in my own home. After a few sips of coffee, I realize I'm hot. From inside my body not the outer layer. Even my forehead is moist. My bathrobe is starting to stick to my arms. This feels awfully familiar. This couldn't possibly be a hot flash already, could it?

I don't drink the rest of my coffee and I don't finish the paper either. I think it might be nice to surprise the boys and make them a big breakfast of blueberry waffles, grits, bacon, and scrambled eggs, something they probably don't get in the dorms. I go back upstairs to shower, and Leon's still out cold. I slip on what I hope will soon be my last pair of baggy sweats. I close the door quietly behind me, and Arthurine almost gives me a heart attack.

"You're up early," she says, standing outside our room in one of her signature jogging outfits with Snuffy on his leash. "You all right?"

"I'm fine, Arthurine. Thank you."

"Can I do anything for you?"

"Nope."

"Well, I'm going to take Snuffy out to do his business and then I was hoping we could have a little talk."

"Hold it a minute, Arthurine."

"I said I'd be right back."

"Please tell me you didn't drive Prezelle home last night."

"No, Lordy. Spencer and his girlfriend took him."

"Good. So what is it you want to talk about?"

Snuffy actually moves. She tugs on his leash. "Can you just give me a few minutes so I can take him out real fast? He needs to go pretty bad."

"Okay," I say, and follow her down to the front door. I watch Snuffy relieve himself in two ways on our front lawn. Arthurine leaves his business right there and leads him back into the house. "I'm going to make breakfast, so come on into the kitchen with me."

"Okay," she says. I'm hoping she's going to guide Snuffy over to his grungy fur bed that I politely moved out of the kitchen to the side of the sofa in the family room where I can't see him when I eat or cook.

But she doesn't. She sits down on a stool at the far end of the island and Snuffy spreads out all four legs and slides down until his underbelly is flush with the floor. He is disgusting. As I pull out frying pans and bowls and gather the other ingredients, I try not to look down. But the waffle iron is on the shelf below us, not far from where Snuffy is sprawled out.

"Arthurine, would you mind handing me that waffle iron?"

"Not at all," she says, and gets off the stool and sets it up here. "Now, I don't want you to take this the wrong way," she says, unzipping her jacket.

"What's wrong?"

"Nothing's wrong. I just think it's about time for me to move."

"Move where?"

"Someplace where I can be with my own kind."

"What are you talking about, Arthurine?"

"I like it up there where Prezelle lives."

"You do!" I say, but try to make it sound more like a question. She just doesn't know. This is music to my ears. "It does seem like a really nice place."

"It's lovely. And exciting. You have your very own apartment. They have activities every single day of the week if you want to participate. They go on bus trips to Reno. Even cruises. It feels more like a resort than a retirement facility."

"Wow, then maybe I should move in with you."

"Oh, stop it, Marilyn! You and Leon could have this whole house to yourselves."

"Wouldn't that be something."

"I've just been so bored being here all by myself when you're at work or running errands and I get lonely. It doesn't feel good to be this lonely."

"I know exactly how you feel."

"How's that?"

"I just meant that I understand because I remember when I've been bored and lonely. Everybody has, Arthurine."

"Well, I'm on the waiting list."

"You mean you've already applied?"

"Yep. Last month."

"Does Leon know about this?"

"No. I don't know how or when to tell him."

"Just tell him, Arthurine. He's not your father or your husband, he's your son."

"I know, but I also know how much you all like having me here and I'm just a little worried that he might not want me to leave, which is why I thought you'd be much more understanding seeing how we're both women and all."

"I certainly do, but I'm sure he'll want what's best for you."

"I don't know. I don't think he truly understands widowhood. What losing somebody you've loved all your life feels like. He just thought bringing me here would fill up that space, but it don't work like that at all. I've been here coming up on two years, and if I hadn't started walking the mall I probably wouldn't have met Prezelle, whose kindness and attention have begun to resurrect me, if you and the Lord can forgive me for using that word this way."

"You don't need to be forgiven, Arthurine. But does Prezelle know you want to move into his building?"

"Of course he does. He was the one that put the idea into my head. I told him I would give it some thought and the more I thought about it, the more excited I got, which is something I haven't felt in a long time: excitement. He said he wants me closer to him and I want to be closer to where he is."

Excuse me for asking, Miss Thang. This is so cute I almost can't hold it in. "Arthurine, are you in *love* with Prezelle?"

She leans forward on her elbows and covers her mouth like a fan with her fingers. "I can't remember what being in love is supposed to feel like and to be honest with you, I don't rightly care. All I know is that I enjoy Prezelle's company and he enjoys mine. That's good enough."

"I think this is great. For everybody," I say.

"Well, it still might be months, and could even be as much as a whole year before I can get in there, because that waiting list is long. Unless of course folks start dying off faster than they thought."

What a terrible way to get an apartment. "Well, just let me know what I can do to help."

"You could help by starting to drop little hints to get Leon thinking about my not being here without being dead."

"I can try, but I'll need to think about this one for a minute or so, Arthurine."

"I've got time. The other thing is if you could help me study for my driver's test because I can't afford to fail it again, Marilyn. If I do, I won't ever be able to drive my car again legally."

"We don't want you to have to do that," I say.

"Thank you, sugar," she says, standing up. "How long before I'll smell bacon?"

"You'll smell it in about a half hour and not a minute sooner."

"Fair enough. Come on, Snuffy, let's go," she says and leads him over to his bed.

"Wait a minute!"

"Yes, Marilyn?"

"Can you have a dog there?"

"No. I want you and Leon to have Snuffy." And off she goes.

At the crack of dawn on Tuesday, Spencer, Brianna, and at least five other spring-breakers all head for our condo on the south shore of Lake Tahoe. I checked Caltrans to make sure the roads were clear and got the weather report online. No snow predictions. Even so, I give my standard lecture: please drive carefully and responsibly up in those mountains and please don't drink and get behind the wheel and please don't destroy the place; leave it the way you found it. Of course they each promise to adhere to my wishes and Spencer tells me he and Brianna—who apparently has never seen snow—will see us late Thursday afternoon.

I'm completely shocked when Leon insists on going with me to have my procedure done. Paulette comes anyway, just because. I also can't believe when Leon tells me he's not just taking today off, but I think he said the rest of this week, too. I'm not quite sure because I was still somewhat out of it when we got home. I sleep through most of the afternoon, but feel pretty normal when I wake up. I'm not in any pain, and have very little bleeding. I have to assure him that I'm okay with the way things have turned out and ask if we could not discuss it anymore. I can tell he's relieved because he has spent all day and night trying to say the politically correct thing until I finally just ask him to be quiet and talk about something else.

I get up pretty early to get ready for work but realize it's Wednesday, and I don't have to be at HC until noon. Leon is in the kitchen drinking coffee. It feels strange seeing him this time of day.

"So, why'd you take off work?" I ask, not pouring myself a cup of coffee. I make a mental note to buy two pounds of decaffeinated Sumatra and Mocha Java later.

"Because I just needed to."

"Well, you chose a good time to do it, with Spencer being home."

"But he's not home. He's gone."

"You know what I meant. He'll be back tomorrow, but we're going to Fresno first thing Friday morning."

"Do you really think it's a good idea for him and his girlfriend to go down there?"

"Honestly?"

He nods.

"I really don't want Spencer to see Lovey under these circumstances, at least not right now, until we can find out what's going on. It seems like Brianna has a good idea what to expect. But then there's Joy."

"Which is precisely my point. His girlfriend shouldn't have to deal with our family's problems while she's here."

"Why are you so worried about her?" I ask.

"I'm not worried about her. It's just a difficult situation to have to be exposed to. That's all I'm saying."

"I'll talk to him about it. I'd really just planned to take Lovey to the doctor because it's going to take up most of the day."

"Why?"

"I told you a couple of weeks ago, Leon."

"I'm sorry. I forgot. I've had a lot on my mind. Sorry."

"Well, she's getting tests done and depending on what time we finish, I was planning to drive back that evening. Spencer's leaving Sunday morning."

"I know."

"The doctor said if Lovey's test results look good, then there's some other mental-state test she should take. But I have to be there with her."

"Sounds like you're going to be doing a lot of running back and forth."

"Somebody's gotta do it. And besides, she's worth it. You understand that, don't you?"

He just looks at me. "What will you do if it turns out she's got Alzheimer's?"

"I'll deal with it when the time comes."

"Okay, then," he says, obviously wanting to switch gears. "So, where do we go from here?"

"What do you mean by that?"

"Now that there's no baby in our future, that space is open again and I was just wondering if you're giving any thought to what you might do with it."

"To be very honest, Leon, I have."

He looks rather surprised by my response.

"Even before I found out I was pregnant I'd been thinking about going back to school."

"Really? To study what?"

"I'm not completely sure."

"You have to have some idea. You used to want to save lost souls."

"I think maybe I should start with Marilyn."

"Oh, you think your soul is lost?"

"No. But it's been in hiding."

"And how's that?"

"I haven't had time to pay attention to what I really feel, what I really care about, or what I honestly think, and it's almost made me numb."

"Well, whose fault is that?"

"Did you hear me blame you?"

"No. Then I don't get it."

"Just about everything I do is for someone else's benefit."

"That's not true."

"Maybe you don't see it this way, but I'm telling you it's how it feels to me."

"So this is the best reason you could come up with to go back to school?"

"No. I feel like now that the kids are all gone, it's not too late for me to find my place out here."

He's nodding his head and if I was able to read him accurately, I'd almost be inclined to think he understands what I'm saying and that he might even agree.

"I really just need a change, Leon."

"So do I."

"I'm tired of doing the same thing the same way all the time."

"Me, too."

"I really want to get out more."

"So do I."

"I hardly ever spend time with my friends and when I do I always seem to be in a hurry, rushing to get home to do something: cook, take Arthurine to Bible study, laundry, something."

"Well you're not completely alone here either."

"I feel like I need to do something I've never tried before."

"Believe me, I understand that all too well."

"Name me one thing."

"Oh, I can't think of anything right now."

"Why not? Just one thing. Not ten."

"You tell me one while I think for a second."

"I've got a journal full of things, but for starters I'd like to go skinny-dipping in the ocean and make love on the beach at night. I'd like to get a tattoo. Yes, I would. I'd like to go to the airport with no luggage and just get on a plane to Paris or Rio. Somewhere, anywhere that lights up at night. Now you."

"Wow, you've given this a lot of thought I see. Okay. Let's see. I've always wanted to learn how to sail. And scuba dive. Drive a motorcycle across the United States. Go on safari with a bunch of guys. Design a house."

"So you have thought about it."

"In passing. They're fantasies, Marilyn. And rather far-fetched."

"I disagree. Totally. What's so far-fetched about going on safari? I'd like to do that one day myself. I want to go to Africa in general. We live in California, Leon. What's to stop you from taking scuba lessons?"

He's thinking. Trying to come up with a bullshit excuse. I just know it. "Well, I've actually applied to the master's program at two art schools."

"Really? To study what?"

"I don't know, mixed media."

"Can't you be more specific than that?"

"Both programs offer courses in all the things I love or want to learn how to do: from metal arts and glasswork to jewelry-making, and even sculpture. I could learn all about textiles and wood and maybe how to design furniture."

"Well, this certainly narrows it down. And what kind of job will the sum of these kinds of classes get you?"

"I don't know. I don't really care. I haven't thought about it that far. All I know is that I have to do something."

"You are doing something."

"No, I'm not. I haven't done anything except be your wife and raise kids for the last twenty-two years. That's what I've been doing. I think it's time for me to do something just for myself."

"I feel the same way."

"You want to go back to school, too?"

"Not really. But I'm seriously entertaining the idea of making a career change."

"What? Since when?"

"Oh, don't ask me that. It's been going on for some time. But to be honest, I think lately it's hit home that life is too short to not spend it doing what you really want to be doing."

"I thought you loved what you do, Leon."

"I used to. But my enthusiasm for my work has waned over the years. I've just done a pretty good job of hiding it."

"Not as good as you think."

"Well, I'll be honest. I'm mentally exhausted. I have no desire to go any further up the ladder in my field. In fact, I don't even know what appealed to me about engineering when I think back."

"You wanted to design buildings so they were safe," is all I can think to say.

"But none of the buildings have ever thanked me."

"The people who work in them do."

"They don't even know I exist."

"So, what are your options, Leon?"

"What do you think they are?"

"I can only speak for myself."

"Well, I could just quit my fucking job and go live in the wilderness for a year to find myself. Sabrina would love that."

"Be serious. And since when did you start using profanity?"

"What are you talking about?"

"You just said the f-word."

"I did not."

"You did so."

"Okay. If I did, it must've slipped out so fast I didn't realize it. I'm sorry. Anyway," he says, and gulps down what now has to be cold coffee, "I'm just bored with my life."

"So am I. But I'm bored with *our* life, Leon."

"So am I."

I'm surprised when he agrees with me on this one. "So what are we going to do about it?"

"I've been wondering about that for a long time, too," he says, "but I think we should wait to finish this conversation after Spence leaves."

"Why? What's he got to do with this?"

"I just don't want you to be upset while he's here."

"What could you possibly say that would upset me so much?"

"I just think our timing is wrong."

"Isn't it always? Go on and spit it out, Leon."

"I probably am going to have to leave."

"Your job?"

"Yes," he says. "And you."

I do not say a single solitary word. I grab my purse, snatch a jacket from the hall closet and storm toward the garage. Leon is trailing behind me.

"I didn't mean I wanted to leave *today*!"

The chime makes its beep-beep sound before I slam the door shut. I get in my car and raise the garage door as Leon comes charging out just as I'm backing out of the driveway. He stands next to his motorcycle, yelling, "Marilyn, I was just thinking out loud! Come back, please!"

I feel like running his ass over. But I don't. I think my tires make that burning rubber sound when I hit the gas. I have no idea where I'm going, but I know I cannot go to work. He wants to leave me? Then go, you son of a bitch! Right now, I just need to be as far away from him as possible. And here I am thinking we're finally having an honest, heart-to-heart talk, something we haven't done in years, when he's probably had his little agenda all laid out for some time but just hadn't planned on making his announcement today.

I'm halfway down the hill when it hits me: he's the one who wants to leave—not me—so why hasn't he? I slam on the brakes, make a U-turn and whip into the driveway and kill the engine. Through the garage I go, and turn off the chime so there's no beep when I open the door. I wish I were a burglar or a serial killer because he'd be shit out of luck either way.

He's on the phone. "She left out of here angry as all hell," he's saying. "Yes, I told her. No. I just said I was tired of the job. No, she didn't understand. I tried. I'm not sure. No. I can't just leave. Because. It wouldn't be fair to her. Or my mother. I was just trying to be honest with her and I can't believe it actually slipped out. I don't think she's devastated. More pissed than anything. She's a strong woman. No, I've told you before, I don't. Yes, I'm sure. Everything in time. This was just dreadful timing. One of my sons is home from college. He went snowboarding with his friends. The condo. Yes, the girlfriend is wife ma-terial. Look, I've gotta go. I need to think. No. Not tonight. I'll try to call you later. I hope she's all right."

I walk into the kitchen and stop dead in my tracks. "I'm fine," I say. "Call the bitch back and tell her you're coming right over, because I'm not going anywhere, Leon. You said you wanted to leave. So leave."

"I didn't mean today, Marilyn."

"Oh, so what am I supposed to do, wait until it's con-venient for you? Is that it?"

"Marilyn, I'm sorry."

"Leon, if you don't get out of this house in the next ten minutes, I'm going to do something I might regret."

"I just meant that a break might do us both some good. I'm going through something, Marilyn, and it scares me."

"Tell that to the bitch on the phone! Is she your secretary?"

"No."

"Does she work in your office? Of course she does, and I bet she's what, in her fucking twenties?"

"Thirties."

"Oh, an old bitch, but not quite as old as me, huh?"

"Marilyn, this is all wrong."

"I'm looking at the clock, Leon!"

"I'm just going to get my jacket. Marilyn, please, please understand that I didn't mean this quite the way it came out. I swear it," he says, as he puts on his brand-new leather bomber. He stops in front of the door and when he sees what must be flames shooting out my nostrils, he takes the hint and leaves. I hope he gets on that stupid motorcycle and rides off a fucking cliff just like Thelma and Louise did. But when I hear him revving up its engine and then taking off at what sounds like break-neck speed, my heart drops because I know Leon doesn't know how to go fast around curves.

Chapter 13

The doorbell rings and I just about jump out of my
skin. It couldn't possibly be Paulette or Bunny
because they always call first. Plus, I haven't had
enough time to even consider what just happened here
to think about what I'm going to tell them. Please don't
let it be those Jehovah's Witnesses because I am not in
the mood for explaining why I don't need to hear The
Word. Especially this morning. But then again, if it is
them, maybe I should just invite them in for tea because
Arthurine should be hopping off of her mall van any moment. Let her deal with them. And they can debate as
long as they want to about whose God is the holiest.

I turn the knob slowly, prepared for battle, but by the
time I step out in front of the door my demeanor
changes. "Gordon?"

"Good morning, Marilyn! Forgive me for just dropping by like this, but I just bought a house not three
blocks from here and as I'm driving down the street I

see your husband's card in the ashtray and for some reason I pull it out only to discover that I'm right in front of your house. I'm not kidding. So I figured this was a sign, and I just took a chance and rang the doorbell. How are you?"

"I'm fine." What else can I say? Plus I'm in shock. Never in a million years would I have thought Gordon King would be on the other side of my front door on any morning. Jehovah may very well have had something to do with this, I don't know. "Come on in," I say, stepping away so he can enter.

"Seriously. I don't mean to intrude. I just wanted to say hello."

"Hello," I say, hoping this is a dream and I can do anything I want to in it. If this be the case, then I want Gordon to read my mind and come closer. I want him to wrap his arms around me like warm vines. I want him to make me forget about every tragic event that's been interrupting my journey. I want him to kiss me slowly and deeply. I want him to make love to me at an angle, on those stairs behind us, so that as he's finding his way inside, I'll slide up so high I'll be able to look down on my world and see it clearer. I want him to dust my heart with hope. Wipe away the cobwebs covering my soul. Open all the clogged-up drains where my energy has been trapped. And then I want to flood. I want him to be the river I seek.

When my eyes are wide open, I want him to ask me what I've been doing for the past twenty-three years. I will tell him the truth. I will not apologize for being a housewife. I want him to be the man to ask me how I'd like to spend the rest of life. What am I willing to do to make the last third of it even more vibrant and fulfilling than the first two. "Finally," he'll say. "You've found your center. Now, let's try this again, but this time we'll get it right. It's the reason why I'm in your dream. But wake up. Because I'm here, right now."

I close the door. "You're not intruding," I say. "Do you drink coffee?"

"Doesn't everybody?"

I don't bother answering. He looks good to me even in work clothes. He's wearing a black bandanna tied around his head like an Indian to keep his locks from falling in his face, I suppose. "Where's your house?"

"You can't miss it. It's the ugliest one on the block. I got a good deal on it and since I've got a little time on my hands, I'm already getting quite a kick trying to make it like new. Might take me about a year or so, but it's okay."

"You're not a principal anymore?"

"Yes and no. I took a year's leave because I got a grant to research and run an outreach program for adolescent boys. There's a lot more to it, but I'll leave it at that. Like I said, I didn't mean to invade your privacy. How's your husband?"

"He's fine."

"He's a nice brother. I like him. Seems really smart and he certainly loves him some Marilyn."

I have to stop myself from saying, "Oh, so he had you fooled, too?" Instead I just say, "He is smart."

"Your home is really nice. Well, would you look at that?"

"What?" I say, looking, too. I thought maybe he might have just seen a mouse or something. But he's walking over to look at a table I sort of redid.

"What's all this stuff on here?"

"Just stuff," I say.

"Where in the world did you find a table like this?"

"It should be obvious, Gordon. Somebody made it."

"You?"

I nod.

"Get out."

"Come on. Let's go on into the kitchen so I can get the coffee started." He follows so close behind me I think I can smell his mouthwash. He sits on a stool at the counter. Looks around. I pour cold water into the clean clear pot. Put a few scoops of real coffee into the gold filter. I don't know if I want this thing to perc fast or slow.

"Then I suppose you made that light fixture over the table, too?"

"Yep."

"Finally," he sighs.

"Finally, what?"

"You found your center."

I'm about ready to have a stroke any second. I need to get him out of this house. I'm too emotionally fragile right now to have this man who I used to not just be madly in love with but even married to, in my kitchen, the kitchen in which moments ago my present husband just told me how bored he was with me and our life and that he was leaving me. In fact, I think the son of a bitch is gone. "How do you take your coffee?"

"Black," he says. "Do you make a lot of these types of things?"

"When I have time."

"Leon told me you guys have a daughter and twin sons, all in college. That's something."

"Sabrina is finishing her last year at Cal. And the twins are sophomores at Moorhouse. In fact, one of them—Spencer—is here this week on spring break but he's in Tahoe snowboarding, and Simeon is playing in a jazz band in Atlanta so he wasn't able to make it."

"This is what I love to hear," he says, taking the cup I'm handing him as I try very hard not to touch his hand. "So do you sell any of your work?"

"No. It's a hobby. I do it because it's fun and it relaxes me. I give most of it away. In fact, I'm sure I can find something in my workshop or the garage to give to you. I need to get rid of some of this stuff."

"I'll take anything you want to give me," he says, taking a sip of his coffee. "You ever thought of selling any of it?"

"Not really."

"You should. Maybe at some of these craft fairs. They're all over northern California in the summer. And those folks sell some pretty amazing things at all kinds of prices. I'm surprised you haven't done it."

"I haven't thought that far ahead yet."

"I'm not sure what you mean by 'yet.' "

"Well, a lot of things seem to be happening at once

and I only seem to be able to focus on one thing at a time."

"Welcome to the human race. Do you work?"

"Part-time at a craft store."

"Oh, so you're still tiptoeing."

"What's that supposed to mean? I just told you this has always been just a hobby. I haven't had to think about 'making a living' before."

"So does this mean you have to think about it now?"

"Maybe. No. I don't know what I'm thinking about doing."

"I'll shut up," he says, taking what seems to be the last sip of his coffee. "Aren't you having any?"

"No."

"You don't drink coffee?"

"Not with caffeine."

"Menopause, huh?"

"How'd you know?"

"Come on, Marilyn. I wasn't born yesterday. I also read."

"Is your girlfriend going through it?"

"Not yet. Your husband told you about Blossom?"

"Blossom?"

"Her real name is Ayanna which means beautiful flower in Swahili, but everybody just calls her Blossom. She's from Kenya but lives in Paris."

"Well, Leon was quite taken by Blossom's petals."

He chuckles. "She's an amazing woman all right."

"If she lives in Paris, how can she be your girlfriend?"

"Who said she was my girlfriend?"

"You did."

"No, I didn't. You did."

Now he's actually laughing out loud. "You have not changed," he says, looking at me in a way that is making me feel so comfortable I'm uncomfortable.

"She imports art, so she travels back and forth."

"Did you ever have any kids, Gordon?"

"Just the ones you didn't have," he says.

I hear Arthurine coming in the front door. Just what I need. I know she saw that black Saab parked out front and she's wondering whose it is. I can hear her sneakers squishing in this direction. "Marilyn, where are you, baby?"

"In the kitchen, Arthurine."

I look at Gordon. "My mother-in-law."

He nods. Stands up. My goodness. I hope Blossom knows what to do with all this. Obviously she must. "Well, now that I know where you and Leon live, I'll stop by every day! Seriously, I'm down on Sequoia and don't ask what color my house is because I couldn't honestly say."

"Why, hello there," Arthurine says to Gordon. She has no idea who he is, but apparently he just turned the wattage up a few amps for her.

"How are you, ma'am. I'm Gordon King. An old friend of Marilyn's and just happened to be in the neighborhood."

"I'm Arthurine and don't let me run you off. Stay!" She's actually leaning her back against the doorway, and it looks like she's about to plié because her right toe is pointing and her heel isn't touching the floor.

"Gotta get to work," he says. "Have you been out jogging?"

Now she's blushing! Even behind those giant spectacles I can see her eyelids fluttering. "I guess you could say that," she says proudly. She ought to stop. Poor Prezelle. Lord help him. I wish I had a scripture for this occasion, but I don't.

"Well," she continues, "I really walk the mall, but I'm getting to be so fast it feels like I'm jogging."

"Well you certainly look healthy and in top form and that's a pretty snazzy outfit you're wearing."

"Why, thank you, Gordon."

"You're quite welcome," he says.

As Gordon gets up and heads out of the kitchen, Arthurine barely gives him enough room to pass. I give her a slight push when I brush up against her.

That's when the phone rings. Hallelujah!

"Good seeing you again, Marilyn," Gordon says, once we get to the front door. "And please give some thought to those craft fairs or eBay. I'd look into some if not all of these avenues if I were you."

The phone rings again.

"Well, it certainly can't hurt," I say.

Ring. Ring. Ring.

"Arthurine! Would you please answer the phone?"

"I was just about to!"

"I'd buy something from you in a heartbeat even though you did promise to give me something and I was hoping it was going to be today, but I'm a patient man. I can wait. And I'll be back."

"Hello. Hold on a minute, please," she says, covering the mouthpiece with one hand. Now Arthurine is standing in the entry. "Gordon!"

"Yes, ma'am?"

"I just have to tell you that we think a lot alike because I've been telling her she should sell some of this stuff, too, but she won't listen to me. Maybe you have more influence. How well do you know this chile?"

"Arthurine, just answer the phone, would you?"

"Okay! Hope to see you again soon!" she says and disappears into the kitchen.

I wave good-bye to him like he's going off to war or something. But before I can get back inside, I hear Arthurine asking, "What happened?"

I run into the kitchen. "Who is it, Arthurine? What's wrong?"

"It's Spencer," she says.

My heart stops.

"Well, it's not Spencer on the phone but the girl telling me he broke his wrist or something or another on that board. Here," she says, handing me the phone. "You talk to her."

"Brianna?"

"Hello, Mrs. Grimes. First off, Spencer's gonna be all right. He's just getting out of surgery."

"Surgery? Surgery for what?"

"Well, apparently he broke his wrist in quite a few places and they couldn't just put a cast on it so they had to go in and make some adjustments."

"What kind of adjustments?"

"I'm not completely sure, but the doctor said something about he might need to put some kind of pins in there to hold his bones together."

"So where are you guys?"

"We're in the emergency room."

"I know that, Brianna, but what hospital?"

"I'm not real sure but I'll get the name in a second. It all just happened so fast, I can't even believe we're up here in these mountains in an emergency room."

"Where is Spencer right this minute, Brianna?"

"He should be going into the recovery room in a few minutes."

"Okay. Where are all the boys?"

"They're sitting out here in the waiting room with me."

"Which wrist is it?"

"I don't know. I have to think a second. It's his right one."

"It would be. Is there any way I can talk to him?"

"Not yet. He asked me not to call you or his dad until after the surgery. And that's what I'm doing. Hold on a minute, Mrs. Grimes. They just called my name. I'll call you back in a few minutes."

She hangs up.

Arthurine's eyes are closed, which means she's praying. "He'll be just fine," she says opening them. "You want me to try to reach Leon at work on the other line?"

"No!"

"Okay. I suppose there's no need to get him all upset until we know what's going on."

When the phone rings again, I answer before the ring finishes. "Hello."

"Hi, Mom! It's Sim. Guess what."

"Hi, Sim. I really want to know but your brother just broke his wrist snowboarding and has had surgery and he's up in Tahoe in the emergency room and I'm waiting by the phone to hear what his prognosis is, so can I call you right back, baby?"

"Sure, Mom. What an idiot. I bet he was showing off for what's-her-name. Call me back later. Love you."

I hang up and it rings again. "Hello?"

"Mrs. Grimes?"

I want to say, don't you recognize my voice. "Yes, Brianna. Is Spencer's wrist all right?"

"Well, sort of. He wants to talk to you even though he might not make a whole lot of sense because they gave him quite a bit of pain medication. Here you go."

"Mom, don't freak out. It was just an accident. But I'm alive. It's just a stupid wrist. But check it out, I look like I might be an alien or something."

"What are you talking about, Spencer?"

"You've gotta see this shit. It's so fucking cool. I've got like metal screws going right into my fucking wrist, man, and I can't even feel it, man. This is so fucking deep."

"*Spencer!* Please put Brianna back on the phone."

Apparently he heard me and understood.

"Hello again, Mrs. Grimes. I apologize for Spencer, but he's really out of it. Anyway, what he was trying to tell you is that they've had to put this apparatus called an external fixator on his wrist and he's got these metal-like rods holding his bones together."

"You mean inside or out?"

"Well, both. You can see where they go right through his skin."

"Oh, my God. And how long will he have to wear this?"

"Eight weeks."

"When can he leave?"

"We're not sure yet if he's going to have to stay here all night, but he's probably not going to be able to do much traveling tomorrow, I wouldn't think. But why don't we do this. As soon as the doctor gets back, which they just told me won't be for another four or five hours because he's got another surgery scheduled, I can have him call you and explain everything and see what he thinks is best for Spence to do. How's that sound?"

"It sounds okay. It sounds okay. How are you holding up?"

"I just want to go home. I don't like snow. It's too cold up here and I hardly saw any black people. I don't like it up here, I don't care how pretty it is."

"I don't much blame you. But thank you for being there for my son, Brianna."

"You're quite welcome, ma'am. Bye-bye."

I hang up.

"Don't worry, Marilyn. A wrist can heal," Arthurine says, which is about the smartest thing I've heard her say in a long time.

"That's true."

"Aren't you supposed to be at work right now?"

"I wasn't feeling very good this morning."

"Well, that's understandable," she says, heading back toward Snuffy's bed. "Considering what all you've been through."

Chapter 14

That's not a motorcycle I hear on the other side of the wall, is it? I'm in my workshop where I've been killing time for the last three and a half hours waiting to hear from the doctor. Where I mindlessly threw together two ridiculous pillows that weren't worth stuffing. I wouldn't even give them away, which is precisely why I tossed them in the trash. I have no idea what I'm sewing now.

When the door from the garage opens, my foot freezes on the machine pedal. That better not be him. My hands drop into my lap and I just sit here. Maybe Leon's going crazy or something. Or he's having a nervous breakdown and needs help. I certainly can't help him.

Knock. Knock.

"Who is it?"

"It's me," Arthurine says, standing in the doorway. "Leon came home from work a little early today. He said he wasn't feeling good either. Maybe you both are coming down with the same thing. I'm staying away from the two of you, that's for sure. There's a trip to Reno next week that Prezelle has invited me to, so I can't afford to get sick.

"I wouldn't miss this for anything. I've never been inside a casino, but I don't think the Lord will mind if I play the slot machines. Anyway, Leon was looking for you, and I figured you might be in here. You look upset, Marilyn. Don't worry, Spencer's going to be all right, baby."

"I'm not really worrying, Arthurine. What are Leon's symptoms?"

"He said he's having pains in his chest and shortness of breath."

"Maybe he's having a heart attack."

"Don't even think that, Marilyn."

"Anything's possible."

"I checked his forehead. He don't have a fever. Why don't you go on up and check on him? See for yourself."

"I will in a minute. I have to make a phone call first," I say, and pick up the portable and press line two.

"Well, it didn't help with me telling him about Spencer."

"I'm sure that would send him over the edge."

"Marilyn?"

"What?"

"He loves all three of his children. You know that."

"Of course he does. He loves them so much he wants to be morphed."

"Wants to be what?"

"Never mind. Did he tell you he'd been at work?"

"Well, no. But why wouldn't he be?"

"Why don't you go back upstairs and ask him where he really came from, Arthurine?"

"What's going on, Marilyn?"

"Go ask your loving, caring, thoughtful, Mac Daddy son."

She looks terribly confused, and I didn't mean to do or say anything to her about any of this before Leon did or at least until the air cleared and I got my bearings. But shit happens. She turns and walks away. I call Paulette on the boys' line. "How you doing?" I ask.

"Marilyn?"

"Yeah, it's me."

"What's wrong? I can hear it in your voice and you know damn well you never call here asking how I'm doing. What's wrong? You haven't gotten an infection or anything, have you?"

"No. It would be nice if it was that simple."

"Is it Leon?"

"You always were clairvoyant, Paulette."

"What's he gone and done? Wait. Let me guess: told you he's leaving because he's bored and now that the kids are all grown-up he realizes he's missed out on the most exciting time of his life because he got married so young and has been overburdened with the demands of it all and now here's his one chance to get it back and have some damn fun before he dies an old man and of course he has met some sweet young thang completely by accident because of course he had no intention of cheating on you but she was the one who put the radar out and came after him and he couldn't believe it when he didn't resist her advances but he was even more surprised when he had to repeat the shit over and over because boy oh boy, she put no demands on him whatsoever, none, and she just appreciates him for who he is and what he does and she makes him feel interesting and smart and desirable and he'd forgotten what this felt like with you and hell, she makes him feel twenty-five again and even though he doesn't think this little interlude is anything serious or if it's going anywhere but all he knows is that he has to leave to see for himself, to fill in the blanks, and he's sorry for hurting you because of course he still loves you. Is that about right?"

I want to cry but I'm laughing too hard. "You've got it just about right. Anyway, first this asshole tells me over coffee this morning that he might need a change of scenery from his job, and I basically tell him that I understand how things can get a little stale, but then when he tells me he thinks he may have to leave, of course I'm thinking he's talking about his job, which he is, but then as a little fucking addendum, he tacks me on, too."

"I've been through this one once and that was all it took. You don't know how many women have come into my store spending money like crazy because they're depressed and feeling hopeless and ugly, like they've outlived their usefulness because their husbands have surprised them this very same way. Like Puff the Magic Fucking Dragon—poof!—they just up and leave: kids and all. I listen to their stories, which are almost all identical, and I take their sad credit cards, and try to make them feel pretty and necessary. Men are just so predictable. This shit must be their rite of passage to middle age or something because they all seem to go a little nuts after they hit their forties. Are you okay over there?"

"Oh, I'm fine. But this is the kicker, Paulette. At first I get in my car and leave and then I turn that sucker around and drive back up that hill and march in here and tell him since he's the one who wants to leave then he's the one who should go. So he does. This is after I threaten him of course, but guess what?"

"What, girl?"

"The motherfucker came back!"

"Home?"

"Yes! He's upstairs right now!"

"Doing what?"

"I don't know. Arthurine just told me he's coming down with something and I hope it's terminal cancer and he just came back so he could spend his last waking hours with his family. I can get the shovel out of the garage and start digging his grave in the backyard."

"Shut up, Marilyn! I know you're just upset. But why did he come back I wonder?"

"Because he's stupid, that's why. He probably doesn't even remember saying it. That's a line he's been using a lot around here lately after he does or says something off the wall. Anyway, I hate his guts and I want a divorce."

"Slow down, Marilyn. Leon's not quite up there with

some of these other sleazebags. Maybe he is going through a tough patch."

"Well, somebody else is helping him get through it."

"It happens. But sometimes it's just a silly fling."

"What if I were to have a silly little fling? Do you think he'd be as understanding? Huh?"

"You've got a point. They can usually dish it out but they never seem to be able to take it. And just for the record. Almost all of these deserted wives take the suckers back after they get tired of playing with Barbies and come to their senses."

"Not me. If you leave, you're gone. Anyway, I don't want to talk about Mr. Corndog anymore. Spencer broke his wrist snowboarding today and I've been waiting by this phone to see when he can come home and oh shit!"

"What?"

"I forgot to call Simeon back."

"He's in one piece I hope?"

"Yeah. I swear, Paulette, when it rains it pours, doesn't it?"

"It's God's way of making us pay attention, so deal with it, Marilyn."

"I'm just not sure how, right this minute."

"Don't worry. It's always the hardest road. Not the easy one. Look. I've got three customers standing here. Call me back if you need me or if anything changes, okay?"

"Okay. And please don't tell Miss Bunny any of this. Not yet. I don't feel like hearing her psychobabble."

"I won't. Just remember, sometimes what looks like the end is really the beginning."

The beginning of what?

I don't want to go upstairs but I go anyway. Might as well see what he has to say. And who knows, maybe he is sick. But even if he is, why didn't he let his girlfriend play Nurse Betty since she apparently has restorative powers. The door to our bedroom is open. He's sitting up on top of the burgundy comforter, on the phone, obviously talking to Simeon. I just stand here and listen.

"Yes, Son, I think that's great! An agent? You guys must be really good. At first I was upset when I heard you were changing majors, but the more I thought about it, the more I realized that you're only young once and you should take all the risks you can right now while you have time on your side. I mean it. What have you got to lose? There are so many roads out here you can take and you can keep changing them until you find the one you want to travel down. I know. Me? Truthfully? I think I may be burned out. Yes, the job and just my life. Well, I've been doing things I can't explain before thinking about who it might hurt. I don't do it on purpose and it's scary because I feel like I'm out of control. Sure, she sees it. No, she can't. I don't think I need a shrink, Simeon. Sometimes you have to step outside of yourself in order to see inside. I agree. Music is a great tool. I just have to do whatever it takes to get hold of myself before I destroy everything I've worked for and the people I love. Yes, I still do. Very much so. Look, Son, your mother's just come in and I'm sure she wants to say hello to you. I'd like to hear your music so don't be surprised when I fly down to check you out. Good. Spencer's going to be fine. He's always been the daredevil."

"I'll call him back," I say, because I don't want to follow up half of what he just said.

"Sim, Mom's a little shook up and out of sorts, so she said she'll call you back later. Okay. I love you, Son."

He puts the phone back into the cradle and looks at me.

I look at him.

"I'm sorry," he says.

"I'm glad to hear it, Leon. That should pretty much fix everything, then, huh?"

"No. But I really didn't mean some of the things I said."

"Yes, you did. You meant every word of it. And it's okay. I meant what I said."

"I didn't intend for this to happen like this, Marilyn. I swear it."

"I already know the whole spiel so don't even bother repeating it for me, Leon."

"What spiel are you talking about?"

"Middle-aged men going through a midlife crisis and using that as an excuse for doing whatever they feel like doing."

"Who said I was going through a midlife crisis?"

"It's pretty obvious, Leon."

"Not to me it isn't."

"Of course it wouldn't be."

"What are some of the symptoms?"

"Overt stupidity. Promiscuity. Regressive behavior. How would I know, Leon? All I know is what menopause feels like."

"All men don't go through it, do they?"

"I just told you, I've got enough to worry about. Look up your own stuff."

"I don't buy into that crap."

"Anyway, I still haven't heard from that doctor."

"He called while I was on the other line."

"What did he say, Leon? I've been going crazy."

"Spencer's fine. He's just in a lot of pain. The doctor said he needs to stay put for at least another day because he has to keep his wrist elevated or his fingers might swell up and get sore and it could cause some kind of drainage and then lead to an infection."

"So, no more surgery, then?"

"No. The doctor said he's giving Spence his X-rays and all his notes to take back to Atlanta."

"Good. I'm relieved to hear this. So they won't be back until Friday."

"That's the way it is."

"Then I have to figure out whether to leave early afternoon on Thursday or early Friday."

"You're still going down there?"

"I can't just change Lovey's appointment, Leon! We've been through this once before so I'm not even going to go there. Spencer's been taken care of. And I need to make sure that the same thing will happen to my mother."

"Well, I'll be here for him."

"Don't you mean 'them'?"

"No."

"So what do you propose we do now, Leon? Just pick it up where we left off this morning?"

"I'm not sure."

"I can tell you right now, that my answer to that question is an unequivocal no."

"Look, Marilyn. I'll be honest with you, okay? I think we could both use a break from each other. A breather. To maybe get a better perspective on what we have or don't have."

"I couldn't agree more. Then why'd you come back so damn soon? I thought you were on your way."

"Because this isn't the right time to make an exit and you know that."

"Then why'd you bring it up if you weren't planning to back it up?"

"Because you insisted."

"Okay, so?"

"I was trying to wait until after Spence left."

"Well, scratch that one. So, are you moving in with her?"

"No. It's not that serious. I'm not in love with her. It's just something that's been fun and frivolous."

"Fun and frivolous, huh? You know Gordon stopped by right after you left and you'll never believe this but he just bought a house right down the street and Lord have mercy he looked so damn good I wanted to lick him. Arthurine got a little worked up over him, too. Maybe after you're gone, or hell, why wait till then? I could give him a little spin in the sack later on tonight for old times' sake. He was good, you know. In fact, maybe I'll video-tape it so you can see how it's supposed to be done."

"Don't do this, Marilyn."

"Why not? You did."

"Okay, you have a right to throw acid on me, but what I want to say is that I accept responsibility for what I've become: a boring middle-aged man who forgot how to live. I could use some lessons on how to recon-struct myself into being the man you married, the man I know I am."

"And just how do you propose to do that?"

"I'm going away."

"Really?"

"On Monday. Frank and I are going to Costa Rica. For four weeks."

"Costa Rica? For four weeks? That's a whole month. Is this some kind of conspiracy?"

"Not at all."

"Well it's been carefully planned, that much is obvi-ous. No worries. Go. Anywhere you want to. Just think. A whole month to spend with your cheating-but-almost-divorced homeboy?"

"Actually, he's back at home."

"You mean to tell me Joyce took his sorry ass back?"

"They do love each other, Marilyn. They've even started going to counseling. In fact, I forgot to tell you that Saturday is Frank's birthday and Sunday is their twenty-fifth wedding anniversary so they're having a big party. We have to go."

"No, we don't."

"It would hurt them deeply if you didn't come. I know you're mad at me, but don't take it out on them."

"I'll give it some thought. We were on our way to Costa Rica a minute ago. Let's go back." He sees how cynical I'm being and I know he's serious but I feel like he wants me to understand his so-called plight but when has he ever taken this much time to give me this much consideration?

"Well, anyway, last year, Frank's brother Abe and a group of his buddies all went down there for a whole month."

"To do what?"

"Find themselves."

"Don't you mean, lose themselves?"

"No, Frank and I are pretty much in the same boat."

"And what boat is that, Leon?"

"It's hard to explain because we don't really under-stand why nothing seems to be making much sense to us anymore."

"So just what are you two going to do down there to find yourselves?"

"We don't have all the details yet. All Abe said was that sometimes you have to step outside of your situation in order to get your perspective back."

"Well, I empathize with you two lost adulterers. So, is it a four-star hotel with a spa?"

"Actually there's more to it than that. But to answer your question, yes, it is, and there's a spectacular spa."

"Oh goody. Wouldn't want you to miss your workout while you're searching for your soul."

"Marilyn, please."

"So, you've been planning this for some time, then."

"Look. I've been feeling confused about a lot of things and this might be the best thing I could do for me and for you."

"Maybe you should just go ahead and take me out of this video."

"Are you saying that you want me to leave?"

"I'll say this much. I've certainly wondered what my life would be like on my own. I can't deny that."

"So, would you want to try being apart for a while to see what happens?"

"Yeah, but what about your mother?"

"I hadn't thought about Mother."

"Of course you haven't. You were just supposed to leave me here with her to continue being Miss Endless Caregiver, was that it?"

"No. But I'll think of something."

"She wants to move out, you know."

"What?"

"She wants to move over there where her boyfriend lives."

"He is not her boyfriend."

"He's her boyfriend."

"Isn't that place more like a nursing home for people who have medical problems?"

"No, it is not. It's an apartment complex for seniors. And according to Arthurine, Prezelle is not handicapped in any sense of the word."

"The thought itself is disgusting."

"Anyway, she's on the waiting list."

"When did all this happen?"

"While you were out being frivolous and hence missing in action, Arthurine's been getting plenty of it. That's when."

"But why does she want to move?"

"Because she's bored and lonely, Leon. Just like the rest of us who live in this house! She's having fun. Something I don't have much of anymore, at least not with my husband. And I'll say this so we can come clean. I just lost a baby I didn't want and I think God did it to shake you up and get you to admit all this stuff, but I'm supposed to do something different, too, and I don't know how I'm supposed to do it or what I'm supposed to do but I can't do it by the book anymore. That much I do know."

"I told you I thought going back to school was a good idea."

"That is not what you said, Leon. But it's okay. I'm not just talking about going back to school. Anyway, I'm exhausted. I'm tired of talking. And please don't even think about sleeping in this bed tonight or any of the remaining nights before you leave."

"I won't touch you, Marilyn."

"I know that. Why start now? But do this, Leon: show your mother some respect and try not to make her feel guilty because she's still got feelings. Prezelle is a nice man. And she would be much happier over there."

"How soon does she want to go?"

"The waiting list is long so it could be months. But

don't let this news stop you from leaving. If I have to, I can deal with Arthurine, or better yet, maybe I could leave and you two could stay here and then you could bring your girlfriend. How's that sound?"

"I told you she's not my girlfriend."

"Then what is she?"

"A good friend."

"Do you sleep with your friends?"

"No, not usually."

I would love to sucker punch him if I could do it hard enough to hurt. "Whatever."

"Whatever you want to do, you'll have my support. Financial and emotional."

"Let's just deal with the first one and see what happens. Okay," I say, turning to leave.

"What are you doing right now?"

"Going back downstairs to fix something I ruined."

"Would you have dinner with me later?"

"I thought you were so sick?"

"I had to tell Mother something."

"Well, think about it, Leon. What would make you think I'd want to have dinner with you after what we've been through today, huh?"

"So you don't have to worry about cooking."

"Excuse me?"

"You can even choose the restaurant."

"Am I lucky or what? Look, Leon. You're missing the point and you know it. I haven't thought about food all day, and I certainly had no intention of cooking."

"Then what are we going to eat?"

" *We?* You aren't even supposed to be here! You left me this morning! Remember?"

He's shaking his head no like a little kid.

"Call your fucking girlfriend back! Have her for dinner."

"That's not funny, Marilyn."

"And I'm not laughing. I think I'll order Chinese."

"I'm not really in the mood for Chinese tonight."

"You're not in the . . . *what* did you just say?"

"I said I don't really have a taste for Chinese tonight."

If I had a shoe on with a thick heel I'd throw it at his stupid ass. "Leon," I sigh. "I don't know how you made it through college sometimes. But read my lips: I don't really give a flying fuck what you're in the mood to eat. Okay? So hurry up and recover and get out of the bed and go eat lobster or lamb at one of your favorite spots. Your mother likes to dine out, so take her. And on the way, you can pick your ho up and see if the two of them hit it off."

"Marilyn, that's not a very nice thing to say."

"Who's trying to be nice? I see you found the nicest possible way to tell me how tired you are of being my husband in one breath and that you were leaving me in the next. So fuck you, Mr. Nice Guy. I've got some research to do."

"That is *not* what I said and it's not what I'm doing. What kind of research?"

"That's really none of your business."

"I'm just curious. I've never heard you say you're going to research anything."

"I'm about to explore my options."

"Good, because that's really all I'm trying to figure out, too. I hope to be a better man when Frank and I get back. Seriously."

"Then you're going to need to stay a whole lot longer than four weeks."

Chapter 15

I do not order Chinese. I do not research craft fairs or how to sell anything on eBay. If I were a man, I'd probably go down on MacArthur Boulevard and get myself a prostitute. But I'm not a man. I'm a woman whose shoulders feel heavier than any man's right now. I have to get out of this house. Arthurine's television is blaring and I pray she's in there sound asleep. The house is dark and I don't want to turn on the lights as I tiptoe down the stairs. At the garage door, I turn off the chime, and get in my car. I roll down all the windows and open the sunroof even though it's cold outside. I don't care.

I drive with the heat off. Play the only CD in here, one I made just for the car. I blast it. And sing along with Jill, Alicia Keys, and Etta James. Santana, Moby, and Ben Harper. In the Caldecott Tunnel everything sounds louder and I scream at the top of my lungs because I remember reading a long time ago that this could do wonders in reducing stress and anger. I've got both, and for a little extra insurance, I give it all I've got one more time for as long as I can. My head hurts like hell afterward. This could be one of those times when less is better.

When Sarah McLachlan sings the song from the *City of Angels* soundtrack, I see Meg Ryan sliding down the end of that bathtub under a trillion bubbles while dreaming about Nicholas Cage. I'm remembering all too well how much she longed for him and how much he longed for her while his ghost watched her bathe. I wish someone longed for me that way. Oh Lord, I'm getting sentimental and don't feel like going there. It's just a song from a mushy movie and plus I can't stand Meg Ryan. I turn the radio on and let her drown.

At the Lafayette Hotel, I get off the freeway. I do not know why. The car seems to be driving me where I'm supposed to go. The hotel looks like a small modern castle, all terra-cotta and white stucco. It does not seem to fit the location it's in because there are hundreds of homes nestled in the surrounding hills. I could pretend I'm in England and before I know it, I'm at the entrance.

"Checking in, ma'am?" a young blond guy asks. He looks like a surfer.

"I am," I say. "Do you surf?"

"Absolutely," he says. "Are your bags in the trunk?"

"No. I don't have any."

"I hear you," he says. "Well, registration's right inside. I'm pretty sure we've got plenty of rooms this evening."

I give him a ten-dollar tip. Rooms are available and I

register for a suite. It has a working fireplace, a view of Mt. Diablo, and it is not cheap. I don't care. When I get inside my room I see what I paid for. I almost don't know what to do. It feels like I'm standing in a photograph of a room in a fancy hotel. The walls are hunter green. White plantation shutters cover the windows. The comforter is fluffy and white. I strike a long match and make a fire. Then I take my sneakers off and lie down on the bed. I look up at the white ceiling and close my eyes. When I open them again, it's daylight.

I have just made history. This marks the first time I've ever spent the night away from home, alone, in almost a quarter of a century. I pray Leon is freaking out. He should know what it feels like to wonder where I am for once. I wish I could live here—or somewhere that wasn't home—for a month without telling him. I have already taken the rest of the week off from work to be with my son who isn't around. In fact, maybe I should find some exotic place to go where I can dig up my soul until it rises to the surface. But then what?

I order breakfast from room service. Orange juice. Decaffeinated coffee. Eggs Benedict. Home fries. Eat all of it and read *USA Today*. The television is waiting to be turned on, and since I'm in a frigging hotel room and don't want to go home yet, I do. Some talk show is on and I can't believe when seconds before they go to a commercial break, the topic of today's show is splattered across the screen: CAN THIS MARRIAGE BE SAVED?

The real question should be, is it worth saving? Or ask if they want to save their marriage because it's the *mar-*

riage they want to hold on to, not the *person*. As if marriage is some kind of all-encompassing entity that can sustain you all by itself. Ask them if they're pissed because they thought they were getting a package deal. Ask them if they feel like they've gotten the short end of the marriage stick. Or do they want to save their marriage because they've just gotten used to being married and don't know what else to do? Ask them that. Ask if they're just afraid of meeting themselves without the veil of marriage covering their face. Ask how tired they are of putting on a good show for everybody to the point where even they fall for their own lie. Ask them what's more important, saving the marriage or saving yourself? And who goes on nationwide television to find the answer to this question? Where do they find these people? Why haven't Leon and I ever gotten a call? I think we qualify.

I turn this silly shit off and take a bath with just as many bubbles as Meg Ryan had but don't feel all dreamy and what have you and I don't see any fucking ghosts or feel any aura in here and if I did I'd open the window and blow him right on out of here. After starring in my own movie for a half hour I get out and put my same clothes back on. Open the shutters and look out at the green velvet hills that seem to go on forever. This is just one of the reasons why I love California. It's not flat and gray. It is not all one thing. And even on a gloomy day it's still beautiful. I'm not half as afraid of earthquakes as I should be, mostly because I feel like a fault line myself. Right now, for instance, I'm rattling inside. My mind is jostling. My heart is shivering. I'm all shook up. I stare at the rolling hills until they become one emerald blur, until an unbelievable calm seems to fall over me and I realize something I haven't thought about before: just about everybody in my life is doing exactly what they want to do. Arthurine is like a college girl, making plans to move out on her own. She's even got travel plans. Who cares if it's to Reno? Arthurine is probably in better shape than I am, too. At least she gets some exercise. Spencer—broken wrist and all—is with the girl he wants to be with right now and loves being a college student whose parents can afford to send him a ticket to come home for spring break and even go snowboarding in Lake Tahoe. Simeon has discovered that playing music is what really moves him. Sabrina is happy and pregnant. She knows I wished she could have waited until after she got her master's but she basically blew me off and is doing it the way she wants to. Even Joy. She enjoys getting high, although I'm sure it's because it's the only pleasure she's found that's guaranteed. And then there's Leon. My so-called husband. He's having an affair but thinks of it as a new form of friendship. And now he's getting on an airplane, flying to a tropical place where he really believes he's going to have some kind of epiphany or a metaphysical experience that's going to transform him. Into what, I don't know. But at least he's finally trying something new. Now it's just me. And Lovey.

Paulette is yakking on the phone when I walk into her boutique. She's heading toward the back where she keeps all of her stock so I say hello to Maya, Paulette's niece, who works part-time. She's walking around this small but wonderful little shop, making sure everything is in its place, and waiting for one of four women to ask for her help. Paulette sells good quality merchandise at reasonable prices: sexy lingerie, cool handmade jewelry, casual-funky clothing, and distinctive evening wear— things you won't find in a department store. She sells soaps and candles that she makes herself. Today it smells like honeydew.

I lean against the counter, which is really a teak table someone made just for her shop, and I have to look up because hanging above my head is the very first chandelier I made. Or redid. It was rusted brass when I found it on the sidewalk in front of a house that was being demolished in West Oakland. But it's red now. Rose red. Paulette loves red because she says it gives her energy. I remember wrapping and gluing the rayon ribbon around each arm so tight my fingers blistered. I added sprigs of hot pink baby's breath and burgundy silk orchids. Each light rises like a white flame from the center of leaves in three shades of green in velvet, rayon, and satin. Each leaf's edges are wired, which allowed me to bend, pull, and twist them to look as natural as possible. It's pretty—but not my taste. Paulette has had so many offers to buy it that she finally hung a NOT FOR SALE tag on it. Because of her I've made about twenty variations for her customers over the past year.

She's still on the phone. Looks and sounds like a heated conversation. One of the women is furiously going through the sale rack. She must be on her lunch hour. She's black and somewhat attractive. But it seems like she's in the wrong store. She's wearing a dark blue suit with matching loafers that I didn't even know they still made. Another woman is trying on something because I can see her bare white feet under the dressing-room door. A redhead with gray roots and probably on her second face-lift tightens the knot of a yellow cashmere sweater that's draped over her shoulders. She is killing time because she's already on her second trip around the store and has not picked up a thing. And then there's a middle-aged blonde still in her tennis outfit and visor, looking through a mountain of pillows in a corner.

I made every single one of them. She picks up one and puts it back. The longer I look at them the more I realize that all of them aren't as attractive as I once thought. In fact, some of them are downright drab. I feel like pulling at least six of them out and dragging them to the back of the store. Friendship can be just as blind as love sometimes, I suppose. I don't know why I'm even noticing things in here I made when I've been in here hundreds of times, and rarely acknowledged any of it. Like those hats on the wall. They're old Stetsons I had blocked and cleaned and just replaced the old rayon bands with outrageous trim so that they're now funky and feminine and one of a kind. I've been in here when someone tried one on, bought it, and never said a word. I made Paulette promise to keep her mouth shut because it was her bright idea to put my stuff in here to prove to me that people would buy it.

"How may I help you?" Paulette asks me, dropping the phone rather harshly on the counter.

"I was just about ready to start shoplifting, but you look like you could use the money, so here." I drop the Platinum American Express and Gold Visa cards on the table. "Pick the one you'd prefer that I use since I don't see a sign anywhere."

"We take *all* major credit cards."

"Good. Because I'm here to shop hard," I say, and we're both trying not to laugh. I wink at Maya. She knows how we do.

"Are you feeling distraught?" Paulette asks.

The other women are now all ears.

"It's my husband. He's deserting me. He's found another woman half my age."

"No?" Paulette squeals.

"Yes, and on Monday he's off to Costa Rica for four weeks to find himself."

"Costa Rica's a pretty nice place to find anything," the tennis player says.

"I'd say so," says the redhead. "Is he going alone?"

"No, he's going with a buddy who's also suffering from the same disease."

"What disease is it they have?" This is the young black girl. She has pulled down one of my hats.

"I call it Mid-Life Crazy."

"Oh, why didn't you say that? My husband has left three times," says the redhead.

"And what did you do?"

"Got depressed. Cried a lot. And then I took him back."

"But why?"

"Because it was easier than living without him. We have the house and the kids almost in college. I didn't want to change my life just because he wanted to chase after those young girls in his office who throw themselves at him and all the other successful married men there. Those women don't care about us. But he always comes to his senses when he gets tired."

"Well, I don't know what to do," I say.

"Kick her ass," a black woman whom I didn't see come in is saying. She's in her early forties and will never find anything in this store to fit her even though Paulette occasionally carries a sixteen.

"Change the locks before he gets back."

"I say wait it out," the redhead says. "If you love him."

"That's a good point," I say.

"Does the name Gordon King mean anything to you?" Paulette finally interjects.

"That's too dangerous, and I'm not out of the danger zone yet if you get my drift."

"How much longer before you can do the cancan?"

The women all get that "the-what?" look on their faces. We have lost them.

"Another week, but it's the last thing on my mind right now."

"That's understandable."

"So, Paulette, is everything going okay in your world?"

"Couldn't be better. Mookie is being released from a special program where he's been studying law for the past two years and now suddenly needs a place to stay since he didn't get his degree the first time he enrolled at this same institution and I'm having a little trouble honoring his request, but other than that, everything's peachy. So, is there something in particular you're looking for today?"

"Yes," I say, with a look on my face that says we'll talk about this later.

"Tell me what you had in mind."

"Something pretty," I say.

"Well, I'd like to think that's about everything in here."

"How much is the chandelier?"

"It's not for sale."

"Why not?"

"Because it was a gift."

"Okay, then. I don't need anything for the house anyway."

"Are you going straight home after you leave here?"

"What would make you ask that?"

"Well, I'm clairvoyant and I know you're bound for Fresno if my memory serves me right and I'm almost positive that little number you're wearing is on day two, so you might want to step over to the casual rack first, you think?"

I give her the finger. "Okay. But I also want something that will make me feel sexy and take his breath away."

"Who?" Paulette asks.

The women are curious again. This is so much fun. Pretending.

"The invisible man with no name who'll most likely take my husband's place one day." Now just about all of the women are sitting in the window seat, apparently waiting to see just what it's going to take to accomplish this.

Spencer still doesn't sound like himself but I tell him that I'm heading for Fresno today and will be back late tomorrow afternoon or early evening. That I would like to make him and his girlfriend a gourmet dinner on Saturday since they fly out early Sunday. This seems to excite him. The boy loves to eat and I love cooking for people who appreciate it. Except of course my husband, who would be fortunate to get a few morsels of Snuffy's dog food mixed in with the gravy I would so gladly pour over his mashed potatoes. I pity the fool. Spencer tells me his wrist is the worst pain he's ever felt, but he's handling it like a man. I tell him not to try so hard, because he'll have plenty of opportunities to prove his manliness. This shouldn't be one of them.

I do not call Leon or Arthurine. Since he's on vacation, he can take her to Bible study. And I'm not going to any party on Saturday. I don't care what the occasion is. Plus, it doesn't really matter. They're all the same anyway. All of our middle-aged friends have the same kind of parties: the music is either jazz or old R&B and is turned down so low you can barely hear it until more than two people get drunk and demand that the hosts "Turn it up!" because they're about ready to "cut up" on the living room but most likely the garage floor. This can happen quickly, much later, or not at all. If it's the latter, we just stand around or sit on the couch and comment on their new piece of artwork—even those of us who have little or no knowledge of art—and then we'll engage in one of the many long drawn-out philosophical and political discussions and you hope for a topic you feel so strongly about that you have to stop yourself from raising your voice. But who is it you're trying to convince and what difference will it make? So you just eat your sushi until it's time for the gumbo that the hostess swears is the best we'll ever have tasted and you just pray it tastes like gumbo and you can find the shrimp and spot a crab claw as we sip on Napa Valley's finest and go home without breaking a glass, breaking up, or breaking down.

Against my better judgment, I pull up to the drive-up window of Burger King and order a Whopper with small fries and no drink. I always have a bottle of water in the car. I eat a few fries then realize I'm almost out of gas. Before I hit the freeway I stop to fill up. I toss my sunglasses in the glove compartment. When I try to close it, it won't shut. To make room, I try moving around the thick wad of napkins I've accumulated from other drive-up windows, a small bottle of hand sanitizer, reading glasses that have recently become a necessity, and a few other things. This time I push it harder but it pops back open and a thick piece of folded paper falls on the floor.

When I reach down to pick it up, my arm hits the glove compartment and it snaps shut.

When the pump stops I get out and am just about to toss this paper when I decide to open it to make sure it's trash-worthy. Of course it's that list of promises I made to myself that I haven't looked at since the day I read it in the doctor's office. I peek at the first point: "Stop swearing." Shame shame shame. I haven't even come close to reducing my usage, let alone stopping altogether. And why was it so important? I believe it was because it made me feel uneducated when I have a vocabulary. Then why haven't I? Forgot. Lazy.

I finish the last of the burger and every single French fry. Put the nozzle back into the pump and get in the car. The smell of fries and ketchup is overwhelming. I grab the bag and twist the top as if I'm trying to break its neck. I get back out of the car and shove the bag into the trash bin. This is where it should be, and I know it. I am ashamed of myself because I have not kept a single one of these promises. Haven't even tried. What was the fucking point . . . I mean, what was the point in even writing it all down if I wasn't going to give it a try? Just to remind myself in my head how much I wish I could do? Change? Isn't this what drug addicts and alcoholics and overeaters do? Promise they'll quit tomorrow but tomorrow never comes? When will tomorrow become today? It's the same shit—I mean thing—when I get right down to it. No angel is coming down here to intervene, to stop me from suffering from what feels like inertia. No angel will help me see my life any clearer than it is right now. No angel will give me the courage to lift my foot and step outside of this emotionally draining circle. Unless of course that angel has just been extremely patient, hoping that sooner or later I'd befriend her and finally let her come out of hiding.

Chapter 16

I take the long route and decide not to call Lovey ahead of time since she might not remember. And there's no telling where Joy is or what she might be doing. Even if she happens to be home, who knows what state she'll be in. By the time I get there, the kids shouldn't be home from school for at least another hour or so and since I'm almost positive there won't be a lot of options when it comes to dinner, I'll see what's there and then go to the grocery store.

When I'm about an hour outside of Fresno I decide to turn my cell on. Of course I've got three thousand messages from Mr. Costa Rica himself. I don't want to hear any of them so I just press the automatic callback. He answers on the first ring. "Hello, Leon."

"Marilyn, where've you been? We've been worried sick about you. You're giving Mom and me a heart attack. Where are you? Are you all right?"

"I'm fine, Leon. Just fine. I'm on my way to Fresno."

"You mean you're not coming home first?"

"Apparently not if I'm on my way."

"Why didn't you come home last night?"

"Because I didn't want to."

"Well, where'd you stay?"

"That's really none of your business."

"Yes, it is."

"I stayed in a place that gave me enough room to think."

"We've got plenty of rooms in this house where you can think without being disturbed, Marilyn."

"I needed to get out of the house, away from you, Leon."

"I'm sorry you feel that way."

"I am, too, but it's the truth."

"Well, I've got some bad news."

"What now? I just hope it's not one of the kids?"

"No, the kids are fine. Mom's fine. It's Snuffy."

"What about him?"

"He's gone."

"You mean he got out? How?"

"No, he's passed on."

"Well, it's about time," I say, before realizing this isn't exactly what I want him to say to Arthurine. "What I meant was, I've been wondering how much longer he was going to be able to hold on. It was his time, I suppose."

"Mother's a mess."

"I know. She really loved that dog."

"It would've been nice if you'd been here with her."

"Leon, don't even go there, okay?"

"What?"

"My being there would not have stopped Snuffy from dying and there would've been nothing I could do to comfort Arthurine that you couldn't do. So stop with the guilt trip. Look, I just wanted you to know what my plans were."

"Well, I'm glad you finally called. Mother is trying to decide whether or not to have a little service for Snuffy."

"You can't be serious, Leon?"

"She's had that dog for sixteen years, it seems fitting to give him a proper farewell. People do it all the time. There's a cemetery just for pets so it can't be that outlandish."

"Is she going to have him cremated or stuffed?" I ask, unable to help myself.

"You really can be crass when you want to be, Marilyn, you know that?"

"Sometimes the situation dictates it, Leon. But this seems a bit silly. Who's supposed to come to Snuffy's funeral besides me, you, and Arthurine?"

"Prezelle has already said he'd come."

"And who else?"

"That's plenty. He's a dog. He didn't exactly have a slew of friends."

"Leon, I'm going to hang up now, okay?"

"Hold on a second! Spencer said they'd be here in a few hours."

"I already know that, and I'm making dinner for him and Brianna on Saturday."

"How can you be in two places at once?"

"I'm not planning on being in two places at once."

"Then let me ask you something, Marilyn, and I don't mean any harm by it."

"I'm listening."

"Do you remember the original reason you went to see your doctor?"

"Of course I do. To get my hormone levels checked."

"Yes, but this was because you admitted that you'd been forgetting a lot of things and having wild mood swings and just being bitchy all the time for no particular reason."

"And your point?"

"Did she ever actually give you anything for it or not?"

"No, she didn't, Leon. I was pregnant, remember?"

"Yes, but you're not pregnant now and you're acting the same way you were before."

"I think I've got a few good reasons for sounding the way I sound and acting the way I act, and I doubt if it has anything to do with my hormonal balance or imbalance."

"Well, you seem to have forgotten all about Frank and Joyce's party and I just told you about it yesterday."

"I didn't forget."

"Then tell me how are you supposed to make dinner when the party's at the same time?"

"I'm not going to the party, Leon, because I don't care if Frank the adulterer is turning a hundred and they're celebrating fifty years of marital bliss, which you and I both know is a big fat lie. Why should I go over there pretending I'm happy for them when I'm not? She should've left him years ago. But that's neither here nor there. I'm not going, Leon. I'm making my son and his girlfriend and any of his friends that want to come over a dinner I hope they'll remember after they get back to their dorms."

"Why can't you make them lunch?"

"You just don't get it, do you? But I'm going to say this since you're obviously oblivious. I have not seen our sons since last Christmas, and right now, only one of them is here. I miss them. I miss washing their dirty, stinky clothes. I miss hearing their raggedy cars pull into the driveway. But most of all, I miss cooking for them. So on Saturday, that's what I'm going to do. If you can't understand this, Leon, then you can just go to hell."

I hang up. I drive with fury for at least the next twenty or thirty miles. Which is when I realize I might have to rethink this no-swearing promise because sometimes no other words seem to do. I mean, come on, a funeral for a fucking dog?

The garage door is up but Lovey's car isn't in it. In fact it's full of all kinds of foreign objects that don't belong in here. For starters: whose treadmill is that? And what about that red mountain bike? The big-screen TV? Is that somebody's brand-new living room furniture? I think that looks like a car motor, but I hope I'm wrong. I can't wait to hear this one.

I knock on the door a few times. When no one answers I use my new key. As soon as I walk in, I smell something burning. It's hair. "Lovey?"

"I'm back here," she yells from the kitchen.

I speed back there where Mrs. Saundra Norman, one of her oldest customers, is slouched forward in a kitchen chair. She is sound asleep. Lovey is standing behind her waving a hot straightening comb through the air. Continuous circles of white smoke billow up and disappear into the ceiling paint. She spits on the straightening comb to test it but it's so hot the saliva evaporates before it hits the iron.

"Lovey, what are you doing?"

She starts slicing the air with the iron comb again. I can already see where she originally tested it, because a patch of Mrs. Norman's silver hair has been singed off about three inches. "I'm fixing her hair. What does it look like? And why did you just come barging in my house like you own it? You don't live here."

"Lovey, that straightening comb is way too hot. Please put it down."

She looks at it for the longest time and then, thank God, apparently agrees. She sets it on an unlit eye on the back of the stove even though the heat-controlled apparatus she's supposed to be using is plugged in and sitting right next to the stove, with a pair of bumper curlers inside it.

Mrs. Norman's head lifts to an upright position as she opens her eyes, looking around the room as if she doesn't know where she is. Her skin is olive black and smooth. Hardly a wrinkle and I know she's pushing seventy. "How are you, Mrs. Norman?" I say.

"I'm fine and you, sugar?"

"Good. I didn't see your car out front. Did you drive over here?"

"No, my son brought me. I don't drive no more."

"Why not?"

"I forget why. I just can't."

"Are you sure you want Lovey doing your hair today?"

"Lovey ain't done my hair in years, why would I want her to do it today?"

Oh my Lord.

"*You* called me, missy," Lovey says, leaning down over her shoulder. "And I wasn't even charging you! I was trying to be nice and doing it as a favor."

Mrs. Norman turns to see who's talking. "Lovey?"

"Don't act like you don't know who I am, Saundra Lee."

"I'm sorry, baby. I thought I was dreaming. How much more you have left to straighten before you can put some curls in?"

"If you could stay awake and keep your head up, I coulda been finished ten or fifteen minutes ago."

"Well, could you at least open a window, it's hot in here."

I go over and crack open the back door because I know the windows were accidentally painted stuck.

"Thank you, sweetheart. Aren't you one of Lovey's daughters?"

"Yes, I am. I'm Marilyn."

"My my my. You getting old and fat just like the rest of us, ain't you, chile?"

"I suppose so," I say, wishing I could curl up in a knot.

"If you ask me, she look better now than when she was in her twenties, so shut up and mind your own business, Saundra. When my baby was in college, she was so skinny I wouldn't even waste the film in my camera on her, but after she had that first baby, she started filling out, and that's when she started looking like a woman. And she don't look old. We look old. How old are you, Marilyn?"

"Forty-four," I say.

"See there. She don't look a day over forty-three."

"Lovey?" Mrs. Norman asks.

"What is it now?"

"Don't make the curls too tight." She closes her eyes again, and as I stand there watching the two of them very closely, Lovey clicks those bumper curlers the way she always did and Mrs. Norman snores the way she always has.

"Lovey, where's Joy?"

"I think she's at work."

"She got a job?"

"I think so."

"Do you know whose stuff that is in the garage?"

"What stuff?"

"There's all kinds of things in there I've never seen before and it looks like they belong to somebody else."

"I don't know what you're talking about."

"There's a treadmill, a bike, and some furniture, to name a few of them."

"Beats me," she says, and pops Mrs. Norman on the head with a hairbrush to signal she's finished. Mrs. Norman jumps up so quickly she almost loses her balance.

"Thank you. How much do I owe you?"

"Ten dollars," Lovey says.

Mrs. Norman digs inside her big brown purse until she finds what appears to be a handful of crinkled-up bills. "Here," she says, pressing them into Lovey's outstretched palm.

"I don't want all of that," Lovey says, searching through them until she finds a ten. I watch because I don't know what she can and can't do anymore. This is a relief.

"Do you know if Joy drove your car, Lovey?"

"That car is gone."

"What do you mean by gone?"

"Somebody stole it or bought it or something, but it's not coming back. That much I do know."

"That simple bitch," I say under my breath.

"Takes one to know one," Mrs. Norman says, and heads out the front door where she stands until her son arrives fifteen minutes later.

I say good-bye to her but Lovey doesn't. She lies down on the couch and closes her eyes so fast, I'm not sure if she's already asleep. I'm sitting in the chair across from her. "Lovey?"

"What is it now, girl?" She doesn't even open her eyes.

"Do you remember that we go to the doctor tomorrow?"

"Is it tomorrow already?"

"No, but it will be after you wake up. Now you can't eat anything after eight o'clock because the doctor wants you to have blood tests done and he wants to see how your cholesterol levels are. You're going to have a physical so we can find out what might be making you forget things."

"That's just fine and dandy," she says. "Wake me up when it's time to go."

I sit here and watch her sink into those old cushions that seem to adjust to accept her big body. I wonder if she's scared at all. She doesn't act like it. But neither do I and I know I'm afraid of what this all might mean.

A few minutes later the kids come charging through the front door. They're clean but the clothes they're wearing could've stood a little steam from an iron.

"You back again?" Tiecey says.

"Yeah, what you want?" LL says.

"Come here," I say, motioning with my finger to both of them. They saunter over and stand in front of me. They are too cute to sound so ugly. "Do you think this is the way you should greet someone when you walk into this house?"

"I just said you back again?"

"And I just said . . ."

"LL, I know what you just said. How about: 'Hi' or 'Hello, Aunt Marilyn'?"

"Hi or hello, Aunt Marilyn," she says.

"Hi or hello, Aunt Marilyn," LL says.

I give. "Are you guys hungry?"

"Yeah," Tiecey says. "LL always hungry."

"You guys want to go to the grocery store with me?"

"Yeah. Can we pick out something we like?" she asks.

"Only if you can say 'yes' instead of 'yeah.' Can you do that?"

"Yes."

"Yes," LL repeats.

"How long has Grandma Lovey been taking her nap?" Tiecey asks.

"She just fell asleep a few minutes ago."

"Good," LL says.

"What's so good about it?"

"Because she always asks us to do stuff we don't wanna do."

"Like what?"

"Clean up."

"What's wrong with helping out?"

"Don't nobody help us," Tiecey says.

"You can't tell me your mother doesn't do anything around this house?"

"Her don't," she says.

"She doesn't," I say.

"She doesn't," Tiecey says. "Can we go right now?"

"Do you two have homework?"

"Yes. Spelling. But I already know how to spell all the words and even the ones for extra credit. I did my math on the bus."

"I got to practice my letters," LL says.

"Okay, but does Lovey stay here by herself a lot?"

"All day," Tiecey says.

"Do you guys know whose stuff that is in the garage?" They both shake their head no.

"Did your mama get a job?"

They both shake their head no.

"Do you know where she might be?"

"Yeah. She in jail," Tiecey says matter-of-factly.

"She's in what?"

"JAIL," LL says loudly to make sure I hear it this time.

"When did she go to jail? And for what?"

"I think yesterday. I answered the phone when she called collect and she told me she might be home today or tomorrow."

"Did she say why she was in jail?"

"Nope. But probably the same reason she was in there for last time."

"What last time?"

"That last time last time," Tiecey says. "For them drugs."

"Let's go," I say to the kids. "So we can hurry back before Lovey wakes up."

We get back in less than an hour to find Joy sitting on the front steps, smoking a cigarette. Her right eye is black. Her left hand bandaged. "I was worried about my kids," she says.

"Is Lovey still asleep?" I ask.

"Yep. I thought she was dead when I first went in there, but she's still warm."

"I don't know what to say to you, Joy. I really don't."

"You could ask me how I'm doing."

"It's obvious that you're not doing so hot. What were you in jail for?"

"Something stupid that ain't even worth bringing up."

"Please, do bring it up."

"I got into a little rumble."

"I can see that. About what?"

"A little confusion about some cash."

"So it got you thrown in jail and beaten?"

"Looks like it."

"Whose stuff is that in the garage and where is Lovey's car?"

"I'm having a garage sale tomorrow. That stuff belongs to me. Somebody owed me. And Lovey's car is still in the shop."

"No, it ain't," Tiecey says.

"Why don't you just be quiet," Joy says. "Did anybody ask you Miss Grown-Ass?"

"She sold it to somebody for some money to buy them drugs."

Joy jumps up and runs toward Tiecey but I mistakenly grab her by her injured hand and she screams and stops dead in her tracks.

"Sit your butt down," I say, pushing her back toward the porch. "Look, I don't know what's going on around here, but these kids need to be supervised and it looks like Lovey does, too. If you aren't responsible enough to do it, then somebody else is going to have to."

"I'm going to rehab," she blurts out.

"What's rehab?" Tiecey asks.

"A place I can go to get off drugs. Does that answer your question, Miss Smarty?"

"How?"

"I don't know, but I hope to find out."

"And just when are you supposed to do this?" I ask.

"I'll know in three weeks, on my court date."

"And what are the kids and Lovey supposed to do in the meantime?"

"I'll be around to handle my business," she says. "Don't worry about them. Who you think been doing it all these years?"

I don't respond. Tiecey and LL insist on bringing all the bags in by themselves. I make a simple dinner: roasted chicken, baked potato, salad, and steamed broccoli— which the kids are afraid to eat at first. We eat together at the kitchen table like a family, something that seems foreign to them. Lovey seems to be herself. Even Joy is cooperative and cleans the kitchen. Later, I put lots of bubbles in the kids' bathwater and remind them how to say their prayers. I give them each a big hug and kiss before turning out the light. They seem to like this. Once downstairs, I iron something for them to wear to school. Joy notices.

"I was planning on doing some ironing before I went to bed," she says.

"I don't mind," I say.

"It may be hard for you to see, Marilyn, but I am trying."

"I wish you would try a little harder, Joy."

"In case you haven't noticed, I've got a problem."

"Oh, I've noticed. So have your kids. I'm just praying you go through with this rehab thing and I hope they can help you get off whatever it is you're on."

"It's crank."

"What's that?"

"It don't really matter. The point is, I know it's gotten out of control 'cause I've been messing up and now that Lovey's got that disease, I can't keep leaving her or the kids in here all day by themselves."

"Who said she's got a disease?"

"Anybody in their right mind can see she's got it, Marilyn. Just wait. That doctor ain't gon' do nothing but tell you what I already know."

"Since when did you get to be so knowledgeable about any disease?"

"First of all, I know it may be hard for you to believe, but I *can* read, Marilyn, and sometimes I do."

I can't believe it. She's crying. I don't think I've ever seen Joy cry. I feel bad for making her feel bad because she undoubtedly already feels bad. I walk over to put my arms around her, to offer her some comfort but she jerks away.

"And second of all, I know about diseases 'cause I've got quite a few myself. Wanna hear 'em? Herpes. Hepatitis C. Pancreatitis. And looka here: Alopecia," she says, snatching off what is apparently a curly wig that I've thought all this time was a bad weave. Most of her scalp is smooth with small islands of black hair here and there. "But wait! I ain't quite finished! The nurse in the emergency room who fixed my hand told me that not being able to stop using drugs even when I try is a disease, too. It's called addiction. So, you see, sista-girl, I know a little somethin' somethin' about diseases. Any more questions?"

I cannot open my mouth. My heart is throbbing like

a bad toothache in my chest. I wish it would stop. I wish I were blind. I wish I were deaf. I wish I could do something to show her how sorry I am for never allowing myself to get close to her. For not ever trying. For never taking time to care or wonder about what or how she was doing because I've always been completely consumed by my own life. I wipe the tears away from my eyes because I'm not blind. I heard everything she just said, because I'm not deaf. And I realize that I have two diseases I hope there's a cure for—selfishness and apathy—because this stranger standing in front of me happens to be the only sister I have.

Chapter 17

I want Joy to be wrong. I want to be wrong. I've read just about everything I could find about Alzheimer's on the Internet. There are plenty of other reasons why Lovey could be forgetting things. She could just be depressed. She could've had a ministroke or a series of them that just haven't been diagnosed. Maybe it's her thyroid. Or kidneys. Or liver. She could have a vitamin B-12 deficiency. I'm crossing my fingers and praying that whatever it is, the doctor can give her a pill to help restore her back to her old self.

We get her blood drawn at the lab right downstairs from Dr. Merijohn's office. Right after her physical, he tells Lovey she can get dressed, and he'll be back with me in a few minutes. The doctor tells me that physically she appears to be fine but her blood pressure is still somewhat elevated beyond the comfort zone. That he's also worried her cholesterol might be too high but he'll know for sure when he gets the results from the lab in a day or so. I hope Lovey didn't sneak and eat anything like I told her not to do. He tells me that when we go back into the examining room, he's going to ask Lovey a series of questions that are his own version of the kind of test a neurologist would give. But because he's known Lovey for a while, he feels strongly that he'll be able to determine whether she'll also need to be seen by a neurologist for more extensive testing.

When he opens the door, Lovey crosses her legs in a somewhat coquettish fashion. The young doctor doesn't seem to notice. I can't believe it when she winks at me. We sit at opposite ends of a small metal table. The doctor sits on a low stool near the wall. It swivels.

"Do you remember me telling you when I came back with your daughter that I was going to ask you a few simple questions?" the doctor asks.

"I do," she says, grinning at him. This time he does notice. He is a handsome man—even Lovey can see behind those horn-rimmed glasses—and he can't be more than forty. His hair is silky black, his skin olive. He smiles back, to humor her, I suppose, because she blushes. Then he gets serious. "May I begin?"

"Wait a minute. How long will this take 'cause I'm so hungry I could probably eat your shoe?"

"Not more than five or ten minutes at most."

"Okay. But what kind of questions you planning on asking?"

"Simple, everyday types of questions. I don't want you to be afraid."

"Do I look like I'm afraid, sir?"

"No, and you don't have to call me sir."

"Okay. Then call me Lovey."

"Thank you, *Lovey*. Are you comfortable over there?"

She nods yes, like he just asked her out on a date.

"Nice and relaxed?"

She nods yes again, and slides down in her chair to prove it. "Why she have to be in here?" she says, pointing at me.

"Because she's your daughter and she wants to hear how you answer the questions."

"Why? When it ain't none of her business."

"Well, because it's good to have a family member here who cares a great deal about you, just in case you should need their help."

"Whatever you say. But I won't need no help, I can tell you that right now."

"Good. Here we go. Lovey, do you know what day this is?"

She looks at him like he's asked her something far too personal to reveal. But in the very next second, she changes her whole demeanor and thinks about it. Then she looks at me. "Do the kids go to school tomorrow?"

I look over at the doctor. His eyes say it's okay for me to tell her because he's already gotten his answer.

"No they don't, Lovey."

"Then it's Friday."

"Good. Do you know where you are?"

"I'm in the doctor's office."

"Do you know my name?"

"Not right this minute. I ain't seen you in a long time, that's why."

"It's Dr. Merijohn."

"You married?"

"I am indeed."

"Happily?"

"Yes. Now . . ."

"That's too bad," she says.

"Lovey, I'm going to say three words and I'd like you to repeat them back to me: Ball. Flag. Tree."

She stares dead at him and says, "Ball," and then pauses like she's trying to make herself concentrate, but it doesn't work. "Can you say 'em one more time, only a little louder, 'cause I didn't quite hear you?"

"Sure: Ball. Flag. Tree."

"Flagtree," she says triumphantly.

"Do you know what year it is, Lovey?"

"We just had a millimeter come. And Oprah turned fifty. It's probably somewhere around two thousand three or four, but I been so busy I ain't paid much attention to no calendars."

"Do you know who the president of the United States is?"

"Of course I do. Jimmy Clinton."

"What month is this?"

She turns to look out the window behind her. "It's gotta be June 'cause I can see the heat."

"Okay. Starting from one hundred, would you count backward by seven as far as you can?"

"What?"

"Count backward from a hundred by sevens. Just do as much as you can."

She's trying to calculate this in her head but I can see confusion rushing to her face. "I ain't never been good in math. Give me a easier one. Please?"

"Sure, Lovey. I'll say a few numbers in sequential order and I'd like you to continue the sequence for three or four more numbers."

She's watching his lips utter every word.

"Two four six eight ten."

She's still staring at his mouth. But I can see she's getting upset and she clams up.

"Okay, we can skip that one. Can you spell the word 'drum' backward for me?"

"Drum," she says, and then as if saying it louder will allow her to see the letters she yells: "DRUM!" But this doesn't seem to be working because she says, "M," and stops.

"It's okay, Lovey. You're doing fine."

"Some of these questions are stupid."

"Which ones, Lovey?"

"You know which ones."

"Do you remember the three words I asked you about a few minutes ago?"

"Do you?"

"Yes, I do."

"Then why don't you say them?"

"Ball. Flag. Tree. Anyway, we're almost finished."

"Good, 'cause this is getting on my nerves and I'm starving."

"Would you touch your left foot with your right hand for me please?"

She looks down at both feet, makes an X with her arms and bends over and taps each foot with the opposite hand.

"Thank you. Would you close your eyes for me?"

"Why? What you gon' do to me?"

"I'm not going to do anything. I'd just like you to tell me what it is you smell when I ask you."

She closes her eyes so tight the lids tremble. I close mine too, just to be fair.

"Okay, what does this smell like?"

"I don't smell nothing," Lovey says. "Wait a minute." She inhales deeply through her nose. "Is it some kinda tea? What is it I'm supposed to be thinking I'm smelling?"

"I smell toothpaste," I say, and Lovey opens her eyes and he shows us the tube from which he'd squeezed about an inch onto a tongue depresser.

"I was just thinking it smelled like Colgate but missy here beat me to the punch."

"It's okay, Lovey." He holds up a paper clip. "Can you tell me what this is?"

"It's not something I use in my house."

"I understand. Lastly," he says, handing her a pencil and a piece of paper. "Would you write down this sentence for me?"

"Just make it quick, would you?"

"Okay. Ready?"

"I'm listening."

"It is a very nice spring day."

"Slow down, would you?"

He and I both watch her struggle with the first word, and then it's as if she's waiting to see if her hand will automatically write of its own will. It doesn't.

"Did you get it all?"

"Say it again. But a little slower, please."

"It is a very nice spring day."

She presses the pencil against the paper so hard the lead breaks and flies into the air and then she stands up and throws that pencil like a dart right at the doctor. "You done got on my last nerve, you know that? We better be finished."

"We are, Lovey. And I thank you for your patience and cooperation."

"You're welcome. Now let's go, girl."

"Who is that girl, by the way?" he asks.

"She's the girl that brought me here and the girl that's taking me to McDonald's. Good-bye and good luck, Dr. Frankenstein," Lovey says, and out the door she goes.

The doctor gives me a referral to a neurologist. Dr. Richardson is African-American and she'll be able to give Lovey a more extensive examination and test. He tells me when he gets the results from the lab that she'll probably order an MRI once she gets Lovey's past medical records which he'll be sending over.

I tell him I'll make that appointment as soon as I get home. I have to run to catch up to Lovey, who's already going down the stairs. When I pull up to the drive-up window, I order her Big Mac with small fries and a vanilla shake, and when I hand her the bag she looks at me and says, "This is mine. Where's yours?" I just tell her I'm not hungry. But the truth is, I can't eat anything because I've sought answers to too many questions at too many drive-up windows and the answers have never once appeared in the sauce or on the bun.

It's hard to believe that Joy is still at home. The radio is on but turned down low because I can hear the washer agitating back and forth. Clothes are hanging on the line in the backyard. Lovey beelines it over to the sofa without uttering a single word. After finishing her meal, the only thing she said in the car was, "They make the best Big Macs in the world." Joy is mopping the kitchen floor because I can see the shiny wet and dull dry spaces. I stand in the doorway and watch her. She seems somber and sober. I can't believe that so much is going on inside her body. Why didn't she tell anybody? I wonder if Lovey knows.

"She's got it, don't she?" she says.

"She has to go to a different doctor and get a brain scan called an MRI. I called already to make an appointment. I'll be back in two weeks to take her."

"I can take her."

"How, Joy?"

"In her car, that's how."

"But Tiecey said you . . ."

"Who you gon' believe, me or a seven-year-old?"

"Well, how would she even know something like this?"

" 'Cause she's too grown, that's why. All I gotta do is give this dude two hundred dollars and I can get the car back. That's why I'm having the garage sale tomorrow."

"I can just give you two hundred dollars, Joy."

"I don't want your money, Marilyn. Especially not today."

"What's wrong with today?"

"I'm taking something that helps stop me from craving. I'm trying to get through *today*."

"Well, this is a good thing."

She pushes the orange sponge forward and the last dry lane disappears. When she slides it back the tip of the metal jabs her in the ankle. I wince but Joy doesn't acknowledge the pain at all.

"I want to take her," she says. "And you shouldn't have to drive all this way to take our mother to the doctor when I'm right here."

"I don't mind," I say.

"Well, I do. I look bad in front of my kids and I don't want them to keep seeing me the way I been acting. I'm ashamed of myself for not telling you about Lovey when she's been like this for almost a year. Maybe longer."

"It's okay. But I just saw her at Christmas and she seemed fine."

"She was putting on. But she can't do it now."

"Joy, I'm really sorry about all the things you're dealing with, but why didn't you let me know?"

"What, and put a damper on your little Cosby world?"

"Have you been to the doctor?"

"Of course I've been to the doctor. If your hair was

falling out in clumps and every time you ate something it felt like you gotta throw up and your stomach hurt like hell and no amount of drugs seemed to make it stop, who wouldn't go to the doctor?"

"Does anything help?"

She just looks at me. "Look, I'll take Lovey to that doctor in two weeks and you can call here every day if you want to check up on me. If it'll make you feel any better."

"I don't have to go that far, Joy."

"How's your husband?"

"He's fine. On his way to Costa Rica on Monday."

"For what?"

"That's a good question."

"You mean you ain't going with him?"

"No, I don't want to go."

"Why not?"

"Because I've got other things I want to do."

"He didn't invite you, did he?"

"To be honest with you, no, he didn't."

"Is he screwing somebody else?"

"I doubt that very seriously."

"Please, Marilyn. Why is it that all women think their pussy is so good that can't nobody top it?"

"Did you hear me say that?"

"You don't have to. How old is Leon again?"

"He'll be forty-six the end of next month."

"He's probably going through that midlife thing. I saw a special on television about it."

"Did you really?"

"Yeah. What? You don't think I'm interested in things?"

"I don't think that at all."

"You act like you can't even imagine me watching no documentary."

"I didn't say that, did I?"

"You don't have to Marilyn. It's all over your face. But I'll tell you something. Maybe I didn't get a college degree like you but I'm not dumb. I do some seriously stupid shit, but I am far from dumb."

"I never thought you were."

"Well, finally we agree on something."

She actually smiles. I smile back.

"So, is Leon tripping hard?"

"He is tripping very hard."

"Ain't much you can do about it, from what that program said, except ride it out."

"Ride it out. Speaking of which, I need to hit the road so I can beat the traffic."

"What about you?"

"What about me?" I ask.

"How you feeling these days? You should be going through something yourself along the female side of things, ain't you?"

"I'd say that's pretty accurate."

"I saw a special on this, too."

"On what exactly, Joy?"

"On menopause and perimenopause. I never knew there was a difference, did you?"

"Yes."

"Then what is it?"

I can't believe she's testing me. The truth is, I'm not real sure what the difference is. "Why don't you tell me."

"It's deep, that much I do know. And I ain't looking forward to going through the peri-part, which is when you get all them symptoms, but the sooner the menopause part happens, the happier I'll be. No period means no more babies. Anyway, what's it really like?"

"Whatever they said on that TV show, assume I'm experiencing all of it."

"Do you take those hormone pills?"

"Not yet."

"You mean you want to?"

"I don't want to, but I might need to."

"Why?"

"Because they can even you out."

"Oh, so you're lopsided or something. What?"

"Didn't they go into this?"

"Yeah, but you the first person I know going through it I can ask. Tell me."

"Why is it so important right now?"

"Because I've told you all my shit, and I wanna have some general idea what you might be feeling. All right?"

"All right. Anyway, sometimes it's hard to concentrate and you're forgetful a lot and it feels like you've been PMSing for about six months."

"Do you still get your period?"

"I haven't had one in two months."

"The doctor on that show said you can still get pregnant, you know."

"I know."

"So what does a hot flash feel like? Seriously? I mean I don't get it. I don't understand what the flash part is all about."

"It just means you feel hot all of a sudden from inside your whole body and it lasts for maybe a minute and then goes away."

"So you sweat and shit?"

"Yes, Joy."

"So you going through menopause and all this shit with Leon at the same time. You thinking about getting a divorce?"

"What would make you ask me that?"

"Because this lady on the show wrote a book about all the shit women be thinking about and feeling when they're going through the change and she said a lot of times after the kids are gone and it's just you and him . . ."

"His mother is still there."

"In-laws don't count. Not like kids do. Anyway she said that once your kids are out the house, a lot of women start looking at their whole life different."

"Like how?"

"Well, she said some women freak out and get depressed and shit but it's just 'cause they done spent so many years taking care of kids and everybody else that now they don't know what the fuck to do for theyself. These are my own words, not hers, but it's what she said, believe me, 'cause at first I was thinking that maybe that's what Lovey was going through when they was talking about being forgetful and shit. But it didn't take me but a minute to realize Lovey was long past anybody's menopause. Don't look at me like that, Marilyn."

"Like what?"

"Like I'm tripping or something."

"I don't mean to. I just can't believe we're even having a conversation. Especially one that's enlightening."

"Everybody can stand to get a little enlightened, especially when they don't expect it. But anyway, she said some women end up taking pills to stop 'em from feeling depressed when they ain't even really depressed."

"Then what else is it?"

"The lady doctor said that they really secretly miserable as hell and full of rage and probably bored out of their fucking minds and just too goddamn scared to admit it 'cause it would mean they might have to make some major changes and some of 'em are too scared to change anything."

"Really."

"I'm serious. But on the flip side of this coin are the women she said that know the shit is fucked up on the home front, that the husband ain't rocking 'em the way he used to—not even close—and basically knows the shit is dead and is just itching to make that leap, but she ain't completely crazy, so she kinda is like taking her time and trying to figure out the whole puzzle first. But deep down inside, she knows somebody gots to go."

"Really."

"Yeah, and they interviewed both kinds. It was kinda pathetic listening to the first group whining about losing their children, like they was really lost or dead, and how now their lives felt like it didn't have no purpose. I'm listening to these simple-ass women, thinking: you left home once upon a time, bitch, didn't you? Anyway, some of these women got so desperate to—what was the word—nature, *nurture* something that they either meddled in their grown kids' life to the point where the kids depended on them for so much shit they wouldn't know how to get by on their own, and then some went and got somebody else's kids to take care of. I said out loud: get a puppy!"

I'm laughing, enjoying listening to my sister talk, and particularly to me. She knows she's telling me something I haven't heard. I'm looking at her with gratitude all over my face and hope she can read it.

"Okay, I know you gotta go and I'm almost finished. But it was a good show. And to be honest with you, Marilyn, you're the real reason I watched it. I mean you the only woman I know in this age group. I meant to tape it, but we didn't have no blank tapes and I was not taping over *All My Children.* Anyway the other group of women was the ones ready to bail out of the whole Suzy Homemaker routine and become real ho's. Just kidding. All joking aside, these women talked about how they actually loved this stage of their life."

"What made them say that?"

"Well, instead of thinking of menopause like it's all downhill from here, they saw it like they was getting another chance to do some of the shit they never started or finished for one reason or another. One lady said it felt more like it was a new beginning. And when you think about it, it really ain't the end of nothing but your damn period.

Some of them went back to college. I'm talking about women in their forties and fifties! Some of 'em divorced their boring-ass husbands, but I can't lie—quite a few of their husbands left their ass in the wind for some young tender skin. And then there was the ones who had careers—they went to college so they could do what they did—but they realized that they didn't like doing it no more, so some of 'em just upped and quit. Went off and did some silly shit they loved, even if it didn't make 'em half as much money."

"Well, your memory is definitely intact, Joy. And thanks for sharing this with me."

"You're welcome." We head for the front door. She's still got that mop in tow. "Them women got me to thinking, you know."

"I can tell."

"No, I mean, about me maybe trying to start over. I mean, hell, I'm only twenty-six. I still got time to go to college."

"But you need to have a high school diploma to do that, Joy."

"I got my GED right before LL was born. I thought you knew that."

"No, I didn't. Right on, then. Do it. Go."

"First I gotta get my head on straight."

"Well, you're not alone on that front," I say, as I walk into the living room and give Lovey a kiss.

When I get outside, I unlock the car with my keys and then give Joy a peck on the cheek. She's standing on the front porch even after I open the door.

"Yep. I saw it all on some cable channel. When our cable was hooked up," she says pressing the spongy part of the mop against the top step so that the last drop of moisture squishes out.

I now have the feeling that either she doesn't want me to leave or she's glad to have had my undivided attention and she's not quite finished. "Wait a minute. You mean you don't have cable anymore?"

"Nope. We had a box and they finally came and took it."

"I thought you didn't need a box anymore."

"This was a gift from a friend that let us get every channel, including HBO and Showtime, for free."

"Nice to have those kind of friends," I say.

"Yep, but tell me something, Marilyn."

"What's that?"

"Between these two types of women I was just talking about."

"Yes."

"Which group you fall into?"

Chapter 18

My prayers have been answered when I don't see Leon's car in the garage. This doesn't tell me who all is here. The chime is still off because there's no beep when I enter the house. I almost freak out when I hear barking. Arthurine is sitting in the family room watching a rerun of that big dog show they have every year in New York. I rented the movie *Best in Show* because I saw it when it came out and laughed so hard in the theater it took a while before realizing I was just about the only one who thought it was funny. When the lights came up I also saw that I was the only black person there. Arthurine barely cracked a smile during the whole twenty minutes she watched it.

"How you doing, Arthurine?"

I can tell that she was just about to smile, but decides against it. I think I already know what I'm in for.

"I'm just sitting here grieving, baby. That's what I'm doing. How you?"

"I'm really sorry to hear about Snuffy," I say, but I don't want to go over to where she is because I can still see Snuffy's disgusting matted fur bed at the end of the couch, which is where she's sitting.

"I know," she says, and then points down to his bed. "He was laying right there, like he always do. Just a-sleeping. I go to put his leash on and give it a little tug like I always do, but Snuffy didn't budge. Sometimes he do this so I'll pick him up, but I wasn't in no mood for bending down and carrying him that morning 'cause it feels like arthritis is starting to settle in my back, so I give him a big tug and when his whole body rolled off his bed, that's when I realized that Snuffy wasn't sleeping." She's not really crying but I can tell she wishes she could drum up some tears to give her story more impact.

"Where is he now?" I ask, praying he's not somewhere being prepped for his funeral.

"I went on and had him cremated."

"You did?" I say, trying not to sound too excited.

"Yes. Prezelle told me that having a service for him would probably make me feel worse. And he's right. He knows a lot about funerals."

"Why does he know so much about funerals?"

"Because he used to be a mortician."

"No shit? I mean, no kidding?"

"His whole family always had something to do with the dead. Prezelle owned six parlors when he retired. He sold three and left the other three to his three kids. Except one of them just died and now they fighting over who gon' get to run that one. Dead people are the reason he can afford to live in such a nice place."

"That's really something," I say. "Are you and Prezelle still going to Reno next weekend?"

"Absolutely. You can't just keep on grieving day after day. You need relief. With God's help, I'm getting there. And I should be all the way there by next Friday afternoon."

"Good. I'm glad to hear it. Is anybody else here?"

"Spencer was upstairs in his room."

"What about his friend?"

"That little girl?"

"Yes."

"I think she up there with him. I haven't heard nobody come and go."

"What about Leon? What's the latest on him?"

"That's what I want to know. Is something wrong with him that ain't nobody telling me about, Marilyn?"

"What would make you say that?"

"Well, at first he acted like he was coming down with a cold, but I waited and waited and he didn't cough not once and his nose never did run, so I asked him what he thought could be ailing him. And you know what he said?"

"I'm listening."

"He said he needed to get away to do some soul-searching. Did I hear him right?"

"I think you did."

"I told him it wouldn't kill him to start going to church again. This way he could hear God's word every

Sunday and he wouldn't have to search. All the answers would be right in front of him. I told him I'm lucky because I go to Bible study twice a week, which is why God speaks to me more often."

"What exactly do you mean by 'He speaks to you,' Arthurine?"

"I've heard God speak."

"And what does God sound like?"

She cuts her eyes at me. "What do you mean?"

"I mean, what exactly does God sound like? Does He have like a Southern or British or New York accent? A deep or high-pitched voice? What?"

"You trying to be funny?"

"No. I've just always wondered about this when people say God spoke to them, that's all."

"I can't describe it. Plus, he don't always sound the same way. All I want to know is how in God's name is Leon supposed to find his soul in Costa Rica?"

"I don't know, Arthurine."

"Are you two having marital difficulties?"

"I think we're reevaluating the strengths and weaknesses of our marriage."

"Then that means yes."

"Not necessarily. Anyway, do you know where he might be?"

"He said he was going to the mall to get some things to take on his trip. Said he didn't have no island-wear."

"He really said that? Costa Rica is not an island."

"I'm telling you that's exactly what he said. I'm not Lovey, sweetheart. How is she, by the way?"

"She's doing fine, actually."

"Good. Does she have that dreaded disease or not?"

"We won't know for a while. But she's in good hands."

"I know she is. We all are. Some of us just don't know it."

I go up the stairs but stop dead in my tracks when I reach the top step because I can't remember what I was coming up here to do. Before I have a chance to backtrack or try to gather my thoughts, coming from Spencer's room at the end of the hall I hear that tiny girl moaning and groaning like a three-hundred-pound woman. I can't believe it when I find myself standing outside his door and actually listening. I think I'm waiting to hear what sound my son makes when he hits his high note, but all I hear next is her squealing in loud short bursts like I did in my Lamaze class years ago. I hope he's not like his father— Quick Draw McGraw—because after Brianna dies off, I don't hear so much as a squeak from behind this door. I just hope he had enough sense to protect his wrist.

As I walk down to our bedroom, it occurs to me that I can't remember the last time I had sex, never mind an orgasm. I could certainly use one now. And then I ask myself: what's to stop me? I forgot all about that battery-operated penis I have hidden in my drawer that I've never used. In fact, besides ordering eight inches of chocolate rubber, the clitoris stimulator also caught my eye in the catalog, so I bought them both.

Four or five months ago, Leon was on one of his long

business trips and I was tired of pretending I had no sexual urges just because he wasn't here. I'd never really given myself pleasure like I'd heard so many other women talk about—including Paulette, but especially Bunny—so one night I decided to watch the adult channel. I was amazed at what I saw. I ordered the video hoping we could watch it together to get some ideas for pumping up the volume in our dwindling bimonthly and very rapid sex life. He fell asleep before I had a chance to put the thing on pause so we could imitate the couple on the screen.

A catalog came with the video. In it was an assortment of sex toys. It was either this or cheat. I used my own credit card, and was assured that they would come in a nondescript package and would show up on my bill as something "normal." Of course who got the mail the day the package came? Miss Nosey Posey. "What's this, Marilyn?" she'd asked, shaking it.

"I don't know," I said, snatching it from her.

She stood there waiting and waiting and I just kept flipping through every piece of mail, making piles for junk, bills, me, Leon, personal, and when I finally handed her the AARP newsletter she snatched it and quickly rolled it up and started tapping it inside her open palm.

"It's personal, Arthurine," I finally said.

"Is it some of those sexual innuendos? My husband used to get them same brown packages. I wasn't born yesterday."

"Well, Arthurine, if it is sexual in nature, wait about

fifteen minutes and stand outside my bedroom door!" I turned and ran upstairs. I was shocked when I touched the dark brown penis and felt how lifelike it was. It even had simulated testicles, which were softer than I ever imagined. But before I had a chance to decide which one to try first, Arthurine knocked on the door and said the furnace repairman was here and she didn't know where the control panels were. So I put the package in a drawer and haven't touched it until now.

To make this penis operate I need a D battery. Which of course I don't have in here. The clitoris stimulator is an odd-looking thing. It's a pink translucent rubber suction cup in the shape of an oval and right in the middle is a cluster of five or six soft tiny tendrils. They look like an anemone you see swaying from the current in a saltwater fish tank. For this type of stimulation I'm going to need two AA batteries. I opt for the clitoris device because I don't feel like running downstairs past Mrs. Shaft to look for a D battery when I know there's something in here I can take two AA batteries out of. I look around the room. I spot the little miniature reading light I use on those nights when Leon's trying to get to sleep. It only has one.

Then I see the alarm clock! I pop them out and put the one back into the small light. It doesn't really occur to me until I put the batteries into this thing what I'm really about to do. I decide to pretend I'm not me. I'm an actress. In a major movie. And this is a crucial love scene except the man is invisible. I close my eyes and fall back on the bed and turn the dial until I hear the thing buzzing and then I find the spot it was meant for and do what I think I'm supposed to do since I didn't read the instructions. I increase the current and the next thing I know I'm starting to shiver all over and I lose my will and I forget the script and the actress screams out Gordon's name. I'm almost embarrassed when I hear myself declare out loud: "Damn, this thing really works!"

What is sad is that Leon has rarely made me reach this level of unrehearsed, unpretentious ecstasy, and especially in such a short time. My fear now is that because of the urgency and immediacy and ease with which I achieved this pleasure that I might prefer this gadget to a real man because it seems like a sure thing. I believe this is probably how most drug addicts get started. I decide to test it again in a few days just to see if it is consistent.

Knock knock. "Marilyn? Who you yelling at in there?"

"Nobody," I say. "I was singing." I open the door like it has springs in its hinges. "I'm fine," I say. "Have Spencer and Brianna made an appearance yet?"

"They went to see a movie and said they'd see you later."

"Okay. I'll be down in a minute."

"Take your time. You go on back in there and finish singing. You sound happier than you did when you got home and Lord knows my spirits need to be lifted so I'm gon' stand out here a minute or so and listen to the melody to see if I know the words to this song so I can sing right along with you."

• • • •

Leon likes to repeat himself, so it's Vietnamese food night again. I don't inquire about his shopping spree, even though he came in with only one bag from Macy's and one from Sears, which I know probably has floors and floors of tropical wear. If I were to open the trunk of his car, I'd bet big money that it's full of things he doesn't want me to see.

I tell him what happened in Fresno and I spend a great portion of the evening in my workshop sanding that rocking chair. When I get tired, I call Paulette and fill her in. I admit to her that I'm scared for everybody I love, but also for myself.

Paulette just listens. And then I listen to her fill me in on her son who has just gotten out of prison. She doesn't trust him in her house, so she has rented a small apartment for him. He resents her for it. Her husband offers him a job, but he said he needs time to adjust to the outside world before he can even think about falling into another routine. She doesn't know how she gave birth to such a bitter child. She cries.

I sit in one spot and listen to an entire Diane Reeves CD, waiting for Leon to turn off the bedroom light that I can see from here. I am also waiting for Spencer and Brianna to come home so I can remind them about our farewell dinner tomorrow. I call Simeon but get his voice mail. I call Bunny and get her voice mail. I get out my old phone book and starting with the As, go down each entry looking for someone, anybody I haven't talked to for a long time, someone I went to college with—even a long-lost relative—anybody I used to really connect with or once felt close to but by the time I get to the Ds I'm ready to give up. So much for that resolution.

After going through tons of cookbooks, I come up with the menu for tomorrow's dinner:

> *Mixed Green Salad*
> *Fried Chicken* (mostly to take home)
> *Thai Prawns, Scallops & Mussels in Coconut Milk*
> *Angel Hair Pasta* (forget recipe, cook in chicken broth)
> *Stir-fried Collard Greens in Olive Oil & Fresh Garlic*
> *Sweet Hawaiian Bread* (direct from Safeway)
> *Bread Pudding*, with some kind of sauce or sorbet

By midnight, I can't hold my head up anymore, so I go on upstairs and ease into bed as close to the edge of my side as is humanly possible. Thank God Leon sleeps like he's hibernating. In the morning, I'm up before everybody. Even Arthurine. I don't even shower, just brush my teeth and wash my face, slip on a pair of sweats. I make a pot of decaf, and turn the chime back on as I leave for the grocery store. When I get back I must have ten or twelve bags. It's not even nine o'clock. Just for the hell of it, I pop open Leon's trunk. It looks like a grave for shopping bags. I shake my head and chuckle. But don't touch a single one.

The house is still quiet, but I don't want to wake Spencer up just to help me lug these bags in, so I carry them in one at a time. The same way I unload them. I hear someone coming down the steps, moving too fast to be Arthurine.

"Good morning, Marilyn," Leon says, appearing in the kitchen in what look like workout clothes.

"Good morning, Leon."

"How are you?"

"I'm fine. And you?"

"Fine."

"You need any help?" he asks.

"Nope. I'm managing okay."

"Well, I'm going to head off to the gym."

"Have a good workout," I say.

"I will," he says. But just stands there.

"What's wrong?"

"Is this how we're going to do this?"

"Look, Leon. Let's not start so early in the morning, okay? I just want to make sure I have everything I need and then I want to find out if my sister's still sober and if so, I'm going to take a long hard walk and figure out how I'm going to learn to live without you."

"I don't want you to learn how to do that."

"You can't have it both ways, Leon. And right now, it's not even your decision. Go pick up some barbells. Sweat. Steam. And then go to your party. And tomorrow morning, I hope you take your son and his girlfriend back to the airport without flirting with her, and on Monday you can make your exodus."

"What are you going to do while I'm gone?"

"You'll see when you get back."

"You will be here when I get back, I hope. Mother can't be here alone. She needs you here."

"Don't worry about Arthurine. She'll be fine."

"I'm not worried. I'm just concerned. I won't go if you're not going to be here when I get back."

"I'll be here," I say, mostly just to shut him up.

"Seriously. I can cancel this whole trip in a split second."

"No, don't do that, Leon. I *want* you to go."

"You do?"

"The more I've thought about it the more I realized that this trip might be the best thing that could happen to us. We could use some time apart. It may even help us get our perspective back. You said so yourself."

"I did, didn't I."

"So go to the gym. Relax. Everything always turns out for the best."

"All right. And you're sure you won't change your mind about the party?"

I cut my eyes at him while pulling the fat and gristle off the first chicken part and flinging it into the sink. This is what finally gets him out the door.

It's a little past noon. Paulette and Bunny are coming around two. Not to help me because neither of them can cook. And neither of them wants to learn. They like to watch me float around the kitchen, pulling out all the spices and gathering up all the ingredients while they run their mouths and keep me entertained. Sometimes they'll get a bowl or a pot or pan out for me, but mostly, they just keep me company so that even though this meal will take at least three or four hours to prepare, it will probably only feel like one.

Arthurine went to a matinee with her van buddies. I

want to call Joy to see how she's holding up, but it's too soon and I don't want her to feel like I'm spying. But I can't help it if I'm worried. I dial the number with chicken fat on my hands. Joy answers on the second ring. She sounds clear. Alert.

"Joy, it's Marilyn, just calling to say hi and see how you're doing and to let you know how much I appreciated our talk yesterday."

"I did, too. And I'm doing good. Still taking my medication, which I plan to keep taking. It works. Lovey is the same. The garage sale is going on right now. I already sold the treadmill and that bike so I'm getting Lovey's car back this afternoon. Does that sound good enough for you?"

"Yes, it does. Where are the kids?"

"Watching the stuff. I just came in to go to the bathroom and check on Lovey. She didn't wanna sit out there with us."

"Okay then. Tell the kids I said hi and kiss Lovey for me."

"I'll do that. Tell Spencer we'll see him this summer. No doubt. Call tomorrow if you want to. If we ain't here, it just means I took the kids and Lovey to the park."

"The park?"

"They long overdue. And if I can get Lovey to sit still, we might see a movie, too."

"Sounds good, Joy. I'm really proud of you."

"I am, too," she says, chuckling, and hangs up.

Spencer and Brianna stroll into the kitchen about one.

"Well well well, decided to join the living, huh?" I greet them both.

"Hi, Mom," he says, kissing me on the cheek.

"Hello Mrs. Grimes," Brianna says and kisses me, too.

"So, how's that wrist?"

"It's better. It only hurts when I don't keep it elevated or I turn too abruptly," he says, pulling up his jeans that fall right back down to his hips.

I think he's worn those same pants every single day since he's been here. I'm not saying a word. "Then you might want to cut back on so much activity."

"That's what I've been trying to tell him," Brianna says. "But he doesn't listen to me either."

"I think he hears you loud and clear," I say. She looks adorable in those hip-hugging jeans and that hot pink T-shirt that has pink rhinestones in the shape of a heart on the front. I slide the bread pudding into the oven.

"What's that, Mom?"

"Bread pudding."

"Are we having company over? What's with all this food?"

I put my hands on my hips and shift my weight to one leg. "I know you know I'm making this dinner for you and Brianna and any of your friends that are still here."

"Tonight?"

"I told you this in Tahoe, Spencer. You guys are leaving in the morning and I haven't sat down with you for more than ten minutes."

"I think that's when he was on that pain medicine," Brianna says.

"Mom, I swear. I don't remember your mentioning this."

"Why, is there a problem?"

"Well, sorta, kinda."

"Like what?"

"Well, Antoine's cousin plays for the Warriors and he got us free floor seats for the game tonight! They're playing the Lakers, Mom. I'll finally get to see Kobe up close, and we have to go or he'll kill me."

"What time is this game?"

"Seven or seven-thirty. But we'll probably need to leave here about six-fifteen or so because of traffic."

"So what am I supposed to do with all this food, Spencer?"

"We'll be back about ten-thirty or eleven. Antoine said there was a little after-party. But don't worry. You cook it. We can guarantee it will get eaten."

"But I wanted us to sit at the table and dine together. I was going to set the table. I haven't even had a chance to talk to you or Brianna, Spencer."

"Mom, look, I'm sorry. But you know what, we can talk on the phone anytime you want to. I'm just glad to see you. You know that."

"Yeah, this makes me feel a whole lot better."

"We'll be back in California before you know it, Mrs. Grimes. We're out of school the middle of May. You'll be sick of us."

"You're planning to come back?"

"Spencer invited me. We might sublet an apartment

together for the summer. I've already got an internship in San Francisco."

"That's great," I say, not really caring enough about what she's going to be doing to know any details. "What are you two about to do now?"

"Well, we're all packed. But Brianna wants to do a little shopping and since she hasn't seen much of the Bay Area besides Oakland, I'm giving her a tour of San Francisco and Marin County. We might not even make it back here before the game. But I'll call you. Is that cool, Mom?"

"It's cool."

"Where's Dad?"

"Beats me."

"Well, we're gonna dash on out of here."

"But you haven't even eaten breakfast."

"We'll stop and get something."

"Then have fun," I say. "I'll see you later."

"Love you. Oh! Wait! Mom, do you have any extra cash lying around that I could borrow?"

"Like how much?"

"If you could spare a hundred that would be great."

"What's wrong with your ATM card?"

"It has a serious negative balance."

"What if I said no."

He suddenly looks lost and confused.

"Look in my purse," I say.

He does just that. Now he's happy. "Thanks, Mom."

"We'll see you later, Mrs. Grimes."

As soon as I hear my truck back out of that driveway I pick up every single piece of chicken one by one and drop them inside the garbage disposal. I listen to each piece grind to nothing. I do the same thing to the collard greens. After the last white stem disappears, I take handfuls of chopped-up sweet potatoes and push them down there, too. I grab both packages of scallops and prawns and the bag of mussels and march outside where I dump their contents into a trash bin one piece at a time. Then I go back inside and put every bowl, every pot, spice, and utensil back in its place of residence. When the bread pudding is done, I don't wait long enough for it to cool, I just dig out two gigantic mounds and blow on each forkful as I gulp it down with my coffee. I'm just about to chuck the rest of it down the garbage disposal when I hear the doorbell. Unfortunately I'm in tears by the time I let Paulette and Bunny in.

"Girl, what is wrong with you?" Paulette asks.

"It's not your husband again, is it?" Bunny asks.

I shake my head no as they follow me into the kitchen.

"I'm not cooking a damn thing," I say.

"Why not? What happened?"

"Well, my son forgot I wanted to make dinner for him and on his last night being at home after a whole week of not seeing him he's going to a basketball game because that's more important than having dinner with his frigging obsolete mother. But you know what? It's cool. It's so very fucking cool."

"No, it's not, Marilyn," Paulette says. "But slow

down, baby. He's growing up. They all do. The hard part is getting used to being on the periphery when we're not their center anymore."

"That's true," Bunny says.

"Shut up, Bunny. You don't have any kids so you don't even know what the hell I'm even feeling."

"I beg to differ with you, sweetheart. My cats are just like kids."

I'm not going to waste my time responding to her silly ass. "The thing that's bothering me the most is that my own child doesn't seem to appreciate how much time I was prepared to spend cooking this dinner. Which means they probably haven't ever considered how many meals I've actually cooked for them. Or how many loads of clothes I've washed. I thought about it one year. I did over two thousand loads of clothes and cooked over five hundred meals: breakfast and dinner. I wonder if they have a clue as to how much time it takes to fold a T-shirt, a towel, a sheet. How much patience it takes to roll up nine pairs of socks, which don't match or are too dirty to wash again. They're ungrateful and I feel like I've been taken for granted big time."

"Feel better now?" Paulette asks.

I throw a dish towel at her. "I could be overreacting."

"You think?" Bunny says.

Paulette opens and closes the refrigerator and then smooths her hands across the empty countertops. The kitchen is spotless. "I thought you said you bought out the store this morning. What did you do with everything? We figured you'd have half the stuff finished by now."

"I tossed it."

"You tossed what?" Bunny asks.

"Everything."

"Not all that expensive seafood?"

"I did."

"Where exactly did you toss it?"

"Outside in the trash bin."

"That's just ridiculous, Marilyn. And I'm going right out there to get it. I'll figure out a way to cook it myself."

"Is that a bread pudding on the table?" Paulette asks.

"Yes it is."

"I know you're not throwing that out. Don't even answer that. I'll take it home if you don't want it."

"Take it," I say.

"It'll be all right, Marilyn. Just try to understand that when they grow up their friends and girlfriends become important to them. But it doesn't mean he doesn't care or appreciate what you do. Believe me."

"What about your son?"

"That's a whole different ball of wax, honey. You know what I'm saying here. Okay?"

"Yeah, well I'll tell you guys something. This entire household is going to be in for quite a few big surprises because they're about to start seeing what's important to me. And they'll probably go into shock when they realize that most of it does not include them."

Chapter 19

After I convince Paulette and Bunny that I'm not so much upset as I am disappointed and hurt and that I'm not having a nervous breakdown, they take their goodies and leave. I put my sneakers on and take that long hard walk. These hills almost kill me. When I get to Sequoia I turn down the street and search for a house that needs work. I'm not looking for Gordon. I'm looking for repairs. In fact, now would not be a good time to see him. I might throw myself at his feet or break down and confess my fears and sins and beg him to save me or something just as stupid. When I spot his place I know it's the right one because I see the back of his car parked in the driveway. I do an immediate about-face and head back toward my house.

I'm just about to get in the shower when the phone rings. I answer it like Tiecey: "Who's calling and what do you want?"

"Marilyn?" Gordon says.

"Oh shoot! I'm sorry. I thought you might be somebody else."

"Are you all right?"

"Actually, I'm a little upset right now but I should not have answered the phone that way. I apologize."

"No need to. There's nothing wrong with expressing a little anger, especially when you're feeling it. Is there anything I can do?"

Why did he have to ask me that? "No, but thanks."

"I thought I saw you walking up the hill a little while ago, was that you?"

"If she was huffing and puffing then that was probably me."

"Why didn't you stop by?"

"I wasn't sure which house was yours."

"I told you, it's the one that looks like it should be torn down."

"Another time."

"Are you sure you're okay?"

"Yeah. It's just a lot of things going on at once and I'm feeling unappreciated and it just doesn't feel very good."

"So what are you going to do about it?"

"I give."

"What's that supposed to mean?"

"It means I'm changing my course."

"Would your marriage be on or off this course?"

"Off."

"Wow. And you're absolutely sure about this?"

"I think so."

"Well, I'm really sorry to hear this, Marilyn. On one hand. But not the other. Would you like to have dinner with me to talk about what you're going through?"

"I don't know if that's such a good idea right now, Gordon."

"I didn't mean today. And I just meant dinner."

"Then I might take you up on it."

"How's Leon dealing with this?"

"It was his idea."

"Oh. Wow. He seemed like such a cool brother."

"Cool is putting it mildly. How about more like an ice cube."

"Sometimes men go through some weird stuff when we're in our forties. So whatever it is might not even be under his control."

"I beg to differ with you. Anyway, he's not the only one in his forties around here nor does he have a cap on being emotionally frazzled or overly sensitive. Half the time I feel like there's live entertainment going on inside my head. Oh, never mind. I shouldn't even be saying this."

"I'm not going to the tabloids, Marilyn. Remember me? We used to have this honesty thing going on. I don't want to take advantage of you because of your situation. I just know what this feels like, so you go on and get in the shower and call me when you need an ear."

"How d'you know I was about to take a shower?"

"Because I can hear the water in the background and I can tell you're not wet. You take care of yourself."

I hang up. And he's wrong about one thing. I am dripping wet.

• • •

I have to get out of this house, so I drive to Sabrina's apartment in Berkeley without bothering to call. If she's home, she's home. I haven't been over here in so long I forgot how difficult parking is. Luckily, I'm not in the truck and I'm just barely able to squeeze into a tight spot. But no sooner do I put the money in the meter and walk up to her building, than I remember that they don't even live here anymore. They moved to a bigger place right after the first of the year. Shit! Shit! Shit!

It's much harder getting out of this parking space than it was getting in and I pray that I don't do any damage when I tap the fender of that Yukon in front of me. I can see that it's still smooth after I'm out. To be on the safe side, when I get to the corner I pull into a bus stop and call her. She answers. "Sabrina, this is your stupid mother calling to tell you that I was thinking of stopping by to say hi but went to your old apartment and I was wondering if you can tell me how to get to the new place."

She's cracking up. "Hi, Mom. Hate to break it to you, but we just moved across the street. Your son and his Southern belle just left here for the city. I heard you were making this big dinner and I wanna know why we weren't invited?"

"I did invite you, huzzie. Don't give me that."

"You didn't, Mom. I had no idea until Spencer told me."

"Really?"

"Yep. But it's cool. We're coming anyway."

"I'm not cooking now."

"Why not?"

"Let me park this car again and I'll be right up, okay?"

"Okay. Nevil's at the library so you can use our spot in the lot—you can't miss it—space AA. See you in a sec."

I do this and press the AA button and am buzzed in. I think this used to be a school or something. Whatever it was is gone but what they put in its place has been completely restored so that it still has that prewar feeling. I can smell the incense or oils before she opens the door. Her head is wrapped like Erikah Badu's, and she's wearing something flowing, as usual, and of course it's an earth tone. Her belly is getting round. I feel it when she kisses me on the cheek. "Hi, Mom. Welcome to our palatial sanctuary."

And that it is. The apartment is huge. The ceilings are high and the windows are, too. This had to have been a school. The hardwood floors are smooth and dark. Plants are almost everywhere you turn. Everything is low to the floor: Futon. Tables. Lamps. Pillows I made. Handwoven rugs are in well-chosen places. "Sit," she says. "Can I make you some tea?"

"No. I'm fine."

"So why no dinner?"

"Where's Sage?"

"At a birthday party at Chuck E. Cheese for the daughter of one of my girlfriends and afterward she's having eight three-year-olds sleep over. She's crazy. But I'm letting her be crazy. So why no dinner, Mom?"

I collapse on the futon and feel my neck snap because it's much lower than it looks. I'll be glad when she buys some real furniture one day. "Spencer claims he forgot and I'm sure he told you about going to some stupid basketball game, didn't he?"

"Yeah. But what has that got to do with anything?"

"The whole point, Sabrina, was to eat together. It was sort of my way of saying it was nice to see him, brief though it turned out to be. Even still."

"So you didn't cook, or what's the deal?"

"I'm not cooking."

"He hurt your feelings, then, huh?"

"He's not the only one."

"What's Daddy done now?"

"Did he tell you he's going to Costa Rica with Frank for four weeks?"

She sits down on two pillows and crosses her legs in that lotus position. How she can do this being three-and-a-half months pregnant, I don't know. "Why is he going to Costa Rica and with Frank of all people?"

"Because he wants to leave me temporarily so that he can get his head together while he's going through some kind of emotional turmoil that perhaps the young woman he's sleeping with isn't able to help clear up."

"Whoa. Hold up. Stop right there, Mom. You are serious, too, I can see that. Another woman? Are you shitting me?"

"No, I'm not *shitting* you."

"You mean he's like having an affair?"

"I think that's what they call them."

"What would a young woman want with Dad?"

"I can tell you one thing she's not getting."

"Stop it, Mom. I don't want to hear this."

"Well, it's real."

"What is his problem?"

"I don't know."

"Wait a minute. Hold up here. How do you leave someone temporarily?"

"Well, he said he's bored with his job and apparently with me, too, and he's going down there to some kind of resort that's also a spa and a retreat or something he said so he can rejuvenate himself and be new and improved when he gets back."

"How do you feel about all this?"

"I might not be there when he gets back, Sabrina."

"What? But where would you go, Mom?"

"I don't know yet."

"What about Grandma?"

"Arthurine is your dad's problem. He's trying to make her my responsibility but I'm not falling for it this time."

"Well, maybe he just needs this time to get his head straight if he's been stressing. It does happen, Mom."

"I know. But what about me, Sabrina? Huh? Lovey's going through something that might be hard on all of us, but chances are I'm the one who's going to have to handle it. My mother is losing her faculties, Sabrina. Joy swears she's on the road to recovery, but I'm not real sure she's got it in her. I'm bored and lonely. And I'm confused. Half the time I don't know whether I'm coming or going."

I'm crying like a little kid, and this is when my daughter gets up and hugs me as if I am. "It's okay, Mom. You've got a right to feel stressed."

"I'm just the caretaker. The wife. The cook. The recliner Leon chills out in. I'm tired of it and yet I can't help but admit that I'm scared to change."

"Do it anyway, Mom. Why not? You did send in your portfolio and those applications, right?"

I nod, while drying my eyes.

"That's a big step in the right direction. You know what you might want to try?"

"What's that?"

"Yoga."

"I already know the benefits of yoga, Sabrina. You don't have to do a hard sell. When I'm ready to be calm, I'll do it."

"There's also a Chinese doctor and herbalist I want you to see, and a book I want you to read. I bought it just for you."

I sink back into this futon that seems to be more comfortable now than when I first fell into it. "Will this transform my life, too?"

"Don't be so sarcastic, Mom. I'll say this. In China, they don't even have a word for menopause. Those women don't suffer through it the way we do in Western culture."

"Is it the rice?"

"I'll tell you what I read. The more stress you're under, the more symptoms you have. This is supposed to be the last great opportunity you and every woman going through this will ever have to prepare your mind, your body, and your spirit to have a long healthy life. This should be the time in your life to flourish in all kinds of ways."

"I'm trying," I say.

"Well, think of this time like you're going on a long car trip across the desert and this is the only chance you're going to have to make sure your car is tuned properly, that it's full of gas and that you've gotten enough rest to drive. But if you're stressed or pissed or unhappy, you won't make it through the desert. If you want to get to wherever it is you think you want to go, you have to be willing to change everything you do that stops you."

"Give me some examples."

"You don't exercise."

"True."

"You could stand to change your eating habits."

"True."

"You could stand to do something different with your hair."

"I like my hair the way it is."

"It's boring, Mom. Go nappy."

"Are you leaving out anything?"

"You might have to tell Daddy bye-bye. There you have it."

I look at my beautiful, healthy, pregnant, and smart daughter. "Thank you for saying this. But tell me something, Sabrina, are you happy?"

This seems to catch her off guard. "Yes, I am. We have our ups and downs like everybody else, but for the most part, we're on the same wavelength."

"Then why are you the one postponing getting your degree and moving to another continent, basically to accommodate him?"

"What's wrong with that?"

"Would he do it for you?"

"I think so."

"Then why doesn't he?"

"Because I never asked him."

"But I thought you were so gung ho about getting your master's."

"I am, but it can wait a year or two."

"Really?"

"Yes. I've always wanted to see London."

"Then why can't you just buy a ticket and go for a vacation?"

"Mom, why is this bothering you so much all of a sudden?"

"It's not sudden. I'll just say it. You remind me of myself twenty-two years ago when I put getting my master's on hold to marry your father and because I was pregnant with you. The next thing I know, here come the twins. And your daddy wanted me to stay home and be a hands-on kind of mother, which I didn't mind doing, but fast-forward the film, Sabrina, and here I am. I don't want this to happen to you. Looks like you're already on your way."

"There's sacrifice in every relationship, Mom, and somebody's gotta make it."

"But why does it always have to be *us*?"

"It's my choice. Just like you chose to raise us. I'm going to come back in two years and my husband will be able to afford to take care of his family while I . . ."

"Your what? I beg to differ with you, baby, but he is not your husband."

"He feels like my husband."

"But he isn't."

"Anyway, I'm going to get my master's in education and I'm going to focus on improving literacy in our communities and I'm going to help change the way public education avoids the issue. And I'll do it with my child in tow if I have to."

"Two children in tow."

"Sage is my daughter, even if I didn't give birth to her. You probably feel the same about Aunt Joy. I'm blessed, Mom. And please don't worry. I'm not going to give up my dreams or my plans for Nevil or any man. He's on my side."

I get up and head for the door. "Look, I didn't mean to come over here and upset your world. I'm sorry." I give her a hug.

"It's quite all right. Let Daddy do his thing, and you start doing yours. Watch and see. Half the things that drive you crazy will cease to even move you." She hands me the yoga brochure, gives me that doctor's business card, and then gives me the bag with the book in it, which of course I do not open for weeks.

Chapter 20

Leon is off to his party, but left behind the brochure for his resort on the kitchen counter. It's a picturesque place to say the least. There are no phones in the individual bungalows. Messages can only be left at the front desk. There is golf. The spa looks like it couldn't possibly be real. I see what is apparently a hot waterfall gushing from nowhere and people standing under it. A rain forest or jungle surrounds half of this hilltop compound. Crashing waves from an emerald green sea seal off the lower side. I wish I could jump inside these photographs for just a few hours.

At least twenty different kinds of "workshops" are offered at this place and Leon has circled the ones I suppose he's planning to take or maybe he did this just to impress me: "Managing Your Stress, Your Heart, and Your Life" (this one lasts seven days); "Rekindling the Spirit" (five days): for those who no longer find their careers rewarding. This course offers suggestions and guidance on how to consider starting new ones; "Accepting Life's Transitions" (five days): this one's got my name all over it. It's hard to believe he's circled these last two: "Essential Peacemaking: Women and Men" (seven days) and "Not Quite Paradise: How to Turn a Troubled Marriage Around" (seven days).

Wait a minute. I see one that makes me wonder why he and Frank didn't think to consider inviting Joyce and me: "Exploring the Power of the Midlife Journey: A Women's Retreat" (five days). As big as this place looks, we wouldn't have even had to see them. Oh, who cares? It's not like I would've gone anyway. And Lord knows I would not have wanted to get stuck in a room with motormouth Joyce who last I heard had gotten her stomach stapled and had lost a hundred and thirty pounds. As far as I can tell, I'm already on the Journey. I'm just trying to find a more reliable mode of travel.

I spend most of the evening reading over the MFA course descriptions again and literally get chill bumps at the thought of being able to take any of these classes. I'm not even sure when they're going to let me know that I'm not getting accepted. It doesn't matter, because I can still take classes without being enrolled in a degree program. Thank God. In fact, I've already decided to take another one over the summer—something more than the beading class—regardless of what happens. I've narrowed it down to three to choose from: metal arts/jewelry, welded and fabricated sculpture, or neon/illuminated sculpture.

Leon gets home around midnight. I pretend to be

asleep. He smells like wine again. I'm sweating so much that I kick the comforter off of me. I wake up an hour later freezing and pull it back. At five a.m. Leon gets up. I don't. Not even when Spencer and Brianna come in to say good-bye. They bend down to kiss and hug me. In fact, Spencer doesn't even ask what happened to all the food. Not even the bread pudding. He does mention that the Lakers won by eighteen points. That Kobe and Shaq were awesome. That the after-party was off the hook.

I go to church with Arthurine. It's a good sermon. She holds my hand on the way out. We have brunch in Jack London Square, which is on the water. We watch the sailboats and yachts cruise by. I tell Arthurine that I need to go the bookstore and I'll drop her off at home first. But of course she wants to go, too. But I might be a while. She says she's in a browsing mood. I look down at her beige pumps. I can see where her bunions are forcing the leather to crack. What about when your feet start hurting and I'm not ready to go? They have chairs in that café. I'll sit and wait. I do not feel like arguing with her.

We go our separate ways once we get inside. I ask the clerk at the information counter where the art section is. Could I be more specific? Books on jewelry design and working with metal and clay and everything in between. He points toward the back of the store. Are there any books that might give me some insight into the business side of selling and marketing fine art and crafts? He points to the same area. I take out my water bottle and sit on the floor for more than an hour, going through book after book.

I've made most of my stuff by imagining it looking a certain way, and through plain old trial and error. But I am awestruck by how much beauty can be squeezed into a book. On the cover of one is a woven basket made of cocobolo wood. I put this on what is the beginning of a pile. On top of it I place another in which fifty artists share their techniques on how they "introduce" color to metal. I just love the "introduce" thing. One cobalt blue and orange object looks like a giant snail: just *one* example of new ways of glazing ceramic art. Copper and pewter satin roses cluster around a hat. I could learn how to make hats, not just decorate them. But I don't want to make them, so I put this one back. I keep the ones on wire magic and fiber art and finally, quilting like I've never seen in my life. I am so excited. I feel like a child who's been allowed to pick out anything they want in the store. For good measure, I add to the pile a book that tells how to sell and market whatever you make with your hands.

The clerk offers to carry them because they're too heavy, and we spot Arthurine in the café. She's drinking tea and nibbling on a giant cookie. I motion to her and she limps over. Says her feet swelled up from sitting here waiting for me for so long. I just cannot apologize.

I refuse to watch Leon pack, so I drop Arthurine off and head for the mall where I spend hundreds of dollars on colorful workout clothes that I don't bother to try on. I pray that the Ls are big enough or at least don't shrink before I do. The salesgirl asks if I'm starting a brand-new program or just gearing up for summer. I tell her it's an old program but with a whole new approach. She wants to know what the name of it is. I tell her it's called exercise. She laughs. Asks me if I've ever thought of trying yoga. Funny you should ask.

Across the aisle is an entire carousel of nothing but Arthurine's nylon paisley jogging suits, but I cannot bring myself to walk over there. Instead, I go downstairs to the Savvy Department and pick out three very nice peach, lemon, and mint green 100 percent cotton outfits with matching pants, T-shirt, and sweater. I pull the pants diagonally to make sure there's at least 5 percent Lycra in them. There is. I buy them for Arthurine because she really needs to update her look and she'll look vibrant in these colors. She just doesn't know it yet.

It's around eight when I get home. Leon's been waiting for me. Wants to know if I'll drive him to the airport. No. I can't. Why not? Because I don't want to. But you always take me to the airport when I'm gone for longer than a weekend. Get a ride with Frank. But his wife is taking him. Yours isn't, I say. Call a cab. Which is what he does.

Just as I'm leaving for work, I hear the phone ringing but I don't feel like going back inside to answer it. I wonder if it's Leon. While I wait a few more seconds before dialing my voice mail, the cell vibrates in my hand. "Hello?"

"Good morning, Marilyn. What time is it there?"

"Close to nine." I have nothing to follow this up with, so I wait to see what he has to say.

"Well, we made it."

"Mission accomplished."

"It's really quite breathtaking."

"You knew that before you left, Leon."

"I know. But it's different once you get here."

"I wouldn't know."

"Anyway, how are things there?"

"Everything is fine."

"Well, look, I just wanted you to know I made it here safely."

"I thought you might be dead and calling me anyway."

"Marilyn," he sighs.

"What?"

"How's Mother?"

"She's packing."

"Packing for what?"

"She's going to Reno for the weekend with Prezelle and a whole busload of senior citizens."

"And where's she staying?"

"I don't know."

"Well, would you at least find out?"

"She's sixty-eight years old, Leon. She's a big girl."

"That's not the point. Is she sharing a room with someone? It better not be that old fella."

"It's none of my business or yours."

"For Christ sakes, Marilyn. You've certainly become apathetic these past few weeks."

"I'm just numb, Leon."

"Well, that's why I'm here. To try and thaw out."

"Do they have microwaves over there?"

"Look, I just wanted you to know I'm here. Our schedule is going to be jam-packed and pretty hectic, so you might not hear from me until I'm on my way home."

"That's fine with me."

"To be honest, they encourage us not to communicate with our loved ones or our jobs at all."

"Say no more."

"Seriously, Marilyn. I told you there are no phones in our cottages, didn't I?"

"I read the brochure, Leon."

"Good. Then you're aware that the only way to reach me is by leaving a message at the front desk."

"I know that."

"And only in case of an emergency."

"No problem. And I hope that you and Frank are able to get as enlightened as you possibly can."

"Me, too. I've gotta go. The first session starts in two minutes. I still love you, Marilyn."

"What? I can't hear you. You're breaking up," I say and hang up. "I don't like the way you love me," I say to the dead phone and then dial the voice mail. It's Dr. Merijohn. He says that Lovey's blood tests look good, but as he suspected, her cholesterol is too high: 290. He's going to increase the dose of her medication but begs me to help her change her eating habits. He's already sent the test results and copies of her medical history to Dr. Richardson, who's looking forward to seeing Lovey in a few weeks. If for whatever reason I'm not able to go with her he asks that it be another responsible family member. I'm praying for it.

I'm surprised at just how glad I am that Leon's gone. I've been going to work early and staying late. Trudy is becoming quite knowledgeable and even skillful in a number of departments. She asked if I'd ever finished that necklace I was making and I was embarrassed but admitted that I hadn't. "Why don't you leave it here and let me have someone have a go at it? I know exactly what you're after. Don't worry." So I don't.

I even drove out to Bunny's health club and got a brand-new membership knowing it was her day off. I signed up for those yoga classes in Berkeley. I treated myself to one of those day spas but left before the "day" was over. On the phone they sounded like an infomercial on how much pampering I was in store for. The massage therapist seemed afraid to use much pressure and after thirty minutes, I gave her a tip and told her I had to go to the bathroom and I felt refreshed. The manicurist's pager kept going off and while I sat in that pedicure chair that was broken, they had to pour the hot water in and then started vacuuming up all the loose toe and fingernails. So much for "self-care," magazine-style.

Every evening before dinner I check in with Joy, who's still sounding good and after dinner I help Arthurine study for her driver's test. She's skipping Bible study this week because she says she can't study two things at once.

I can't believe it's Thursday already, and here she comes limping into the house with a Nordstrom's shopping bag full of mail. "Most of this look like it's for you. I think I saw something in there from one of those colleges but I don't have on my glasses, so I could be mistaken."

My ears are ringing. But maybe it's my cell phone. Or the second line in my workshop. "Arthurine, do you hear that?"

"What is it I'm listening for?" she asks, leaning toward me.

"Do you hear a phone ringing?"

She tilts her head so her ear points toward the ceiling. "It ain't coming from my room, my phone is turned down so low I can't hardly hear it when I'm in there."

"Is there a TV on somewhere?"

"Not that I know of, but I ain't been in your room."

"Never mind," I say. "I don't hear it now."

"You might want to get your hearing tested because you don't wanna look up one day and be deaf."

"I just thought I heard something ringing, that's all."

"That's how it starts. A little ring here. A little ring there. Then no ring at all. I know what I'm talking about. And speaking of ringing, I forgot to tell you your sister called and said that that neurology doctor had a opening so she's taking Lovey to see her this Tuesday instead of two weeks from now."

"That's great! How did she sound?"

"Like she was your sister."

"Did she seem happy?"

"She wasn't exactly bubbling over, but she certainly

didn't strike me as being depressed. What are you driving at?"

"Did it sound like she could possibly be drunk?"

Arthurine pauses for a minute to remember. "No, not at all. But she was chewing on something which I thought was rude."

"Then I'll call her later."

"She said not to worry. She'll call you after they get back from the doctor."

"But that's five whole days from now!"

"So? What you so worried about?"

"My mother."

"The girl is taking her to the doctor, Marilyn. You think she'd let something happen to Lovey?"

"Not on purpose."

"Oh, chill out, girl."

"Chill out? When did you get so hip?"

"They say it a lot on BET. Oh, shoot. There was another message you might not want to know about but I think I should tell you anyway. Your doctor said that if you'da had the baby, it would've been a little girl."

"Thank you, Arthurine, for being such a good secretary." A little girl? I rub my arms up and down to brush the chill bumps away and to erase the image of a baby girl.

"You're welcome. Anyway, did you get the mail yesterday?"

"No."

"Me neither. Did you get it on Tuesday?"

"No."

"Me neither. Well, here. You go through it. I'm going on upstairs to pack."

"Did you tell me you get back on Sunday night or Monday morning? I can't remember."

"I don't think we ever discussed the coming and going part. But they said we should get back here on Sunday night somewhere between eight and nine. They have to leave a window open because the brochure said the tour company cannot be responsible for the weather or heavy traffic."

"I'll wait, Arthurine, so don't start worrying about it, okay?"

"Do I look worried? No. Do I sound like I'm worried? No."

"Okay you made your point! What time do you need to be over there tomorrow?"

"Prezelle said the bus is leaving that parking lot at one o'clock sharp, so we can't be late or I'll get left."

"Don't worry, you'll be there in plenty of time. But let's just say hypothetically speaking, if you were late. Do you think Prezelle would really go on without you?"

"That's a question I don't have the answer to and do not want to have to find out. I'm just so excited, I hope I can get to sleep tonight."

"And you're still planning on taking your driving test in the morning, right?"

"Of course I am. While it's still fresh in my mind. And then can you drop me off at Prezelle's, if that's all right with you?"

"I said I would, and I will. We're taking your car."

"Why?"

"Because that car needs to be driven. And tomorrow is as good a day as any. What hotel are you staying at?"

"The Nugget. How many times do I have to say it?"

"Don't get cute, Arthurine, or you'll be hitchhiking down to the DMV."

"You still ain't heard a word from Leon?"

"Just that he had arrived."

"Do you miss him?"

"Nope."

"That's a shame. I'm praying very hard that the love you two once shared will come alive again, you know."

"Don't pray too hard, Arthurine. God has already made his decision."

"And how do you know that?"

"Because He spoke to me."

"What? When? What did He say?"

Her eyes look like glassy marbles that are just about to pop out and roll all over the floor.

"He said it's time to get this party started."

She recoils. "He ain't said no such thing and you know it. Sometimes I think you trying to be witty but you ain't a very good comedienne, Marilyn, because you don't have no idea what's funny. And you should not be throwing God's name around like He's a human being or a real person when He ain't."

"I'm sorry, Arthurine."

"All is forgiven."

She goes on upstairs and I walk over to the red table in the entry and start making the usual piles. Arthurine was right. Here's a white envelope from the Academy of Art College with my name typed on the front. I can't open it. Not yet. I slide it all the way down to the end of the table all by itself and continue sorting through the rest of the mail. Shit! There's one from the California College of Arts and Crafts, too. Now I'm having heart palpitations and then it feels like I can hardly breathe. I go over to the living room and sit down on the couch. This feels like a mistake, especially if my heart wants to stop beating and I'm suffocating at the same time. I stand back up. But this time I feel light-headed, so I sit back down. Now I feel hot. I take my sweatshirt off and sit here in my underwire bra and jeans that are too damn tight. I undo the snap and the fat that I hope to lose in the near future expands causing my zipper to unzip itself. I can't open those letters right now. I just can't.

"Marilyn!" Arthurine yells from the top step. "Can I borrow one of your suitcases?"

"I don't care."

"Can I take that black one with the wheels that I can hang my things up in?"

"I said I don't care."

"Can you bring it up here for me?"

"Only if you come down here and do something for me first."

"My feet hurt. I'm seriously thinking about getting these bunions cut off either right after we finish with Lamentations or before start-up with the Song of Solomon in the New Testament."

"The Song of Solomon is in the Old Testament, Arthurine."

"Look, you don't need to correct me when it comes to the Bible. I may get some things out of order, but it's all in there somewhere, so what difference does it make?"

"You're right, Arthurine."

"I don't say nothing about this mishmash you make and call art, now do I?"

"No, you do not."

"Then we're even. Now. Whatever it is you wanted me to do, can I do it up here when you bring me the suitcase?"

"I suppose so. I'll be right back."

I run to the garage and get the garment bag, but by the time I get back into the house, I seem to have conjured up the courage to open the letters myself. After all, there are really only two possible answers: come or stay home. What I'm finding to be more surprising is how much this obviously seems to mean. I just don't want to put so much weight on this that it feels like the only key that can unlock the door.

I take Arthurine the bag and turn to go back downstairs.

"What happened to your blouse, chile?"

"I was burning up."

"Flashing again, are we? Lord, don't I remember. So what was it you wanted me to do?"

"Never mind. It was nothing."

"What was it? Now you done got me all curious."

"I can do it myself."

"Do what yourself?"

"Open these letters I got from the two colleges that will tell me whether or not some of this mess I make confuses the hell out of them, too, or if it's good enough to get me accepted."

"Oh, come on, Marilyn, I was just kidding with you. Oh ye of so little faith. Open them letters, girl, so we can both have a reason to celebrate."

I open them without reading them, then unfold each one and simply look at the first few words of each letter. They're pretty much the same: "It gives us great pleasure . . ." and "We are pleased to advise you . . ." But instead of jumping for joy like I was praying I'd be able to do, I am truly humbled by these letters of acceptance. Because I finally realize that not only do I have to make a choice but that I've always had them.

"What do they say? I'm dying of curiosity."

"You don't really want to know do you, Arthurine?"

"Don't make me snatch them letters from you. What do they say?"

"They basically say the same thing."

She stamps her foot. Which is a bad move.

"Well, they both seem to be saying, 'Let's get this party started!' " I take hold of her right hand and slide my left arm behind her back and I waltz her all the way to her bedroom without even coming close to kicking her bunions.

Chapter 21

don't feel like driving just yet," is what Arthurine says right after she passes her test and I attempt to hand over her keys. She crosses her arms then squeezes them so tight that it pushes her breasts almost up to her chin. The keys hit the pavement.

"I was just thinking that you might want to drop me off and drive yourself over to Prezelle's," I say, reaching down to pick them up once I notice that we're standing in the line of fire of a nervous teenager about to take his driving test. When we get over to Arthurine's white Cadillac, I dangle the keys in front of her one more time for good measure.

"I need more than five minutes to get used to the idea that I can get in this car in broad daylight and drive right past the police without breaking into a cold sweat, plus, go anywhere I want to without sneaking like I'm some-body's criminal." She pivots and rushes over to the pas-senger side of the car and stands there.

I feel like making her wait. "You look very nice in mint green, Arthurine."

"I do, don't I. Thank you," she says. "Now can you hurry up and open this door, I don't have all day."

I drive. As promised.

The slick silver bus is already there when we pull up. A parade of senior citizens is dragging suitcases without wheels as if they do have wheels across the concrete and abandoning them in front of the open baggage compartment. Prezelle is standing between an avocado green overnight case and a brown plaid bag bursting at the seams. It's big enough to hold clothes for a family of four. He appears to be looking for his woman because his face lights up when Arthurine steps out of the car.

"I was getting a little worried," he says, and to my surprise, gives her a quick kiss on her lips. Prezelle is— needless to say—decked out. However, it appears that he may have gotten his seasons a little mixed up. He's sporting a brand-new straw hat and when he bends over to give me a peck on the cheek, I see the price tag and separate bar code still stuck to the underside of the brim. He is also camouflaging a Hawaiian print shirt that I know only comes in short sleeves beneath the tweed suit jacket that most people would consider a separate, especially when it doesn't match the pants that happen to be brown corduroy. I'm afraid to look at his shoes.

"I passed," Arthurine exclaims.

"I knew you would. I told you you would. Congratulations."

"Thank you, Prezelle."

"So now you're legal, huh?"

"I am indeed."

"Then why didn't you drive over here instead of making Marilyn go out of her way to bring you?"

"She insisted. Didn't you, Marilyn?"

"I did. I wanted to see you both off and wish you a good time."

"Well, that's awful nice of you. Is that a new outfit you're wearing there, Reeney?"

"It most certainly is. I can't believe you even noticed."

"I've never seen you in a solid color before, that's why."

"Do you like it?"

"I do. It is downright flattering. But I hope you brought a few of the ones you always wear that I like."

"Of course I did. I'm planning on wearing the purple and gold one to dinner."

"Did you know it's a buffet? All you can eat?"

"Don't tell me that, Prezelle. I don't need no buffet to eat all I can." She chuckles.

"Can I get your bags out of the trunk?"

"I only brought one," she says.

"I'll get it, Prezelle," I say.

"No no no. Let a man do a man's job."

I smile at him as I pop the trunk open and then at Arthurine who looks like she knows she's already hit the jackpot. Prezelle lifts the black garment bag up and starts to carry it toward the bus. I want to tell him it's got wheels, but I just keep my big mouth shut.

He hurries back. "Come on, Reeney," he says, reaching out to take her hand. "Or we might not get to sit together."

"Prezelle, don't worry yourself for no reason. We'll be closer than a bus seat tonight and tomorrow."

I think I'm hearing things. "Wait a minute. I mean, excuse me a second. Arthurine?"

"What?"

"Do you mean to tell me that you and Prezelle are staying in the same room?"

"Of course we are. What a stupid question, Marilyn."

"What's so stupid about it?"

"I don't think it's a stupid question," Prezelle says. "I can see how you might wonder why we would choose to go this route."

"And what route is that?" she asks, looking at him.

"We save eighteen dollars in a double."

"That ain't the reason we talked about, Prezelle."

"Look, I'm not implying that there's anything wrong with the two of you . . . I mean, it's your business and you're both consenting adults. I just didn't know it was going down like this."

"Well, it is going down like this and we gots to go," she says, this time grabbing Prezelle by the hand and pretty much dragging him over to the bus entrance. "Bye, Marilyn," she says, as he helps her get up that first step. "Try to have a good weekend without me."

"That's impossible," I say. "I miss you already."

"Bye-bye," Prezelle whispers to me.

Part of me wants to wait until they're seated safely on

the bus and long after it disappears from sight, I'd stand here a few more minutes to make sure that if they forgot something that would cause them to have to turn around and come back, I'd be here to go get whatever it was they needed. But Arthurine and Prezelle are not on their way to camp and they are not my children. Every tinted window on this bus has a smiling senior citizen behind it, two of whom are waving to me like they're leaving for their honeymoon.

I didn't call to tell anybody about my news yesterday. I wanted the reality of it to sink in first: I'm going back to school. Just like my children. I needed to really weigh what this is going to mean. I also have no idea if Leon will pay the tuition or if I'll be taking out a student loan. This even sounds odd: me taking out a student loan for myself. But I'll do whatever I have to do. I'm going.

I meet Paulette and Bunny for a shopping lunch in San Francisco. Bunny—much like Prezelle—doesn't seem to know it's the end of March and not August. She's in a tight, white, hip-hugging sweat suit that you wouldn't dream of sweating in, even though there's a matching jacket that doesn't quite reach her waist, and under it she's wearing a white satin camisole that's obviously too small. Paulette, on the other hand, looks like a grown-up having lunch on Maiden Lane on a sunny spring afternoon. Her braids look unbelievably good, which tells me that her daughter didn't do them. She's in black leather pants, black boots, a white shirt with a great collar, and a red blazer. I'm not commenting on what I'm wearing. But I'm presentable. I also don't bother telling them my news until after we order. Neither one seems surprised to hear it.

"I don't mean to be a pessimist but just because you got in doesn't mean you're actually going to go," Paulette starts in.

"I'm going," I say.

"I won't believe it until I see it," Bunny says.

"I'm going," I say.

"When you walk through the doors and sit your behind behind a desk, that's when I'll believe it."

"Look, I can't lie. I'm scared as hell."

"Scared of what?" Bunny asks.

"That my life is about to change."

"Hallelujah," Paulette says, after she finally swallows what apparently is very doughy sourdough bread. "But all change is scary. Like it's supposed to be."

"Why should it have to be scary?" Bunny asks on my behalf.

"Because there's safety in sameness and predictability. But when you're not quite sure what's around the corner it gives rise to a little trepidation. Some people freak out and get stuck right there. But like they say: 'Opportunities just don't keep knocking at your door.' Especially when you get to be our age."

"Whose age?" Bunny says, looking over the top of her tinted sunglasses even though there's no sun in here.

"I'm doing this. I swear I am."

"I believe you," Paulette says, and leans back in her

chair. "You're long overdue, girlfriend. The biggest debt you owe is to Marilyn."

I nod while trying to convince myself that I'm enjoying this Caesar salad when what I'd really like to do is snatch a few of those fries off the guy's plate sitting at the next table and ask if I could just take the first bite out of that thick juicy hamburger he's about to bring to his mouth. "Did Aretha braid your hair like that, Paulette?"

"You know Aretha can't do this. So don't be cute. This girl in Oakland did it and she's cheap. I can get you her number."

"Great. I could use a new look."

"Took you long enough to realize it."

"Bunny, you should chill with the negative comments."

"I'm just trying to be a motivating instigator. How's Leon doing in Costa Rica by the way?" she asks.

"I'll be honest. I want to know what the deal is, too," Paulette says. "I mean I'm not trying to get all into your Kool-Aid—yes I am—but you gave us a sip and now we want to drink the whole glass. What's the latest word?"

"He called to say he got there, but that's it."

"Get out," she says.

"Aren't you just a little paranoid about this whole thing? I mean, come on, Marilyn. Four wife-free weeks in the Caribbean with his buddy?"

"I'm not really worrying too much about Leon these days if you want the honest to God's truth. It's weird, but I don't even miss him."

"Then I'd file those papers and put them into his

sunbaked hands as soon as he walks in the house. Sort of a welcome home present," Bunny says.

"You can be one cold broad," Paulette says, "which is one reason you're by yourself. And it's not that simple."

"Sometimes you have to be cold to make your point because they certainly go out of their way to make theirs, don't they? And if you happen to get your feelings hurt while they do it, sorry Charlie, tuna's not for cats. That was a bad analogy. Forget I said that."

"Consider it forgotten," I say, "whatever it is you think you just said. Anyway, who's on your plate these days, Bunny? We haven't heard you spit out his credentials or possessions so you must be on empty."

"Thank you very much for reminding her, Marilyn."

"I'm in the early no-name stage. Don't worry. You'll know when it's time to know."

"What *did* you just say?" Paulette says.

"Nothing," Bunny says, leaning on her elbows and staring at me. "But I have a different bone to pick with you, Marilyn Manson."

"What now?"

"What's the big idea coming to the club and signing up for membership when I wasn't there?"

"I didn't know it was your day off. And I don't want to go to the same gym as Leon."

"I could've gotten you a discount, but you're not going to come anyway. You should just call the business office and get your money back."

"Are you PMSing today or something?" Paulette asks.

"No. But Marilyn's been talking a lot of shit about all

the stuff she was going to do after her kids left for college and I haven't seen her start—let alone finish—a doggone thing. So to think she's actually going to go back to college *and* go to the gym, too, it's just hard for me to believe."

"Oh ye of little faith," I say. "I've been looking over the schedule but was hoping you'd help me with a course of action. I'm serious. I need to do this."

Bunny holds out her hand, palm up. "How long do you think you'll last?"

"I'm making a lifestyle change, Bunny. I'm not going on some little stupid diet so I can lose twenty pounds in six weeks and kill myself at the gym to get into a string bikini. I want to make exercise be a regular part of my day-to-day life so it's just as important as breakfast."

"But it *is* as important as breakfast, girl. That's what I've been trying to tell you lazy Negro women for years."

"Don't look at me, Bunny. I walk three times a week around Lake Merritt and lift my grandbabies at least twice a week, and plus I still do my Jane Fonda tapes."

"She's serious, you know that, don't you?" Bunny says to me.

"Jane still works."

"Anyway Marilyn. I don't mean to be so cynical, but here's the deal. The first thing we need to do is get you a fitness evaluation."

"I'm out of shape. I already know that."

"We measure your entire body and determine your body fat."

"I can show you where the fat is right now."

"Seriously. We can tell you what your target heart rate zone is so when you do any cardiovascular work—like running, spinning, jogging, the treadmill, climber . . ."

"Okay, WE GET IT!" Paulette says. "Now get to the damn point would you, Bunny?"

"Anyway if you . . ."

For the next ten minutes, Paulette and I eat and watch Bunny exercise her lips.

". . . and let me just give you something to think about until our consultation."

Paulette's eyes are going up in her head and I kick her under the table. But it's not her leg, it's Bunny's.

"See I told you, you aren't serious! I'm going to Neiman's to find something pretty to sleep in." She raises her hand for the check.

"Okay, I'm sorry. What should I be thinking about until we meet?"

"Set yourself a goal and write it down. Not your ideal weight. Say you're a fourteen and you want to get back down to a ten. Is that a realistic goal, you might ask?"

"Yes, that is the question."

"Go to hell, Marilyn. You have any important stuff coming up that you want to look good for?"

"Divorce court."

"Aren't you going anywhere this summer?"

"I hadn't exactly thought that far ahead."

"Well, since your husband's taking four long ones, you should give yourself at least a week's worth of vacation and so you won't feel lonely, Paulette and I will be more than happy to go with you. Let's say around the end of August after you finish your class."

"We haven't done that in a long time, have we?" Paulette says. "We're overdue."

"Sounds good to me," I say.

"And by then you should be able to slide into a size ten swimsuit without rupturing those thighs."

"A twelve will suffice."

"But where can we go?" Paulette asks.

"Any place that's cheap," Bunny throws in.

"Somewhere outside of the U.S.," I say.

"But not Mexico! I've had enough of Mexico," Paulette says.

"We're getting off the subject," Bunny says.

"Wait a minute, Bunny," Paulette says. "I don't think we should wait until August. That's when I go to Vegas for the Magic Convention and you guys know I can't miss that. If I had nothing but time, I'd kill to go to Greece for the Olympics."

"Me, too," I say. "I've got a Greek Isles calendar that's so unbelievably pretty it doesn't even look real. Hey, why don't we go to a swank spa or something?"

"I wouldn't mind going on that black cruise," Bunny says.

"No way," Paulette says. "I did it once and that was enough. Too many horny and ugly men trying to get laid and there's no place to hide unless you jump off the damn ship. And do I look Puerto Rican? I don't think so. They can't have any more of my money."

"Okay, we'll figure out somewhere to go but for right

now, let's forget about it! Anyway, Marilyn, back to the subject?"

"No, we're finished! I'll give all of this some thought."

"Are we ready?"

"One last thing and this is really important."

"We've heard enough! Are we going shopping or not?"

"I forgot what I came over here to look for," Paulette says.

"I just need a good pair of running shoes."

"To do what in?" Bunny asks.

"Don't let it worry you. Now whose turn is it to pay?"

"You really need to stop asking such silly questions when you already know the answer," she says, and walks off. Paulette has the nerve to follow her.

Chapter 22

You always know when you're in Berkeley, that's all I have to say. What did you think of it?" Paulette says, waving to everybody in the room like she's on a float in a parade.

"I liked it."

She rolls her eyes at me. "I didn't like that oily flower smell in the room and I didn't like that creepy swaying-in-the-wind music they played, and the sound of that water oozing through those little rocks got on my damn nerves. And I don't like walking on nobody's floor without something on my feet, and I certainly didn't like Luna touching my ass. All in all: it's just too slow. I'll stick with Jane."

"Did you know that Jane gave up aerobics for yoga?"

"She did not."

"She did so. Anyway, to hell with you and Jane. I liked it and I'm going to do it again."

"Knock yourself right on out. The next thing I know

you'll be burning incense and candles and eating tofu and drinking soy milk and wearing gauze and those flat sandals with no heel and no socks even when it's cold as hell outside. Watch."

"Shut up, Paulette. I can't help it if you don't know how to be still and quiet at the same time."

"And I'm going to keep it like that. I could sure use a cappuccino. There's gotta be a Starbucks on one of these corners and yes I'm a sucker so don't start in. All this inhaling and exhaling mess doesn't work half as fast as caffeine. Plus I've got too much on my mind to be squirming around on a hard-ass floor."

"Is this about Mookie?"

"Girl, one of his ex-girlfriends, who's got two kids she swears are his has been calling the house all hours of the night looking for him since he's been out, even after I've told the girl ten times that he doesn't live here. Cleopatra is a dope-fiend, just like all of his other women. But when she told me I need to stop lying to her, I finally cussed the bitch out."

"You did say Cleopatra, didn't you?"

"I did. And she looks just like Mike Tyson. Even built like him. Except she's only five-two."

I'm laughing, trying to picture her. "So you cussed her out, now forget about it."

"But this child is crazy. She ran her car into this dude's Lexus while he was in his house sleeping after she found out he'd been dealing with somebody else. This is when Mookie was still locked up of course."

"Did she get hurt?"

"Not a scratch. I'm not exaggerating, Marilyn. Roscoe told me to give the phone to him the next time she calls."

"I would do just that. Can't you block her number?"

"She doesn't have one. She calls from a pay phone."

"Then I'd talk to Mookie. Make him set her straight."

"It's on my list of things to do today. What's on yours?"

"It's fitness day for me. I had that evaluation already."

"From Bunny?"

"No. I can't deal with Bunny under these circumstances. She agrees. Anyway, I almost had a stroke doing all the stuff they made me do to figure out my fitness level."

"And what was it?"

"Low. Very very low."

"What did they really say, Marilyn? Is there any hope for your old ass?"

"My body fat is like thirty percent. Which is high. They said eighteen would be ideal and I said yeah, but twenty-two makes a whole lot more sense."

"What percentage do you think mine is?"

"I don't know. They have this thing they squeeze all over you and then do some math and that's how they figure it out."

"What do you think mine might be? Look at me."

"I can't guess, Paulette."

"Guess, bitch."

"Okay. Twenty-two."

"I knew I was in better shape than you. It's Jane. I'm telling you."

"Bunny's is probably ten or twelve."

"Speaking of bunnies. What are you doing for Easter?"

"I'm actually going to church with Mr. and Mrs. Goodenough. You will not believe this but Arthurine went and eloped with Prezelle in Reno! I love it! Leon's probably going to have a stroke when he finds out! Anyway, I got them matching jogging suits as a wedding gift: chocolate brown and beige no less. And, Paulette, I meant to get that girl's number that braided your hair."

"I'll leave it on your machine. But let me warn you right now. She's a talker, as nice as can be, but strictly ghetto. And her duplex isn't in the greatest neighborhood, but it's safe. She's fast, too."

"Okay. So what are you doing?"

"Probably taking my grandkids to Sunday school because they can't sit still long enough to stay in church and then we'll take them on an Easter egg hunt."

I can tell Trudy's been waiting for me to walk through the door. "Here you go," she says, and hands me Bunny's necklace. It's finished. The ends are done perfectly, hidden inside the same silver cones I was looking at in *Bead & Button*.

"Thanks, Trudy. Don't tell me you did this?"

"I did indeed. I have branched out, sister."

"But this is *real* jewelry."

"Don't I know it? You were right about glass, but there's lots of folks out there who still love plastic! You should check out my Web site or log on eBay if you want to see some of my handiwork. If it keeps up, at the rate I'm going, I'll be opening up Trudy's Treasure Box a year or so from now."

I give her a bear hug and tell her how proud I am of her. And I am. She suggests we sign up for some craft fairs and if we're lucky, we can get booths side by side. I might take her up on it.

After work I go to the gym to meet with my new trainer. I ask the guy checking our membership cards if he would see to it that Bunny gets the box I give him. He tells me that he has to check it first. It's the rule. Since 9/11. No worries, I tell him. He holds it up in front of the scanner. "Nice," he says. He'll put it in her office on her desk. It's safe, he says.

My trainer's name is Ming. She is six foot three. She is Malaysian. She is also a lesbian and an ex-Olympic volleyball player. She has on a yellow polo shirt with the club's logo on it and black warm-ups. I can tell that her hair was short but it looks like she's letting it grow out. Her smile is warm. I like her immediately when she extends her long arm out to shake my hand. "So," she sings, "you are ready to get into the best shape possible, then?"

"I am."

"I read over your application. I read your goals—your fitness evaluation. I know everything. You said you are hoping to make a lifestyle change, and this is true?"

"This is true."

"Then let's go sit and talk and I can tell you what my feelings are for achieving these goals and you can tell me if you want to try. That sound good?"

"It does."

"Follow me," she says, using her head.

This place is awesome. Stainless steel is everywhere: corrugated pipes snake their way throughout the ceiling; the rails that lead to the second level are smooth and sleek. Most of the equipment is silver and white. The walls: purple. Mustard yellow. Orange. The sound system pumps and thumps Top 40 hip-hop music while at least sixty people ride, pedal, walk, glide, and run on various cardiovascular machines as they listen with headphones to their own music or to one or all of the six TVs on six different channels that hang from the ceiling.

There are very few fat people in here. But I do see quite a few out-of-shape folks so I don't feel so bad by the time Ming and I sit down. She basically tells me the same thing Bunny told me at lunch last week. She's just more specific. She says that I need to concentrate on getting at least four or five days of cardio in a week if I want to burn fat and calories. That she'll start me out easy— just thirty minutes—but the goal is to get up to an hour in my target heart-rate zone five or six days a week.

"Are you serious?" I say.

"Yes. It's not hard. Wait to see how much energy you have. How good you feel. You won't be mad at me."

"But what kind of cardiovascular exercise are we talking about?"

"Do you like to run?"

"I don't know."

"Let's be safe and start you walking on the treadmill. Do you know the treadmill?"

"Not personally."

She doesn't laugh. She doesn't get it.

"I actually have one at home, but I couldn't tell you how to turn it on."

This she laughs at. "Well, it's just one machine. But it's the easiest for most peoples to start out on. Later, we can make it harder and you will appreciate it. But if you don't like, there are other machines you can try. And we can change them so you don't get bored."

"What if they all bore me?"

"That's too bad. You said you are making the lifestyle change, so you won't be bored. You will benefit. Besides, every twelve weeks we change your program. How boring could that be?"

"Good point."

"Anyways, I will show you how to use the treadmills and then you will arrive at the club for about forty-five minutes before we begin the strength training."

"So you're not going to stand there while I do my cardio?"

"No. You would be wasting your money. And I would be bored watching you walk walk walk, get it?" She laughs.

"I see."

"We divide the body into sections. One day we will do work on the back. Then the chest and arms. And day third is lower body."

"Okay."

"But not so fast. All of these days we will do abs."

"Can't wait."

"You will love it. We will use those balls up there," she says, pointing to at least three different sizes of rubber balls that look like they belong on the beach.

"I don't get it," I say.

"You will see how good they are soon enough. You will want one to have for home. It will be a good idea. But not today."

"I'll take your word for it."

"Now, you will promise to eat a good breakfast like something on the sheet we gave you?"

"I'll try."

"You don't want to work out on empty stomach. It's not good. And breakfast is very important."

"I know, I've heard."

"Bunny gave you the spiel, huh?"

"Yes she did."

"She's a smart woman and good boss. Anyways, shall we go to start?"

"You mean right now?"

"Yes, right now."

"I thought we were just going to talk today."

"We talked. But you came here to exercise and get into the best shape, right?"

"Right."

"Then today is the day of your new lifestyle. Let us go."

I do everything she shows me. As soon as I start to sweat I worry that I might be having a heart attack, but Ming checks my heart rate and assures me that I'm not. I push and pull on the arms of these machines and lift the handheld weights like I'm Miss Olympia. I'm much stronger than Ming thought I was. But she isn't the only one surprised. I slide and slip off two of those big balls, but Ming promises that I'll catch on. By the time I walk out of here, I wipe my face dry and toss my towel into the basket and just stand here for a few minutes looking around. I feel good. Because I've finally done something I've been meaning to.

Arthurine has been here again. I think she deliberately comes when she knows I'm not at home. I also know she's trying to get everything out of here before Leon gets back. As if he might reprimand her and make her put everything back if she weren't quite finished. It's amazing how our roles change as we get older.

Dinner is broiled chicken breasts, steamed broccoli, and a salad. I read the mail, flipping through at least four catalogs of no interest. I look up at the clock. It's after nine. I've waited as long as I can. I want to know what that doctor had to say about our mother. Joy could've called to say something. Bitch. I grab the phone and dial the number with far too much hostility. "Joy?"

"I was planning on calling you tonight. As soon as I got the kids in the bed."

"You want to call me back?"

"They're in the tub. They can soak a few more minutes."

"So how did everything go?"

"Everything went just fine."

"Just tell me what happened at the doctor's office."

"Okay. She was very nice."

"Who was?"

"The doctor. Lovey was a different story. But anyway, she gave her some mental test that she didn't do so hot on. But she got a few answers right."

"Yeah."

"Yeah, anyway, the doctor . . . did you know she was black?"

"Yes, I did. Keep talking."

"Okay. Anyway, she said she couldn't say right on the spot if Lovey had Alzheimer's or not. But she might not have it."

"Did she actually say that?"

"Not in those exact words, no."

"Then why are you saying it?"

"She said she couldn't come right out and say she had it 'cause she needed to take maybe one or two more tests first."

"That's different than saying she doesn't have it, Joy."

"Whatever. Anyway, she had me walk Lovey across that hot-ass parking lot and get her a MRI."

"So you took her?"

"I just said I did, didn't I? It was a bitch trying to get Lovey to lay down inside that thing. She thought she was going into space. I musta spent twenty minutes trying to convince her that she wasn't going nowhere. That they needed her to be still so they could take some pictures of her brain."

"And did she?"

"Only after I promised to take her to McDonald's and get her a Big Mac with large fries."

"She has to stop with the French fries. Her cholesterol is too high."

"You know good and well she ain't eating her Big Mac without no fries."

"When will the results be back?"

"Not for a week. But the problem is the doctor is going on vacation tomorrow for two weeks."

"And? Does that mean we have to wait until she gets back to get the results?"

"That's about the size of it."

"Did she say anything about her having a PET scan?"

"She said a lot of shit that was kinda over my head, to be honest. But I do remember her saying that after she looks at that MRI, if something looks shaky then Lovey won't need to have no PET scan. Plus Medicare don't pay for that test and it's expensive as hell."

"How much?"

"Three thousand dollars. I'm serious."

"So now we just have to wait. Okay. How's Lovey?"

"The same."

"And you?"

"Nervous as hell."

"About this?"

"This, and my court date next week."

"I thought you said you'll probably just be going to rehab?"

"Well, I talked with the lawyer and he said if the judge cuts me some slack on that other minor offense last year, I might end up doing a twenty-eight-day stint in a rehab program or they could make me do the one that last six weeks, but then again, there's still a chance I could get a little time."

"Are you serious?"

"Dead serious."

"Like what kind of time?"

"Two years."

"In jail?"

"Prison. I'd probably be out in six months."

"But what about your kids? And Lovey?" I say, thinking out loud.

"Why you think I'm tripping so hard?"

"Well, look. Right now. Don't worry about them."

"Somebody's got to."

"Then let it be me," I say. "Do you want me to come down there and go with you for your court appearance?"

"Would you do that, Marilyn?"

"Sure. I don't see why not."

"Thank you. I'm still taking that medication, Marilyn, if you worrying about it. I'm clean. I swear it. I'm even going to meetings."

"What kind of meetings?"

"AA and NA."

"What's NA?"

"Narcotics Anonymous. They meet in the same place. It just depends on my mood which door I walk through."

"Well, I'm just glad to hear you're walking through one," I say. "Joy, let me ask you something that might sound silly, but it's not meant to."

"I'm listening."

"I know you've heard of yoga, right?"

"Of course I have, girl. I saw a documentary on that, too. Why?"

"Would you ever consider trying it?"

"No."

"Why not?"

"Because I just don't buy some of this new age shit, that's why. Bending and stretching is supposed to make everything feel better. I bend over when I clean out the tub and I stretch when I hang clothes on the line and I still feel like shit. And that meditating goes hand in hand with the yoga. Hell, I been breathing every single day of my life, but they claim if you breathe a certain way—and how many fucking ways can you breathe is what I'd like to know—but listening to them, you'd swear you get a buzz or something. Why? Don't tell me you into it?"

"I just started. But it calms you down. And they say it can help you relax."

"Then you bend and breathe for both of us. I gotta go. I hear the kids up there screaming and running around, which means Lovey probably be next."

"Bye, Joy. Give Lovey and the kids a kiss for me, and I'll see you next week."

After I hang up, I remember that today is also the first day to register for classes online. I head straight to the computer and log on, using my personal ID number. I click and press every button and check all the appropriate boxes, including the space that asks which session, and I hit the one for summer. When I finally get to the one that asks for the course number, I take a deep breath and punch in the numbers for the metals/jewelry class. I go back over the entire form to make sure I did it all correctly, and realizing I think I have, I hit ENTER. My heart is beating faster than it did on the treadmill and I know it has to be past my target zone as I push the chair away from the keyboard and wait and watch for a message that will tell me if I've been confirmed. And there it is.

Chapter 23

Paulette lied. You can't get much deeper in the 'hood than this. She didn't tell me you couldn't see the damn place from the street. I must've ridden up and down this avenue five or six times looking for the address until I finally stop and ask a woman if she knows a girl around here that braids hair. She was sitting on the front steps smoking a cigarette. "Hell, just pick one. Everybody braid hair now days. Shit, I'm available," she says and starts laughing to herself. She is stoned out of her mind on something.

I back into a driveway to turn around again, and from my rearview mirror I see purple. The side of this apartment building is what's facing the street. It looks more like a deserted motel, because two old cars are parked in two of the four parking spaces. One is rusted out and the other has three tires and no passenger door. The plants on the balconies have been dead a long time and bright broken toys are scattered on one. I get nervous when one of the splintered wooden doors flings open and a black guy about thirty comes charging down the stairs right past me as I'm backing right on past this place which I realize is my destination.

One side of this stucco house is definitely purple and the other side lime green. I look at the numbers, and park in front of the dark door. A patch of grass is the size of my bathroom, but someone has planted beds of petunias and zinnias. Loud rap music is coming from the other side of the duplex, thank God, and then I hear growling. I look to the right and behind a metal fence are two pit bulls. I knock on the door since there's no doorbell.

At first, I didn't believe Paulette when she told me the girl's name was Orange. I tried calling the next day to make an appointment just in case Orange might have been getting booked up since Easter was less than a week away. Her phone was disconnected so I called Paulette back to make sure she'd given me the right number. She had. "Try this one," she said. "It's her sister."

"Where does she live?"

"In the same duplex. You know how it is."

"I'm almost afraid to ask what her name is."

"It's Blue. Both of them braid and both of them have kids."

"Anything else?"

"They aren't the tidiest housekeepers in the world."

"Do you mean they're junky or nasty?"

"You'll see. But it won't kill you for one day to come down out of those hills to get a taste of the real world."

"Do you hear me complaining?"

"Call me whenever they finish."

I knock again. I hear kids running through the house. A little chocolate boy about four with big bright eyes opens the door. "Hi," he says. "Who you?"

Before I get a chance to answer, a girl about eight comes up from behind and pushes him away from the door. "How many times Mama done told you just don't be opening the door unless you know who it is. Now get over there and sit down somewhere." She turns her attention to me. "You here to see Orange or Blue?"

"I think Orange."

"I gotta go wake her up. She was braiding late last night. Come on in and have a seat. She be out in a minute."

It's hard to digest what I'm seeing. The floors in this living room and down the hallway that were once hardwood have been painted over many, many times but the latest with the ugliest shade of brown I've ever seen. The color our cabins at camp used to be. There are two couches in this small living room. One plaid. The other is some kind of wild print whose colors are fading. A great deal of food has been spilled on both, but at least it doesn't smell like it. A toddler who looks like he could be a year or so is sleeping on one of them. He has rows of thick braids in his hair and is sucking his thumb like it's breakfast. A fake zebra rug is underneath a glass table that's begging for some Windex. The curtains on the picture window are sheer, but tacked to the wall above them are two dark sheets that are closed at the halfway point of the window with two safety pins, I think to control the light.

I don't know where to sit. I hear giggling and then yelling coming from a few doorways down the hallway. "Marilyn, this Orange! I'm sorry to be running a little late, but just sit tight. I'll be out in about ten or fifteen minutes. I gotta make sure my kids get to school on time even though they already late."

"No problem," I say. My appointment was for eight o'clock. It's eight-thirty.

"Did you figure out yet what kinda braids you want?" she yells again.

"I think individuals."

"Human or synthetic?"

"I don't know."

"All I got here is synthetic, unless you want to run down on San Pablo and pick up some human hair but they don't open till ten. You driving ain't you?"

"Yes, but synthetic is okay."

"I thank Paulette said you was closer to a six or a four."

"I really don't know. But take your time. I can come back a little later if you want me to."

She finally stops yelling and I can hear the wood creaking from the weight of something. I imagine it must be her. "Naw, don't do that. I got somebody coming in here right after you. Here I come now." The house actually feels like it's trembling. In fact, it looks lopsided when I look down the hall and see a six-foot girl who can't be more than twenty-three but weighing in the neighborhood of three hundred pounds coming down the hall in tight gray leggings and a Lakers sleeveless jersey. Her thighs look like Christmas hams. She must have a thousand thin braids in her hair, half of which are struggling to cover breasts that are bigger than my head. She turns around to reprimand the cute little boy who met me at the door, and I see the other half covers more than half of her back, which is pretty long and wide. "Go brush yo' teeth, boy. Don't make me come back there and say it again. And tell Ray Ray he better be outta here before I count to ten."

When she sees me, she smiles. Now I see that even though she's a *Glamour* "Don't" it's obvious that she's not only pretty but also one of the sexiest big women I've ever seen. "I'm Orange, and I'm sorry for the wait and all this mess. It's hard keeping a house clean when you got kids running through it all day long and you trying to braid hair, too. Come on over here in the kitchen."

I follow her around a half corner, and it's a kitchen all right. Pink and gray linoleum on the floor. The sink hosts its share of unwashed dishes. Pots on the stove just like at Lovey's: one with hard rice, the other with string beans that have been cooked so long they're brown. A frying pan is full of cold white chicken grease. On the floor over by the kitchen table are mounds and mounds of hair that look like black cotton candy with an occasional cluster of red vines running through it. "Blue?" she yells again.

"What?" a voice that sounds almost like an echo sails around the corner from that hallway.

"Get your ass in here and clean up this damn kitchen. You said you was doing it last night. I told you we had a early appointment."

Orange grabs the broom and sweeps the hair up so fast I'm mesmerized just watching her do it. She then calls the little girl, "Brittany, get in here and clean off this table before you walk out that door and it better be now!"

Here comes Brittany, who does exactly what she's told. Her hair is braided thicker and shorter. I think it's hers. She removes the plates and bowls and dirty glasses and grabs a bottle of Fantastik, sprays the table so it's spotless, and then says, "We need six dollars for lunch."

Orange lifts a pound of hair and flips it over her shoulder then reaches inside her jersey under a soft mountain of brown flesh and pulls out a ten-dollar bill. "And don't act like you don't know what change is. You hear me?"

"I hear you," Brittany says. "Did you call the school and tell 'em we was gon' be late again?"

"Do we have a phone here that work?"

"Aunt Blue do."

"Marilyn, would you mind dropping these kids off at school. It ain't but five blocks. I'll take the gas money off your hair."

"It's no problem," I say and get up.

"Wait. Never mind. They can walk. They already late, so what's five more minutes. Hurry up, Ray Ray, or you gon' get left." And out comes Ray Ray. He must be six or seven. Rather pudgy and clearly on his way to being big like his mother. "He ain't mine. He my sister's. Go!"

"I'll call the school in a minute. Have a good day and don't talk to nobody you don't know. Understood?"

They both nod like they hear this every day. Through the front door I hear Brittany telling the dogs to shut up. Although it was more like "Shut the fuck up."

"Blue say her be out in a minute." This is the little boy who was at the front door. But now he is dressed to the nines. His T-shirt, jeans, and sneakers all bear a designer label. His face is shiny from too much Nivea lotion. I wonder where he's going so early. Preschool, probably.

"Go get my cigarettes, Lexus. Sit," she says to me, pointing to a chair that's got crushed cereal flakes in it. I wipe them off into my palm and start looking for the trash.

"Don't even worry about that. Throw it right down there on the floor. It's getting mopped later."

I follow her instructions. "I'm allergic to smoke."

She looks at me like I might be making this up. "Then we got a problem. What happen, you can't breathe or something?"

"Pretty much."

"Five years ago you could smoke anywhere and wasn't nobody complaining, but now all of a sudden everybody's allergic and worrying about secondhand smoke. But I'll open the window and blow it in that direction. Can you handle that?"

"I guess."

"Look, I ain't no chain-smoker. So don't freak. You drink coffee?"

"Just decaf."

"What's the point in drinking it?"

"I just like the taste. And plus I'm perimenopausal and caffeine brings on hot flashes."

"Peri-who?"

"Perimenopausal. It's the year or two or five before your actual period stops when you have a bunch of unpleasant symptoms."

"That's about the nicest fucking way I've ever heard anybody put it. My grandmama and all my aunties all said the same thing: for about three or four years they thought they was losing their goddamn minds, they sweated like pigs, couldn't remember shit, couldn't sleep through the damn night, their hands and feet was always ice cold and the straw that broke the camel's back as they say was when they had to start using K-Y jelly. How old are you?"

"Forty-four. I'll be forty-five the end of October."

"You look damn good for your age. I'da never put you past thirty-eight. That's how old my mama is. Blue, get your ass out here!"

Orange goes over to a closet and pulls out about ten long cellophane packages of synthetic hair that looks real. "You wanna keep your same dull brownish-black or you want me to pump it up a little bit?"

"Like how much pumping?"

"How long you want it?"

"Maybe to my shoulders."

She rips open one of the bags and the hair is a reddish-brown. It's pretty. "This ain't too much for you, is it? I hope not, 'cause you look like you could stand a new look. No offense."

"None taken. It's fine."

"You said you wanted microbraids on the phone, didn't you?"

"Whatever's the fastest."

"Why, you gotta be somewhere at a certain time?"

"At six."

"Girl, we'll have you outta here by two o'clock, three at the latest, if Blue would ever get her lazy ass out here."

"Are both of you going to do my hair?"

"Yeah. We work faster that way."

"How much more will it cost for two people?"

"Didn't Paulette tell you how much we charged her?"

"No. She just said you were reasonable."

"Reasonable. Try cheap. For all these braids it ain't gon' be but one-twenty, plus twenty for the hair. Is that a problem for you?"

"No, that's fine."

"You got cash, I hope."

"I do."

"Good. Anyway, let me get a cup of coffee and you make yourself comfortable."

I hear the baby whimpering.

"Lexus, bring Baby Benny in here so Miss Marilyn can hold him." She turns to me. "Do you mind? He a good baby."

"No, not at all."

I hear the house shaking again. I already know who it is. These two could be twins. "Hi, I'm Blue."

"This is Marilyn," Orange says. "And she ain't got all

day. Now get them dishes cleaned up and if you wanna get paid today you best to step on it."

"What time is the phone company supposed to be here?" she asks. She's taller, not quite as heavy as her sister, and wearing baggy jeans and a big white T-shirt. Her hair is jet black and bone straight. It stops at her shoulder blades. She also sounds like she may have spent some time in class when she was at school.

"Between whatever and whatever. You can't change your day around for them motherfuckers," Orange says.

"I tried calling you and the recording did say your phone was out of service."

"It was cut off. It wasn't out of service. But it'll be back on later today. When did you last wash your hair?"

"Yesterday."

"You married?"

"Yes."

"Blue, put some hot water in a clean cup and put it in the microwave for a minute and a half and then put two teaspoons of Folger's crystals in it with three teaspoons of sugar and then hand me the milk, I'll pour it in myself. How many kids?"

"Three."

"Wait a minute. Blue, go unlock your damn phone and call the school and tell 'em Brittany and Ray Ray is on their way."

Blue obeys.

"How old?" she says to me.

"My daughter's twenty-two and the twin boys nineteen."

"They live with you?"

"Nope. The boys are in college in Atlanta and my daughter goes to U.C. Berkeley and lives with her boyfriend."

"That's so nice. You musta done something right to have all your kids end up in college."

"I just tried to love them."

"It takes more than some damn love, and you know it. What do your husband do for a living?"

"He's an engineer."

"What do he do being a engineer?"

"He makes sure buildings don't fall and crumble during an earthquake."

"Shit, what do he do between earthquakes?"

"Good question. I'm trying to figure that out myself."

"This must mean you about ready to say fuck it then, huh? I can see it all over your face. Ain't but a few of 'em worth a damn and I ain't met one of them yet. They stupid. Selfish. And most of 'em is thugs. Don't get me started, girl. So this is why you need a new do, ain't it?" She's laughing. And so is Blue, who's now back and working at the sink.

"How many of these do we get a month, Blue?"

"A lot. Get a brand-new hairstyle and trade your old husband in for a new model. They go together."

"Are either of you married?"

"Nope," Orange says, wrapping a towel around my shoulders and then a black nylon cape on top of that. "I'm waiting for somebody in particular to ask me. And not my kids' daddy. I hate his ass."

Lexus is walking the struggling baby boy in my direction and gives me his hand. "Here you go."

"Thank you, Lexus. Is this your little brother?"

"Yeah."

"Both of you are quite handsome."

He blushes.

"How old are you?"

He holds up four fingers. "This many."

"Are you on your way to school?"

"Yep."

"You ain't. So stop lying, Lexus. You get to go in September to be in kindergarten."

"In September I get to go," he says to me.

"Well, he sure looks nice not to be going to school."

"He don't like to be dirty. He'd take two or three baths a day if I let him. And he likes to look good at all times. He got it from his daddy. But he ain't going nowhere."

Orange eats three doughnuts with sprinkles from a Krispy Kreme box and washes them down with her white coffee. Lexus watches cartoons on TV. The baby stares at me for about an hour and my arm feels like it's about to fall off. When he gets a serious look on his face and begins to grunt, I smell what he's doing. I mention this to Orange and she tells me she'll deal with him in a minute. That minute lasts an hour, and then she just gives him a bottle and sets him on the floor. He crawls over to the wall and holding on, stumbles over to his brother and lays his head on his back.

At noon, they're not even close to being half finished

but Orange has to run to the grocery store. I remind her that the baby's diaper needs to be changed. She tells Blue to change it. Blue continues to braid but not as fast as she talks on the phone. Orange walks in the door close to an hour later and I help her bring in six grocery bags and watch her put them away in slow motion.

"The baby still needs to be changed," I say.

"Blue, why come you didn't change him like I told you?" But Blue spreads her fingers and pushes her hand against an invisible wall.

At one o'clock, Blue stops to make the kids a peanut butter and jelly sandwich. She eats two herself. She's not as talkative as I thought she was, not until she walks outside to get some fresh air and comes back fifteen minutes later with an entirely different disposition. "Is your mama dead or alive?"

"Alive."

"We just found out that our mama is a dyke. Can you believe that shit?"

"I can believe it."

"You got a big mouth, you know that, Blue. Don't nobody care what our mama is or ain't."

"She don't think we know it, but we do. She been living with her girlfriend and her husband for going on five years—right after she put me and Orange out—but her girlfriend's husband sleep in his own room. I finally got to thinking and I said to myself, 'Hey, what's that shit about?' So last week I just came on out and asked her. I said, 'Mama, you're a dyke, ain't you?' and she said, 'That ain't none of your goddamn business now, is it?'

"Which was a yes. I've been trying to figure out how Orange and me even got here. Mama never would tell us who our daddies were and we just assumed they were the same man since we look so much alike. But one day we look up and our mama done started dressing like a man. Talking like a man. Walking like a man. And I think she believe she is a man. I thought Orange told you?"

"I just met the woman a few hours ago. Why I wanna tell her some shit like that?"

"I think somebody should change that baby," I say.

"Orange, he your baby. Anyway, I still love her. Or him. She changed her name from Lurlene to Lawrence. That's some deep shit. Do you love your mama?"

"Yes, I do."

"That's good. Was she a good mother?"

"Yes, she was. Still is."

"Some of 'em need lessons. Myself included. But at least I try."

At three, Blue has to make a run. Orange has to go to the bank to get a money order. I babysit. I ask Lexus to find me a Pamper and I take the baby in the bathroom. His diaper is full and soggy but that doesn't bother me half as much as knowing he's been sitting in this mess for five fucking hours. I wash his little behind and then I change him.

By four, my hair is just barely half done. "What time do you think you guys might finish?"

"Two more hours. Maybe less."

"Are you sure?"

"I'm sure," Blue says. "I ain't got nothing else to do but your hair."

"Cassius is coming over here about five and I promised him I'd fry him some chicken. Blue, go turn the eye on low under that grease and get that bag of chicken wings out the refrigerator. Good thang I seasoned 'em last night."

"Would you mind if I make a quick phone call?"

"The phone still ain't working unless the phone company came and didn't tell us." She picks up the wall phone and places it back in the cradle. "They ain't been here yet."

"You can use mine," Blue says. "I just need to unlock it."

"It's okay. I have mine. Thanks."

"And what is it you do for a living?" Orange says.

"Not much."

"And do you get paid a lot for doing not much?"

"I make stuff."

"Like what?"

"Like chandeliers and pillows and I redo old hats and furniture and occasionally make a piece of jewelry."

"No shit. Why didn't you bring us something? You can see we could use a pillow or something around the crib. Ain't this some of the ugliest shit you done seen in a long time?"

"It's not bad."

"Yeah, right. Find a page in *Metropolitan Home* that look like this, okay? Anyway, we do the best we can with what we got. So you make creative shit then, huh?"

"I suppose."

"You sell it?"

"Sometimes."

"So you ain't got no real job?"

"I work part-time at an arts and crafts store."

"You sound like you could be a rich white woman."

"Blue, shut up and turn on Oprah would you."

And she does. When I go outside to call Arthurine, the kids are coming down the driveway back from school. Her new husband answers. "Hi, Prezelle. This is Marilyn."

"I know who this is."

"I wanted to know if it would be a problem if I'm an hour late because I'm getting my hair braided and they're running a little behind."

"Take your time, baby. We'll wait. Oh, and by the way, we got your wedding gift. We love it!"

"Good. See you in a bit."

"Hold on a minute! Arthurine wants me to tell you that she heard from Leon!"

"What? When? You mean he called her over there?"

"No. She was at the house getting the last of her things and her private line in her bedroom was ringing so she answered it and it was Leon calling to see how she was doing."

"Oh, really." That motherfucker.

"She'll tell you all about it when you get here," he says.

"Did she tell him you guys got married?"

"No, not to my knowledge. She's saving that for when he gets home."

I go back and sit down and close my eyes until I hear one of the sisters say, "We hope you like it."

I get up to go look in the bathroom mirror. The kitchen smells like fried chicken and burned grease. The man Orange was expecting is sitting in the living room eating and watching BET. He looks like a thug. He's bigger than her. I say hello to him and he just nods. I step in front of the mirror and stare. I don't look like me. I look like the "me" I was about five or ten years ago. I like it.

"You work out?" Orange says when I come back.

"What would make you ask that?"

"You look like you do something."

"I just started."

"I been saying I was gon' start exercising for about two or three years now but I just ain't never got around to it."

"It makes you feel good."

"You do look good," Blue says, dropping the last of the wings into the smoking grease.

"What exactly do you do?"

"Walk on the treadmill and do weights. And I just started doing yoga." I'm prepared to be laughed at or made fun of, but I don't care.

"I heard that shit can do wonders for you. Where you go? Anywhere near a bus stop?" Blue asks.

"Right off Shattuck in Berkeley."

"We might look into that. I need to get up off my big ass and do something."

The guy in the living room who wasn't listening says, "Then you should start today."

Orange just rolls her eyes in his direction.

"Me, too," Blue says. " 'Cause if I can look like you when I'm your age, I won't mind getting old half as much."

"I'll take that as a compliment. But girls, forty-anything is far from old. I'm just getting my second wind." They don't get it and I don't feel like explaining it. I go through my wallet and count out two hundred dollars and hand it to Orange, who is obviously the cashier.

She counts it. Smiles. "This is too much."

"There's a tip in there."

"A tip? We don't usually get no tips."

"Keep it. You earned it. And I really do love this. Thanks a lot."

"We sorry for making you a little late for your appointment, but sometimes it's hard to guess right when it come to these micros and your head is bigger than it seems."

I look at my watch. It's a little past eight o'clock! Shit! I mean, shoot! "It's okay. You did a great job."

"Cool. So you should come back for a touch-up in three or four weeks. We won't charge you nothing. And tell Paulette hi and tell all your friends."

"Do you guys have a business card?"

"Just give 'em our name and number. I promise the phone won't be cut off and this house will be spotless when you come back. And please bring us a pillow. We don't care what color it is."

"I'll do that. Promise. Tell Brittany and Ray Ray I said good-bye. Bye, Lexus."

"Bye-bye," he says, walking outside with me. "Can I go home with you?"

"Maybe another time," I say.

"Get your little butt back in here," Orange says. "That lady don't want nobody's little kids when she done been there and done that. I pray the years go by fast. Blow Miss Marilyn a kiss, Lexus," and he does exactly what she tells him to, including slamming the hell out of that front door.

Chapter 24

I call Arthurine and Prezelle as soon as I get away from these barking dogs and this dark-ass driveway.

"Arthurine, look. I'm sorry for calling you so late, but they just finished braiding my hair. It took forever and they totally underestimated the time. Can I please get a rain check?"

"No, we just been sitting and waiting, sitting and waiting, so you better get your behind on over here. The food is cold, but we can heat it up in the microwave. You ain't got to stay but a minute."

I decide to try whining. "But I'm tired, Arthurine. Can't we have leftovers tomorrow?"

"Tomorrow is bingo night."

"Not even Saturday?"

"We bowl on Saturdays."

"Since when?"

"Since we started bowling on Saturdays, that's when.

You have to drive right past here on your way home, so come on!"

"Arthurine, wait a minute. Aren't we going to church together on Sunday?"

"God willing."

"And I thought you said you were making Easter dinner?"

"Don't go putting words in my mouth. I don't cook on no holidays. Especially on the day He rose."

"Then I misunderstood you."

"It won't be the first time. And won't be the last. But I had the impression that you was planning on surprising us by making a reservation at a restaurant like that one me and you went to on the water."

"Well, I can try. But what about tonight?"

"We'll be listening out for you. And just so you know, Jesus is my final answer," she says and hangs up.

That woman! When I get there, I park in one of the many empty spots for visitors. A white-haired white man with gigantic teeth opens the door for me. "Hello there, young lady!"

"Hello there, young man!" I say back. "And thank you for holding the door."

He blushes. His eyes look glazed. "My pleasure," he says and literally bows. I look for "Goodenough" on the pad and press it. After I'm buzzed in, I realize that the gentleman is still standing at the door. In fact, he's looking outside to see if anybody else might be coming. I wonder what it feels like to be that lonely. I hope I never have to find out.

The lobby is nice. Tiled. It looks just like a regular apartment complex, actually. I don't know what I was expecting. There are a few older folks sitting in what looks exactly like the lounge area at a ski resort. There's even a fireplace, but it's not lit. They all notice me and wave. I wave back. I take the elevator up to the ninth floor. Before I can even get close to #903, Arthurine is poking her wigless head out of the door and motioning me to hurry. "Come on in, chile! And just look what you done gone and did to your hair!"

I give her a hug. She's in one of those mumu-type things. Her wardrobe is going from bad to worse, I swear. "I told you I've been getting it braided all day, Arthurine. Why are you acting so surprised?"

"I just didn't expect it to be so many of 'em," she says raking her fingers through them over and over. "And this ain't your real hair color, neither."

"You're so observant!" Wow! From over her shoulder I see San Francisco and what everybody in these hills covets: a three-bridge view! "I am sorry for being so late. And I won't stay long."

Prezelle comes out of nowhere. Walks over and gives me a hug as well. He's in a red plaid bathrobe with green plaid pajamas underneath. At least he's consistent. "Hello there, Marilyn. You can stay as long as you like but I'll be asleep by ten. That means I've got about forty-five minutes to enjoy your company. I like all those plaits in your hair," he says. "How in the world are you ever going to get those things out?"

"It took all day to put them in. And right now, I

don't want to think about how long it might take to get them out."

"I have to get used to it," Arthurine says. "You look too young. Come sit," she says, waving her arm like Vanna White does when she's showing contestants what the showcase prize is.

I sit on my second plaid couch of the day, but this one is modern and clean. The cocktail table is some kind of veneer, as are the two side ones. The lamps are white porcelain with clusters of spring bouquets on the front and back. The base is gold. I saw them at Target. Everything in here is shiny and clean. The floors are a pale gray tile. The walls a warm white. The kitchen is L-shaped. I don't think two people could walk by at the same time. In fact, as I look around this feels a lot like a hotel room. "What a nice apartment," I say to them both.

"Thanks. I liked it a whole lot more until Arthurine came in here complaining about everything." Prezelle is now sitting in his blue recliner. Arthurine's is right next to it, except hers is burgundy and has ruffles. She's over at the refrigerator, taking Tupperware containers out and placing them on the smallest countertop I think I've ever seen. But it fits in with all the other round corners and right angles and smooth surfaces.

"It is a nice place, but we just too cramped up in here."

"But I told you that would be the case, Mrs. Good-enough, now didn't I?"

"Yes, you did, Prezelle Goodenough, and all I'm say-ing is that I got a house full of lovely furniture in storage and nowhere to put it. Nice things. And as you can see, this place came furnished. Ain't it boring?"

Of course I agree with her, but I can't agree with her. Prezelle seems quite proud of his home. "Well, I think it's quite livable. Can't you guys get a bigger apartment in here?"

"We're on the waiting list," Prezelle says.

"But we also looking at other complexes. This ain't the only nice one out there."

"But you just got here, Arthurine!"

"She can't sit still for moving," Prezelle says. "But I'm on her side. She wants to get a bigger place. We'll get a bigger place and that's all there is to it."

"You hungry?" Arthurine asks.

"Honestly?"

"No, tell me a big fat lie."

"I'm not hungry."

"No problem," she says, and puts the containers back inside the refrigerator. "You want something to drink?"

"I'm fine. I just really wanted to stop for a minute to say hello."

She takes about five steps and is sitting in her chair. They push their wooden levers back and are immediately reclining. I swear they look like they're about to take off. But what a couple. What a delight to find love at this stage of their lives. I envy them.

"The more I look at 'em, the more I think I like them braids," Arthurine says. "But something is different about you. Stand up."

Without even thinking, I'm standing up. She looks me

up and down. I look down to see what she might be looking at since I'm just in jeans and a pink T-shirt, the neckline of which is full of hair particles that are starting to make my neck itch. "You losing weight?"

"I don't think so."

"Don't she look like she done lost some weight, Prezelle?"

"I can't really tell," he says. His eyes are starting to droop and his head is headed to the right.

"Well, I can. I been around you long enough. Your face look thinner."

"Maybe it's the braids."

"You ain't over there depressed and can't eat are you?"

"No, Arthurine. And I'm not depressed. I've been going to the gym. I'm working out with a personal trainer and I started doing yoga."

"Well then, that's it! I knew you was doing something. Sometimes one or two pounds can change the way a person look, especially when they wasn't fat to begin with."

"I'm not too far from it."

"Don't make me get out of this chair and slap you, girl. You can't be but a what? Twelve."

"On a good day."

"Enjoy it while you can."

"So, are you still going to Bible study?"

"Not like I was. I don't enjoy driving as much as I thought I would. And traffic is so bad, I'm scared somebody might hit me from behind or head-on and sometimes I feel like letting that steering wheel go and just pray that car will drive me right on through it. I don't trust myself all the time. It's just entirely too stressful when you old."

"We do read scriptures to each other before we turn in," Prezelle—back from the dead—says.

"That's sweet."

"So you heard my son called."

"I heard."

"He sounded good. Too good if you ask me."

"What's that supposed to mean, Arthurine?"

"Well, he wasn't really talking about the things I thought he shoulda been talking about."

"Which was?"

"You. And him. Your marriage. What the heck is going on? I asked him if he had found his soul yet and he said in a manner of speaking, yes. I asked him how in the world did he manage to find it so soon when he still got more than a week left before he comes home. And guess what he said?"

"I can't, Arthurine, not tonight."

"He said he learned that he's free to move on if he wants to."

"Really? He said that, did he?"

"Wait a minute. So I said, 'Move on to what, son?' And he just said, 'To a higher level.' I still didn't know what he was talking about. He ain't at one of them cult-type places, is he?"

"Not even close. Did he say anything about me? Like why he hasn't bothered to call?"

"No. He didn't mention your name. Which I also

thought was strange. He just said he needed to do this, and he'll be a new man when he gets home."

"And that's it?"

"Oh, he said he wants to have a birthday party."

"A birthday party?"

"That's what he said. He said it's time for him to start celebrating his life."

"No kidding."

"I ain't making this up. You don't think Leon could be using any kind of drugs, do you, Marilyn?"

"Of course not. He'd have found his soul by now if he were. But maybe he should. Since he's been such a frozen little flower who needs to thaw out. Forgive me, Arthurine," I say and stand up.

"The bathroom is over there," she says, pointing to a white door. "I know you just upset."

"I'm not upset and I don't need to go to the bathroom. I'm tired. But more than anything, I'm tired of your son and his bullshit."

"I might have to agree with you on that one," she says. "Tell me something, Marilyn. Do you want a divorce?"

I stop dead in my tracks and then turn to look at her. I wonder what she wants to hear. I wonder what I should say. I wonder what I honestly feel. I wonder what difference it will make one way or the other. My mouth opens and out comes: "I think I do." I can't believe what a relief it is to hear myself say it. To finally admit it. And to the woman who happens to be my husband's mother.

"But what would you do without him? Have you thought about that?"

"I've been giving it some thought. Yes."

"You think you won't mind being by yourself?"

"What difference does it make? As things stand, I feel like a pot of water that someone left the fire under and now it's all evaporated."

"Well, I certainly know what that feels like. But do me a big favor, baby? Don't go doing something you might regret."

"Well, I'm going back to college, I can tell you that much."

"That ain't got nothing to do with your marriage, do it?"

"I think it does. You don't know how many years I've spent doing everything for everybody and neglecting myself."

"Yes, I do. We all do it."

"We?"

"Women. We give up entirely too much for men, and in some cases, for even our children."

"I'm not saying I regret what I've given them. I just feel like nobody really cares what I'm doing as long as I keep doing what I've always done for them."

"I don't know how true that is, Marilyn. But I care."

"And I appreciate that you do. I'm also not claiming that my feelings are based on facts, but acts, or I should say the lack of them. Ever since the twins left, I've just been existing, somewhere between one day and the next. I never had to think about how to fill up empty space before. I've always been concerned about the kids. Leon. My mother. And out of nowhere Leon tells me he needs a break. And then you up and get married and move out without preparing Leon or me for it. My kid comes home for spring break and I'm like an afterthought— and a bank—and now here I am all by myself and I'm just beginning to understand why I've felt sad, but I think I need to pay attention to all the signs."

"What kinda signs you talking about?"

"Don't you remember how you felt after your husband died?"

"Of course I do. Like I was in quicksand and didn't care if nobody tried to save me."

"But you didn't sink to the bottom. It just felt like it. And eventually you didn't need to be rescued by anybody, you just had to keep on living until it felt good again, didn't you?"

"I guess. But it was a little at a time."

"Well, that's all I'm doing. I've lost a baby that I didn't want in the first place and I truly believe that God did that to shake me up because between that, this whole menopause business, and my husband and kids not really needing me to mother them anymore, I've come to see that I'm all I have left. And that's not a bad thing."

"You can still count on the Lord. He don't have no Plan B and He never lets you down."

"I know that, Arthurine. But sometimes the Lord gives us gifts we don't use or opportunities we ignore simply because it's easier. I need to start taking better care of Marilyn, as well as I have of everybody else. I may have to learn how to live alone if that's the only way I can do it. People don't usually die from loneliness."

"But sometimes folks just need to get reacquainted. Like me and Prezelle did. Right, Prezelle?"

He is out cold.

"Anyway, when Leon gets home, I think you two need to go off somewhere quiet and try to figure out if what you got is worth saving instead of throwing it all away."

"Or, maybe I should go somewhere exotic for a month or so—all by myself—to see if I can find my center."

"Now you starting to sound like Leon. Just try to do this: write your plans in pencil but give God the eraser. Be still and stay put."

"I'm not going anywhere anytime soon except to Fresno to check on my mother. But I'll give what you said some thought." I give her a kiss on the forehead.

"I will say this. Regardless of what happen, you gon' always be my favorite daughter-in-law. You understand me?"

"I do and as your *only* daughter-in-law, I do love and care about you, too, Arthurine. I miss you. I even think I miss Snuffy!"

"Now why you have to go and bring him up? If we move out of here, I told Prezelle I want to live someplace where we can have a dog. But of course he likes cats. I told him we could get one of each. They'll just have to learn to get along and accept their differences. Anyway, you be careful."

"I will. And tell Prezelle I said good night. I'll see you two on Sunday." I head down the hall and press the button for the elevator. The doors pop right open. As soon as I get inside, I hear Arthurine yell: "What time you picking us up?"

I just shake my head and hold the doors to stop them from closing, and yell back: "In plenty of time."

Chapter 25

unny loves my hair. And her necklace. Which she is wearing in broad daylight even though it's an evening piece. We decide to stop by Paulette's shop after leaving the gym to see if we can find something new to wear to church tomorrow. She's actually going with her new fellow, whose name she insists on revealing to me in her very special way—it's called guessing—while I attack the treadmill. "Next to Vietnamese food, what's Leon's favorite restaurant?"

"Hell, he's got too many to choose from."

"Just pick one he loves."

"Chez Panisse?"

"It's black-owned."

"Then why didn't you say that?" I'm sweating like a prizefighter and finally up to an incline level higher than one, walking at a pace of three miles per minute, which for me is equivalent to running the 100-meter race under twelve seconds. To put it another way, I can't think. "Just tell me who it is, Bunny, and stop playing these silly games."

"You've got six more minutes to go plus the cool down, so keep walking and let me give you another hint. Does chicken and waffles mean anything to you?"

"You're not talking about that nice-looking brother with the mixed gray hair. Avery-what's-his-name . . . the owner?"

"I am."

"I thought he was married?"

"He's separated and getting a divorce."

"How do you know that?"

"Trust me. I know. It's about to get ugly because there's money and property involved, which is why I've had to keep my mouth shut."

"How long have you had to keep it shut?"

"Five or six months."

"No kidding. And what makes him different from all the others?"

"Stop making it sound like I've done the football team or something, Marilyn, damn. I want to keep this one."

"You wanted to keep all of them, Bunny."

"That's not totally true. Some of them were only good for a much-needed lay and we both knew it."

"Whatever. I'm not even going to bother bringing up any names. How old is this guy?"

"Fifty."

"And that's not too old for you?"

"Not by a long shot. He's a good man, Marilyn. I've finally met somebody who's got integrity and knows what he's doing and what he wants."

"And what is he doing and what does he want?"

"He wants me. And he wants to sell his business and move to Napa and grow grapes."

"I can just picture you out in the fields now, Beulah."

"Seriously, Marilyn. His kids are grown and paid for. His wife is just a needy, greedy, spoiled half-white bitch who hasn't worked a day in her married life and isn't about to start now."

"Sounds like I share some of her attributes."

"Stop. You're not even close. I mean, would you try to take Leon to the cleaners?"

"I wouldn't try to take anybody to the cleaners. And to be honest, I haven't actually thought that far ahead."

"What if he comes home new and improved but wants a divorce? Have you thought about that?"

"Yeah. But what if I want one, too?"

"Then we're back to my original question. Would you want half?"

"No."

"But you deserve it."

"Look, I'm done," I say, grabbing my towel and hopping off this thing. "I think Leon has worked very hard all these years. He's been a good husband. A good father. He's invested wisely. And he's always been a good provider. I've never really had to worry about money before."

"Well, you need to start. If the needle swings to the right or left, you're still going to have to live, and how do you think you're going to be able to do that without his help?"

"I didn't say I wouldn't ask for something. But. If things get to that point, I just want to do what's fair. I don't want to break him."

"Well, this is precisely why I went to college. Even being a country girl from Mississippi my mama always told the girls not to grow up depending on a man for everything because one day when they ain't nowhere to be found, all you've got left is yourself."

"I went to college, too, Bunny."

"I mean, aren't you worried just a little about what you're going to do if this all goes down?"

"Yes! Now, does that make you feel better?"

"No, it does not. I just wanted you to know that Paulette and I got your back, that's all. Leon isn't the only one who's heard of Smith Barney, okay?"

"Okay. And this is nice to know, because if the tables were turned, I'd do the same for you both. But guess what?"

"What?"

"What do you think I've been doing with my little part-time paychecks all these years? Spending them at Nordstrom's and Neiman's?"

She gives me an I-don't-know look.

"I'll just say this. I prefer Merrill Lynch. Enough said?"

"Enough said. And right on. Now let's go rob Paulette."

We walk in together even though we drove here in separate cars. We are surprised that no one's in here. This is a first.

"Yes, I'm looking for something subtle to wear to church tomorrow," Bunny says to Paulette, who's steaming a really nice pale-yellow-and-blue pinstriped suit.

"You wouldn't know subtle if it jumped on top of you," she says. "How are you two huzzies doing? Fit, I see. And love the braids, Marilyn. They were a trip, weren't they?"

"That's putting it mildly."

"Did they talk you to death?"

"Yes. And I had to babysit and change a shitty diaper."

"But isn't that little Lexus edible?" Paulette says.

"You didn't say anybody's name is Lexus, did you?" Bunny asks.

"Yes, it is," I say. "And he is a sweetheart. He even asked if he could go home with me."

"He wants to go home with everybody that comes over there. Did he blow you a kiss?"

"Yes, he did."

"He'll probably end up in juvenile hall in a few years and grow up to be a ladies' man if his mother doesn't change her lifestyle."

"Orange wasn't doing anything strange that I noticed."

"Orange?" Bunny says. "I've heard it all now."

"No, you haven't," I say. "Her sister's name is Blue."

"Oh, I'm getting them mixed up. She's the one with the problem. She sells marijuana between doing weaves and braids."

"Now that I can believe, because she was talking out the top of her head. What size is that suit?" I ask.

"It's too small for you. They did a good job, though. I love the color."

"I do, too. What size is it?"

"It's a twelve, but they run small. Believe me."

"Would you mind if I tried to try it on?"

"Knock yourself out. But if you rip one of those seams you're going to have to hand over Leon's credit card again."

"I have my own credit card, Paulette. I only use his when I'm mad."

"When is he ever coming home?"

"A week from Monday."

I take the suit into a dressing room. I love the way she's draped the door. And it smells so good in here. "Bunny, are you having any luck?" I yell.

"No! All the stuff I see that I like I'd be struck down if I walked into church with this shit on."

"You've been struck down before, haven't you?" Paulette says.

All three of us are cracking up.

"Oh, shit," I hear Paulette say.

"What's going on out there?"

"Here comes this bitch."

"What bitch?" Bunny says.

"Is it that Cleopatra?" I ask, as I pull the skirt up slowly and with a little struggle it slides up over my hips. When I fasten the waistband, I'm happy.

"Yeah, that's her getting out of somebody's car and she's got those kids with her!"

"Who is she?" Bunny whispers, loud enough that I hear her.

"One of Mookie's exes who had two of his kids and now that he's out he's blowing her off and she's been bugging the hell out of me. I wonder what she's doing coming to my store. That's what I'm waiting to see."

"Where's the blouse that goes with this?" I ask.

"That is one homely child," Bunny says. "And so are those kids. Are they both girls? Whatever they are why doesn't she comb their hair? Look at them."

"They're both girls and supposedly they're my grandchildren, but they don't look anything like Mookie to me. And you're right, they are different."

I hear the door open and close.

"What can I do for you, Cleopatra?" Paulette says while she sticks her arm through the drapes with the blouse on a hanger.

"I came here to see you."

"I assumed as much because you're here. But what is it you want?"

"Ain't this a store?"

"What do you think?"

"Don't you want to know who these kids is?"

"I know who they are."

I'm trying to get this blouse buttoned so I can go see, too, but there must be at least ten of them and the buttonholes are so tight I have to push hard to get them to go through. Shit, I want to poke my face between the curtains but there's no way I can do it without being tacky or looking nosey. Lord knows I don't want to do anything to provoke this woman and I hope Paulette doesn't either.

"Go say hi, Quenella and Shante. That's your grand-mamma over there."

"You don't have to push them," Paulette says. "And just what is it that you want me to do?"

"I want you to spend some time with 'em."

"Right now?"

"Why not? You make time for your other two grand-kids every chance you get, why not mine?"

"I'm trying to run a business here."

"So? They won't be in the way."

"I don't even know these kids!"

"That's why I bought 'em over here. This is Quenella. She'll be three next month. And that's Shante. She just turned two."

"Is it now possible to make babies from prison?"

"Why you asking me?"

"Well, Mookie's been behind bars for three years. Go figure."

"I ain't got to justify nothing. He they daddy and he know it. He just don't want to be bothered with 'em either."

"I didn't say I didn't want to get to know them. I'm just not completely convinced that they're my son's kids. And even if they are, I don't think today is the day nor is this the appropriate place for me to entertain them."

"They ain't monkeys."

The jacket fits. I walk out, hoping to break up some of

this tension. "Check this out," I say and do a little turn. "I told you it would fit!"

It doesn't work. Paulette doesn't even look at me. Nor does Bunny, but again, if it looks like drama, she's all eyes. "Look, Cleopatra. I think you need to take these kids home and get in touch with Mookie so the two of you can figure out a way to make other arrangements."

Bunny is pretending to be interested in a dress she would never buy.

"I ain't taking them nowhere."

"Then what are you trying to say?"

"I just said it. I ain't taking them nowhere. They gon' stay here with you."

"No, they aren't."

"Oh, yes, they is."

She turns and heads toward the door. The person in the car has apparently been waiting.

"You should take these kids with you," Paulette says again.

"You don't tell me what to do," she says.

"Well, maybe you'll listen to the police." And just as Paulette is about to pick up the phone, that girl takes something out of her purse and comes charging toward Paulette. Before I know it, Bunny and I are rushing to stop her and that's when we hear a gun go off. The kids are screaming and hide behind a rack of skirts. We all freeze for a moment. But I don't see any blood.

"Paulette?" I yell, as I pull Cleopatra away from her and snatch that gun out of her hands so fast I don't even realize I've done it. Bunny helps me restrain her, but I really don't need it. I have her arm twisted so hard it's almost in a knot. If she moves, it'll break. And if this bitch has hurt my friend, I swear, I'll kill her myself.

"Paulette?" Bunny wails.

"I'm all right," she says, and gets up slowly. She walks over to the little girls and takes them to the rear of the store. She's clearly as spaced as we all are because she doesn't even acknowledge Cleopatra.

"I missed this time, bitch, but I know where you live! And I know where you work! All I asked you to do was be a grandmother to your fucking grandkids. But you couldn't do that?"

"Paulette, get the police on the phone," I say.

"And who in the fuck are you?" Cleopatra turns to me.

I do not know where my strength is coming from, and even though this girl is strong as hell and steadily trying to move, she can't. "Say one more word, bitch, and I'm going to do to you exactly what they do in the movies. Just one more word."

"Fuck you, ho."

I can't help it. I guess I'm on automatic response from all the anger and frustration and rage that's been mounting these last couple of months because I take that gun and with all my might whack her dead in her goddamn mouth. She falls back against the wall mirror but it doesn't break. Now I see blood. Bunny covers her mouth because she can't believe what I just did. But neither can I. Cleopatra is cupping her mouth but can't get up. The person outside in the waiting car has sped off. We hear sirens. I loosen my grip and back away from this girl and hold the gun out in front of her. Just like they do on TV except this isn't TV. It's so real it feels surreal. I look Cleopatra dead in the eye. She is trying to stare me down but her eyes are full of tears and they look sad, not evil. Something has been done to this girl to cause her to act like this. It's both terrifying and heartbreaking to see so much at once in a person's eyes. And especially a young woman. And one whose skin is the same color as mine.

When the police arrive and Paulette explains the whole scenario, they ask if she would like to press charges. She tells them that this all happened so fast she needs time to think about the best way to handle this. For a fleeting moment Cleopatra's eyes lose their icy glare. As a police officer leads her outside to their waiting car, she turns and says, "But what about my kids?"

"Are you a blood relative?" one of them asks Paulette.

And Paulette looks down at the little girls who have seen far too much horror to be able to process it and says, "Yes. I'm their grandmother. And right now, they're in good hands."

As soon as they leave, Paulette closes the shop. It takes us all a while to regroup and settle our nerves. We just sit on the floor. Looking around. At nothing. And everything. Mistakes are always made. But who ever accepts responsibility for them? Who has to bear the burden, the weight? There is blood on this jacket. I was going to buy this size-twelve suit and wear it to church tomorrow. I want so much to close my eyes and just go to sleep to undream this and start from the time Bunny and I walked in the door. I wish we could just erase this and every unwanted painful experience from our minds. "This did really just happen, didn't it, you guys?"

"It was real as hell to me," Bunny says. "This was like being on the evening news except there were no cameras."

"I've seen worse," Paulette says. "But these kids shouldn't have had to see something like this. No child should. I have to figure this out. I need to call my husband. I need to go home."

"Hold it, Paulette," I say. "I don't think you're in any shape to be driving anywhere. Call your husband. And you need to find Mookie and tell him what position he's put you in because he's not handling his business."

Bunny slides close and whispers to me: "They aren't so homely up close."

I look at these children sitting so close they appear to be one. If I blinked they could be Tiecey and LL. I worry about them, too. What they've seen. How much they already know that they don't need. I worry about what I might have to do if Joy does go to rehab for a month or what if she ends up going to prison. What will I do with these kids for six whole months? And Lovey? She's going to need care. I don't care what the name of her disease is. But I can't live in Fresno. Not for a week. Not for a month. I'm going to be a graduate student. I will have classes. Maybe I could bring them up here. But the kids will still be in school. When one of the girls starts sucking her thumb, I snap back.

"Are you girls hungry?" I ask them while Paulette makes her call.

They nod their heads yes.

I look at them in a way that seems to cause the fear on their faces to leave. They don't know any of us but they know we're not the enemy. They know we won't hurt them.

"What do you like to eat?" Bunny asks, bending down to their level.

"McDonald's," the oldest one says.

"What do you like at McDonald's?" Bunny asks.

"A Happy Meal," she says.

Which is probably what we all need.

Chapter 26

The next morning I'm so sore I can hardly move. These braids are too damn tight. It feels like they're pulling my brains right through my scalp. I look at the clock. It's a little past eight. I pick up the phone to call Arthurine and Prezelle.

"Hello," a voice that I don't recognize says.

"I'm sorry, I think I dialed the wrong number. I'm trying to reach Arthurine or Prezelle."

"Marilyn, this is Arthurine! Hold on a minute." She starts coughing so hard I can hear her chest rattling. "Hold the line, I'll be right back." Now she's blowing her nose and it must be Prezelle I hear coughing in the background now. "Marilyn?"

"I'm still here. You sound terrible, Arthurine."

"I know. Me and Prezelle done caught something ferocious and we can't hardly breathe. You didn't catch it, did you?"

"No, I didn't catch that," I say. I hate to admit it, but

I'm relieved to know that I can stay home. "Can I do anything for you guys? Do you need anything? I can come over."

"No, you won't. We don't want you catch this. We'll be all right. We just gon' stay in the bed and rest. We got all kinda tea and plenty of soup to hold us. Sometimes people come to bingo when they know they sick and spread their nasty germs. It's very inconsiderate. But anyway, you have a Happy Easter and call us later. If we don't answer the phone, it's 'cause we asleep."

"Okay, but I'm sorry you guys are sick. And call me if you need anything."

"We'll do that. But the Lord knows what he's doing."

The verdict is still out on Cleopatra. Paulette tells me that she managed to get in touch with Naomi, Cleopatra's older, saner, civilized, and more responsible sister who explained that her younger sibling has quite a few serious issues, most of them unresolved. Naomi works in the biology department at U.C. Berkeley and lives up in the Oakland Hills not too far from me. Naomi also has a husband with a job and they have a one-year-old son. Paulette says she is so unlike her sister that she was tempted to ask if they had the same parents. Naomi says she was lucky. That she somehow managed to escape the lure of the streets and the pandemonium they grew up in called home. She says her sister was not so lucky. That Cleopatra is so broken she probably can't be fixed. Naomi comes and gets the children. Takes them home with her. She says her husband will help her take care of them. That he loves children. She begs Paulette not to press charges, but to get a restraining order instead. It will work, she tells her. They always have in the past.

I haven't talked to Joy in days. I have this urge to call. Like I need to hear the kids' voices. Lovey's, too. After yesterday, I just want to know that they're all safe.

LaTiece answers. "Who's calling?"

"It's Aunt Marilyn. Happy Easter, Tiecey."

"Happy Easter to you, too."

"Did you and LL go on an Easter egg hunt?"

"Nope."

"Not even at school?"

"Nope."

"Did your mother make you a nest?"

"Nope."

"You mean the Easter bunny didn't come?"

"Nope. It ain't no real Easter bunny. Don't you know that?"

"I thought there was one. I saw him last night."

"You did? Where?"

"Dropping off jelly beans and Easter eggs at my house."

"But you ain't got no little kids."

"I think he left them for you and LL."

"Can we come over and get 'em right now?"

"Well, that might be hard to do today. But I'll tell you what. I'll bring them when I come down there this week."

"Okay. Did he leave us a lotta eggs?"

"Yes."

"All different colors?"

"Yes."

"LL. Come here! Hurry up! Aunt Marilyn said the Easter Bunny is real and he left us some candy and eggs at her house and she say she bringing 'em when she come!"

I can hear him jumping up and down and howling with pure joy in the background.

"Where's Lovey?"

"Her sleep."

"How's *she* doing, Tiecey?"

"*She* still be just doing the same old thing."

"What's that?"

"All she do is eat and sleep and watch TV."

"Where's your mother?"

"I don't know."

"She's not there?"

"Nope."

"Where'd she go?"

"I don't know."

"She didn't tell you what time she'd be back?"

"Her just said it would be late."

"What time did she leave?"

"Late."

"Well, when did she leave?"

"I just told you. Late."

"So you mean this was last night?"

"Yeah. I mean, yes."

"And she hasn't called at all?"

"Nope."

"Did she ever get her cell phone turned back on?"

"Nope."

"Tiecey, don't you ever get scared?"

"Scared of what?"

"Of being there by yourself?"

"I ain't by myself. LL here and so is Grandma Lovey."

"Do you know what to do if there's an emergency?"

"What emergency?"

"Like if the house caught on fire or Lovey got really sick or something happened to LL and you couldn't help them. What would you do?"

"Call 9-1-1."

"That's right."

"But what if *I* got drowned or something, who would call 9-1-1 for *me?*"

That's a good one. I know LL doesn't know how. And Lovey might not remember. "As soon as you felt like you might be drowning, you could tell LL to call 9-1-1 because he always listens to you, doesn't he?"

"He would if I was to be drowning."

"Okay. Enough about drowning. Especially since you don't have a pool, hallelujah."

"Hallelujah, hallelujah," she sings it.

"Is there something there for you guys to eat?"

"We already ate. We had cereal. But LL used up all the milk."

"What about Grandma Lovey?"

"Her had oatmeal."

"Okay. I'm going to do this. I'm going to wait a few

hours and then call back to see if your mother comes home."

"Okay."

"But if she gets back before I call, would you have her call me?"

"Okay."

"Wait a minute. I changed my mind, Tiecey. You know how proud Aunt Marilyn is because you're such a smart little girl, don't you?"

"I do now," she says.

"Well, this is what I need you to do. I need you to write my phone number down."

"Just a minute," she says, and I'm waiting for the phone to hit the floor like usual, but it doesn't. I hear her running away and I hear her running back. "What is it?"

I give it to her and ask her to repeat it. Which she does.

"Okay, Tiecey. As soon as your mother walks in that front door I want you to take the portable phone into the bathroom—anywhere she can't see you—and call me. Can you do that?"

"Yes. But why you don't want her to see me call?"

"Well, I'm a little worried that your mother might not be feeling so good and I don't want to make her feel worse."

"You mean she on them drugs again. I ain't stupid."

"I'm just concerned."

"Me, too. That's why come me and LL don't like her when she act crazy. We know it's from them drugs. They told us at school what drugs do to people's minds. I told her what they said. I showed her the piece of paper they gave us, but I don't think she read it, 'cause she just won't stop."

"It's hard for some people to stop."

"That's what her always be saying. But if *she* don't like doing something *she* should not do it. Ain't nobody making her. Just say no!"

"That's true. But sometimes people need to get a little help and then that makes it easier for them to stop."

"Well, help her then, Aunt Marilyn."

"I will. So you and LL just stay right there in the house, and keep an eye out on Lovey to make sure she doesn't do anything to hurt herself."

"Okay. But Grandma Lovey ain't *crazy*. She just old and can't remember stuff. Me and LL always help her remember."

"That's nice," I say. "Give her a kiss for me. And I'll call you in a few hours. Or you'll call me, right?"

"Right. Bye."

After I hang up I just sit there. My heart is beating too fast. I hope Joy hasn't gone off the road again. For some reason, it feels like a good idea to go to church, even though Easter is my least favorite Sunday to go because it's always packed with extra sinners, and most of the women's faces are hidden by big bright hats, their bodies adorned by just-off-the-rack spring suits. They come late, and walk down the center aisle searching for a seat as if they're vacationing runway models. I look for something churchy in my closet that fits and a hat that barely makes it over these braids.

Allen Temple is packed not simply because it's Easter, but because it's Allen Temple, one of the biggest Baptist churches in California. The minister preaches from his heart. I feel his energy travel over the ocean of hats and penetrate mine. I pray for my sister. That she be allowed to discover grace and find peace without drugs. That her hair grows. That some of her pain be driven from her and given to me because I think I can handle it. I pray for her kids. That they find they have a chance to grow up knowing they were loved. That Joy learns to surrender long enough to show them. I pray for my mother. That if she can't ever recover what she's lost or what she's losing, that she not feel like she's lost. I pray that we make her feel necessary and valued as long as possible. That she comes to know comfort, even if I can't provide it myself. I pray for my children. That they stay safe and make good decisions. That they be happy, thoughtful, and caring human beings. That they have the strength to get up if they fall down. I pray that Arthurine and Prezelle live longer than they ever expected and love each other like they're nineteen. I pray for Leon. That he finds what he needs. And for myself, all I want is for You to understand that even though I may not appear to be listening to what You're whispering in my ear or seeing what should be obvious, know that I am trying to find my way, even when it appears like I'm deaf and blind.

I wait until I get in the car to check my cell phone for messages. I don't have any. I start the engine. The phone remembers the last number I called, so I press SEND. It rings once twice three times, and by the fourth, I'm worried. I hang up. Dial manually this time. On the first ring, Tiecey picks up. "Is she there?"

"Who?"

"Your mother, Tiecey."

"Nope. Not yet."

"What took you so long answering the phone?"

"I was washing Grandma Lovey's hair in the bathroom."

"Oh. Where's LL?"

"Playing video games."

"Is that *all* he ever does?"

"Yep."

"Can he read?"

"I don't know."

I know this is not the time to ask these questions but I don't know what else to ask right now. I can't sit around the rest of the day in that big-ass house waiting by the phone. I just can't. "I'm driving down there," I hear myself say.

"Will you bring our Easter egg candy?"

"Yes. Now, if your mother comes home and she's acting like she's been doing something, don't tell her I'm coming, okay?"

"Okay. Do you have the candy right there?"

"I certainly do."

"Goody goody. I'ma run and tell LL right now!"

"Wait!"

But she's already hung up.

Of course I don't have any Easter egg anything. But

before I hit the freeway I stop at home and get out of this corny dress. I put on my lavender sweats, a pair of sneakers. I stop by the drugstore and buy three big bags of shiny green nests, a few bags of jelly beans, some with little white speckled eggs full of malted candy, and two giant chocolate bunny rabbits. I run inside the nearest grocery store and there are a few cartons of dyed eggs left. I buy one with glitter and one that's plain pastels.

It's almost four o'clock when I get on the freeway not far from my house. The first hour is bumper-to-bumper because all the folks are heading back to L.A. When I hit the stretch of highway where I got caught in the parade, it feels like smooth sailing, until I get to the 99 and I'm right back in the holiday traffic again. I'm only about forty or fifty minutes from Fresno, but at the rate I'm going, it might take two hours. My temples are jumping. I'm trying not to be so impatient, but something in me is making it hard. I pick up the phone again. This time I hear Lovey's voice. "Hi there, Lovey!"

"Hi there to you, too!" she says.

"How are you feeling?"

"I'm feeling just fine. And you?"

"Lovey, this is Marilyn."

"I know who this is!"

I think I hear some kind of commotion or something going on in the background, but I can't tell what it is. "Lovey, where's Tiecey?"

"Oh, she's back there crying and what have you, talking to them policemen."

"What policemen?"

"The ones that's in the house. The ones that came to tell us that Joy done went and got herself kilt but this time it's for real."

"Lovey you don't know what you're saying so let me speak to Tiecey or one of the police officers, right now!"

"*Kojak?* Come get this phone and tell this girl that my daughter is dead as dead can be. Wait a minute. I forgot to tell her how it happened. She was walking across the street and . . . wait a minute. Here, Kojak. You tell her."

I pull the car over onto the emergency lane and put my flashers on. I'm praying that this is either a bad joke or a big fucking mistake. That Lovey is really just hallucinating because she used to love watching Telly Savalas: "That is one sexy white man," she'd say week after week after week, each time sounding even more astonished than the last.

"Hello, ma'am. And you are?"

Hearing a strange man's voice on the line is startling. "I'm Lovey's daughter and Joy's sister, Marilyn. Who are you?"

"I'm Officer Daryl Strayhorn, and I'm here with your mother and Ms. Dupree's two children. The little girl told me you're on your way here, driving from Oakland."

"Wait a minute. What are you doing there? And tell me what my mother just said isn't true. She's got some kind of dementia so she probably got this all wrong. Now please, tell me what's really going on."

"Well, unfortunately, what your mother has told you is pretty accurate. Your sister was crossing the street when a drunk driver ran a red light."

"A drunk driver hit her?"

"Yes. He was going about sixty miles an hour. I'm very sorry, ma'am."

"So you mean my sister is really dead?"

"I'm afraid she is, ma'am."

I sit here and watch the blur of speeding cars whiz by. It feels like I'm at the movies. The drive-in. But I don't like this ending. And why do taillights have to be red? I roll the window down to let some air in. I inhale deeply and then slowly blow it out. "When did this happen?"

"Last night, about nine."

"And we're just now finding out?"

"Well, your sister didn't have any ID on her. But someone at the scene told us later what he thought her name was. It took some doing to locate your family."

"And who was this person?"

"Well, all I know is his name is Earl. Your sister was leaving a Narcotics Anonymous meeting but apparently a couple of people knew her."

"And my sister is dead?"

"She is."

"Where is she right now?"

"Well, she's at the morgue."

"The morgue. So she's not in jail. Not in rehab. Not at the store. Not at McDonald's. But at the fucking morgue!" I hit the steering wheel so hard that my palm stings and immediately starts throbbing.

"For what it's worth, I can say that she didn't suffer any even though the impact of the vehicle at that speed threw her more than thirty yards, her death was instant. I'm very sorry."

"How are the kids?"

"They seem to be holding up okay. I know this is tough, but we're going to need you or another family member to go down to the morgue to identify her as soon as possible. How long before you get here?"

"I don't know. An hour. Or less. Traffic is bad. I don't know."

"Well, would you mind stopping there first to get it over with?"

"You mean go down there tonight?"

"You won't have to see her physically if you choose not to. They can show you a photograph from her shoulders up, probably just her face."

"I don't think I can do this tonight. It's too much."

"Based on my experience, ma'am, the longer you have to think about it, the more difficult it gets. I know it's like a bad dream, but these kinds of tragedies always are."

"I don't believe this shit. She was trying."

"I don't know if this will make you feel any better, but there were enough witnesses who saw the whole thing and apparently the fella who was driving tried to flee the crime scene but some good citizens actually followed him because the front end of the ambulance was pretty messed up and his tire was flat. They called us and that's how we were able to apprehend them."

"You mean an ambulance driver hit her?"

"Yes."

"Was their siren on?"

"Witnesses claim that was the case."

"So they were on their way to go help someone, then?"

"Well, that's not quite clear to us at this moment. It's being investigated."

"You mean they weren't going to save someone's life?"

"I'm not in a position to confirm or refute that, ma'am. But you'll find out the truth soon enough, believe me."

"So there were two of them?"

"Yes. The driver is a paramedic and the emergency technician with him is female."

"Where are they now?"

"They're both in custody."

"I don't believe this."

"I know it's a lot to handle all at once, but there's no easy way to tell someone."

"I'll try to get there as soon as I can."

"Please don't rush. Pull over and take some deep breaths if you need to."

"I've already done that."

"Good. Do you know how to get there?"

"Isn't it downtown by the courthouse, near the Fulton Mall?"

"That's correct. We'll have one of our officers stay here with the children and your mother until you get here."

"Thank you. May I speak to the little girl, please?"

"Yes. Here she is right now."

"Tiecey, Aunt Marilyn is so sorry to hear about this. I'll be there as soon as I can. Are you okay?"

"Yes. So Mama ain't coming back then, is she?"

"No, it doesn't look like she is."

"I knew this was gonna happen one day."

"And just how could you know it, Tiecey? Please tell me."

"I just did."

"Well, you go try to comfort LL and Lovey and I'll be there as soon as I can."

"You didn't forget our candy, did you?"

"No, I didn't."

I hang up and for the next ten minutes I drive like I'm drunk. But I can't afford to lose it. Not out here. And not right now. The farther I go, the more I realize that I can't afford to lose it anywhere or anytime.

"Get a grip, Marilyn," I say out loud as I pull over again and take a series of deep breaths to slow my heart down. When it seems like it has, I open the ashtray and feel for the piece of scrap paper I scribbled the number to Leon's resort on one day when I was thinking of calling him but changed my mind. I dial it, but nothing happens. I'm out of range. I get back on the freeway and drive a few more miles. Try again. Still no service. I do this every few miles until I hear a ring and to my surprise, a young woman with a Southern drawl answers, apparently from the front desk. "Yes, hello, I need to get in touch with Mr. Grimes, please."

"Excuse me, did you say Mr. or Mrs. Grimes, ma'am?"

"I said mister. I'm Mrs. Grimes."

"But I just saw you in the gift shop across the way just moments ago, didn't I?"

"What did I look like?"

"Pretty. Tall. A body I'd kill for."

"And how old would you guess me to be?"

"Thirty-two or four tops."

"It wasn't me. I'm his wife calling from California and I'm overweight and forty-four years old so would you mind relaying this message to him for me, please?"

"Oh, my! I sincerely apologize for my error in judgment. I may very well have made a mistake."

"No worries. Just tell Mr. or Mrs. Grimes—I really don't give a shit which one—that Leon's mother eloped in Reno last week and married her seventy-one-year-old boyfriend, Prezelle, a retired mortician, and she moved out of the house and now lives on the ninth floor of a senior citizen complex with a three-bridge view. He'll just be thrilled."

"What great news! I'll get this to his bungalow right away, although I think he's in session right now."

"Wait. I'm not finished."

"I'm sorry, Mrs. Grimes. Go on. I'm writing this all down."

"Good. You can also tell him that his real wife's sister has been in a fatal accident so I will not be home when he gets back."

"I'm so very sorry, ma'am. I think I should interrupt him because this certainly qualifies as an emergency."

"No, please don't."

"It's perfectly all right. He's on the last day of 'Accepting Life's Transitions: Letting Go, Moving On' and I doubt that he'll miss anything at this late hour."

"Wait. Is his buddy Frank there with his wife, too?"

"Yes. They all came together."

"Lovely! Then do pass this one last thing on to Mr. Grimes for me, too, would you?"

"I surely will."

"Tell him that the real Mrs. Grimes is so fucking happy he was able to find his missing soul that she's going to see if she can locate hers, too. And you, Miss Thang. You should really consider getting into a different line of work—one that doesn't require you to think." I press END and toss the little phone over to the passenger seat.

Chapter 27

I pass the exit that takes me to Lovey's and get off at the one that takes me straight to the county morgue. My heart is beating so fast I wish I didn't have one. Once inside, a leathery Hispanic woman with a skunklike white streak in her black hair leans on the information counter as if she's been waiting for me. Either these light green tiles have recently been waxed or there has been little foot traffic. As soon as I hear myself say, "I'm here to identify my sister, who's been killed by two drunk paramedic drivers," it feels more like I've really just come here to pick up something: a hot pizza or dry cleaning or could she check to see if maybe you have a shoe in my size. All I know is that I should not leave here empty-handed.

The woman, whose badge reads CARMEN, slams her palms down on the counter. "Aye yae yae. I'm so sorry. She makes five drunk deaths this week! Through those doors," she says, pointing at a blue metal door. I open it slowly, afraid of what I'll find on the other side. It's a waiting area with yet another counter. Behind this one a blond kid who doesn't look old enough to buy alcohol asks me my name and who I'm here to identify. I tell him. There are three people sitting in chairs. I sit, too. Wishing we were all here to pick up pizzas or shoes. But I'm here to point out my sister. Not in a lineup. But lying down. I don't know why I'm not crying. I don't even know why I don't feel all that sad. In fact, I'm more pissed than anything that two fucking drunks can change so many lives by making one wrong move. The next moment I'm ashamed because I realize I'm actually relieved for Joy.

"Yes, ma'am. I'm very sorry about your loss. Someone will be out in a few minutes to greet you. Can I get you anything? A Coke, coffee, water, or anything?"

"No, I'm fine."

"I'll take a Pepsi," a Hispanic woman says. She's wearing a royal blue floral dress that's too tight. She looks to be in her early forties but I bet she's in her late thirties. Regardless, she's been crying.

"I'll see if we have one in back. Be right back."

She looks at me like she needs to confess but I'm not sure I want to hear it. "I'm here to pick up my son's personal effects, as they call it. Everything he had in his pockets. They took his wallet."

"I'm sorry," I say.

She nods. I feel like I'm supposed to ask her something I really don't want to know, so I do. "How old was he?"

"Eighteen. Gang doings. I want to go back to Guadalajara so bad. Every week more and more kids just dying for silly reasons or no reason at all. I hear you say your sister is back there from drunk drivers hitting her?" She uses her head to point to another blue door. "How old was she?"

Was is past tense. "She's twenty-six."

"Did he have insurance?"

"Who?"

"The drunk who hit her."

"It was two of them. Paramedics."

"You mean those ambulance drivers?" The woman covers her mouth and her shoulders go up to her ears. "How could they did this to her?"

"Well apparently they needed a few drinks in order to do their job."

"Did your sister have any kids?"

"She has two."

"Terrible for them to lose their mother. So my son he has a six-month-old. Guess who gets to raise it now after eight of my own? We grandmothers get to do it."

It's precisely at this moment when I realize that Tiecey and LL don't have a grandmother on either side that can raise them. I don't know where their father is. I don't think Joy ever met his parents. They were from Kansas City or one of those flat middle states. But what these kids do have is an aunt. And that would be me. It has to be me. Doesn't it?

"But truthfully," the woman is saying, "I don't mind. My son will live on through his son."

"Marilyn Grimes," a man in a blue surgical-looking uniform says. I raise my hand and stand up.

"Well, one good thing," the woman says. "The lawyers will make sure their college tuition is paid. Small price for a life, hey?"

"That's putting it mildly. You take care, and I'm sorry for all of our losses."

She waves as the young man brings her a can of Diet Pepsi.

"Hello, Ms. Grimes. I'm Paul Jackson, the medical examiner, and I'm here to give you the option of looking at a photo of your sister, or to escort you in to see her. It's your choice."

"Is she back there?" I say pointing at the door.

"Yes, she is. But if you're not up to it, we can—"

"I want to see her," I say.

"Okay, but you don't have to go in alone."

Mr. Jackson leads me through the blue doors and then into a small room no bigger than a laundry room. There's no place to sit and nothing to even lean on. A big picture window takes up most of one wall. Drawn drapes prevent us from seeing what's behind them. Of course I know my sister's back there. I wonder if she knows I'm out here. I wonder exactly who it is I'm going to see. Which Joy? The one I was beginning to know or the one I never knew? And what is it going to feel like? Looking at her and she can't look back. I don't think I can do this. I take a deep breath, and as soon as Mr. Jackson takes two short steps and taps on the glass, I yell, "Wait!"

But it's too late. I watch those drapes open like King Tut is behind them. But lying on a gurney, wrapped in white flannel blankets like a baby in winter is the sister my mother gave me. Her brown face is facing me. She looks like she's sleeping. I find myself moving so close my breath fogs the glass. A tall Middle Eastern man in gray steps out from behind the drapes and around the end of the gurney where Joy's legs should be. I keep my eyes on her face. I'm so sorry this had to happen to you. You deserved a chance to live a full life. You were on your way, Joy. And I was rooting for you. I know that Lovey's love wasn't enough to make up for what you carried in your heart. That somebody didn't love you enough to keep you. Or care for you. I can't imagine what you do with that kind of pain. But we tried to show you we cared; even when we were mad, that was the reason. You are the only sister I've had and I just wish we could've gotten closer sooner. I wish I had been more comforting to you. But don't you worry. I can promise you one thing: your kids won't be abandoned. And they will be loved.

Mr. Jackson makes a facial expression that says he is sorry. Mine responds with gratitude.

"Is this your sister, Mrs. Grimes?"

"Yes, she is."

"My sincere condolences. This kind of loss is a tragedy for all of us. We know it's tough, believe me. If you'd like to stay a bit longer, I'll be happy to step outside if you prefer to be alone."

"No, don't leave, please," I say. "I'm ready."

"Are you sure?"

"I'm sure," I say. I hate this. It feels like a bad dream. But I know it's not.

I see Mr. Jackson look over my shoulder. He is apparently giving the other examiner the eye-to-eye signal to close the drapes, which I hear swoosh close behind me. I head toward the door. "Can you tell me where the closest restroom is?"

"Sure," he says when we come out into the hallway. "It's right down there on your left. I'll just go on down to the front desk and get the paperwork together for you."

Paperwork?

When I arrive at the house a police officer has taken the liberty of ordering a pizza for the kids and hot wings and garlic chips for Lovey. I reimburse him, then thank him, and he leaves. All three members of my family are eating at the kitchen table. I stand in the doorway. The kids look sad but not as distraught as I thought they'd be.

"Aunt Marilyn, did you remember to bring our Easter eggs and jelly beans and stuff?" Tiecey asks.

"Yes, I did. It's all in the car."

"Can we go get it?" LL asks.

"I don't care," I say and sit down.

They toss the crusts of two slices into the empty box.

Lovey finishes sucking the meat from a wing and then slides it out of her mouth and tosses it onto the pile of crusts. "I say good riddance," she says out of nowhere. "She was getting on my nerves anyway. Now I ain't got to be bothered. I gave that chile too much when she didn't even have none of my blood. And when she come back next time, maybe she'll be more grateful and know what to do. Maybe she'll be nicer. Maybe she'll finish high school. Go to college. Time will tell. Can we go now?"

"Go where, Lovey?"

"Anywhere but here."

"Did you find your papers?"

"What papers?"

"Your medical papers. You said you put them in a safe place."

"You can't believe everything I tell you."

"I know where she put it," Tiecey says standing there with a handful of jelly beans.

"How do you know what I'm even talking about?"

" 'Cause Grandma Lovey showed me a long time ago where she keep her important stuff. I'm the one who always having to keep moving it. Come on, I'll show you."

"Moving it, why?"

"That girl talks too much, sometimes," Lovey says as she gets up and heads for the living room.

" 'Cause Grandma Lovey said people is too slick. She told me to move it to a new place every time it's a holiday."

"I did not say no such thing!"

"Yes she did," she whispers. "Grandma can't remember a lot of stuff, but you know that already, don't you?"

"Yes, I do. And have you done what she asked you to?"

"Yeah, but I couldn't keep thinking up new places. This house ain't all that big. So I went back to where I think I hid it the first time."

I follow her to Lovey's bedroom. It smells bad in here. Funky and sour. Like a window has never been opened. Like Lovey hasn't been bathing the way she used to. Tiecey lifts the mattress up about six or seven inches away from the box spring and pulls out a thick envelope. She opens it and takes out some papers that have been folded like a letter. She hands it to me. But before I open it, I ask her: "When did Lovey start sleeping on a twin-size bed? It had to have been recently because I was just here a few weeks ago and there was a queen-size bed in this room. What happened to it?"

"Mama traded her 'cause Grandma Lovey said the bed was getting too big and she didn't like it no more. That's why she always be sleeping on the couch. I betcha she on it now. Wanna bet?"

"No, I don't feel like betting right now. Did your mama ever see these papers?"

"Yeah. Grandma Lovey gave her one just like it but she told me not to never let my mama get a holt of this one."

"Why?"

"I don't know. Read it and see."

She is too grown. I unfold what apparently is a legitimate California power of attorney for health-care form that Lovey has filled in all the blanks, giving me the authority to make any and all of her health-care decisions if she becomes unable to do so on her own. There was space for an alternate appointee, but she left it blank. I flip to the last page. It's been signed by her, witnessed by two people I've never heard of, and notarized. This was a little less than two years ago: August 2002.

"I wonder why I never got a copy of this," I hear myself say.

"Well, Grandma Lovey put one in a envelope with your name on it. I saw her write it 'cause she asked me if I knew how to spell your street and I couldn't. And she asked my mama to put a stamp on it and mail it."

I stop reading.

I get it now. What did you think I'd do, Joy: wait until something terrible but not as tragic as this happened and I'd run down here and kidnap Lovey and drag her back to Oakland and just leave you and the kids here to fend for yourselves? I mean, did you really think I was that shallow or callous? That I wouldn't care what happened to you and the kids? I wished you'd have given me more credit.

"Mama got one, too."

"How do you know that?"

" 'Cause . . ."

"It's because, not 'cause, okay?"

"Because. First of all, I was with Grandma Lovey when she asked two people she didn't even know to be a Jehovah's Witness and sign they names on the paper and they was nice and did it even though that lady behind the desk at the bank said they didn't need to but Grandma Lovey said it was space for them to witness so it couldn't hurt and then that lady put this silver thing on a black spongy thing and pressed down real hard with it on three of 'em *bam bam bam* and then she blew on 'em I guess to make sure they was dry and then she made Grandma Lovey put her thumb on something and then she wrote her name three times on each one. I know 'cause I liked the way that ink smelled. After that we went to Target 'cause Grandma Lovey was buying me something nice for school and she bought me a cherry Slurpee and I spilled it on the front seat of her car but she didn't get mad. When we got home she gave one of them papers to Mama and told her to mail it to you and she made me hide this one."

"And what about your mama's?"

"I gotta make sure she didn't move it, but can't I do it tomorrow, please?"

"Yes, Tiecey. But do you understand what has happened tonight?"

"Yeah. My mama done got kilt and she ain't never coming back. I might see her one day in heaven. If she made it."

"She made it, believe me."

"How you know?"

"Because God spoke to me, that's how I know. He told me she was welcome up there. In fact, He said she was going to be happier up there because she wouldn't be needing any drugs, her hair would grow as long as she wanted it to, all of her problems would go away, and she could watch what good kids you and LL were going to grow up to be."

"Did God really say all that?"

"Unless I heard Him wrong, and there's nothing wrong with my hearing."

"Well, God supposed to know everything, so He must know what He talking about then."

"Tiecey. You know, I know your mother made you and LL mad sometimes, and I know she disappointed you from time to time, but you also said that she only got on your nerves when she took drugs, didn't you?"

She's nodding her head in agreement.

"But can't you think of something she did that made you happy? Anything?"

She's thinking.

"Just one thing."

"Oh, yeah! When she took me and LL to Disneyland that time and we got to go on all them rides and eat cotton candy. That was so much fun."

I sit here listening to her think out loud.

"And I forgot all about that time she showed me and LL how to do cartwheels."

"Joy didn't know how to do a cartwheel."

"Yes her did! She could do backflips, too. LL can do it, too. But I can't."

"Now see there. I bet if you thought about it a little longer you could probably remember more things your mama did that showed you how much she loved you. You understand what I'm saying here, Tiecey?"

"Yes."

"I'm going to miss her even though we didn't spend all that much time together and we never really got to know each other. Lately it was starting to feel like we were. She was the only sister I had."

"And she was the only mama I had."

"Well, there's probably going to be some things around here that's going to change."

"Like what?"

"Well, I have to figure a lot of that out."

"Like what?"

"Like which bedroom I should give you and which one I should give LL."

"I don't want to sleep in my mama's room."

"In my house," I say.

"You mean we get to come live with you and Uncle Leon?"

"Well, Uncle Leon might not be living with us."

"Where's he going?"

"I don't really know."

"You mean he didn't tell you where he was moving?"

"He hasn't moved yet."

"Y'all getting a divorce, ain't you?"

"I'm not sure what's going to happen right now, Tiecey."

"Well then, maybe he might could stay until we get there and then if you be nice and we be nice and don't get on his nerves he can pretend like he our daddy."

"You know, you have quite a lot going inside that little nappy head that needs to be washed, don't you?"

"Can I get it braided like yours, Aunt Marilyn?"

"No. This is too much hair for a little girl."

"I told you I'm almost eight."

"And if I have anything to do with it, you're going to act like it, too."

"Do we really get to come to your house and live?"

"It might be the way it's going to have to be."

"Don't you like me and LL?"

"Of course I do."

"Then why you always be making us say things over and over, like we get on your nerves?"

"You don't get on my nerves. It's just that sometimes, I get upset when it seems like you guys haven't learned your manners or if you're speaking like you've never learned how to speak proper English."

"What you mean by proper English? We speak English."

"We'll talk about it another time."

"Why you don't like LL playing video games? All kids play video games."

"I know that. But it seems like all he does is play video games and watch cartoons."

"What's wrong with that?"

"There's more interesting things to do."

"Like what?"

"You can read a book."

"He can't read."

"Then I'll read to him."

"I can read but I wouldn't mind you reading something to me, too."

"I can do that."

"What else is interesting to do?"

"You can make things: jewelry."

"I don't know how to make no jewelry."

"I can show you."

Her eyes light up. "Then we both can change."

"See, that's what I mean: at *almost* eight you shouldn't be thinking about changing anything. But don't worry about it right now. You two will come and live with me before I let you go into foster care."

"We don't like foster care homes."

"How would you know?"

" 'Cause we had to go to one before."

I'm learning far more about everything and everybody tonight than I had expected. But I can't ask any more questions. I know more than enough. "Well, you won't be going to another one, I can tell you that much." When I hear these words come out of my mouth I can also feel them vibrating on my tongue. But this is the way it is. And this grown but resourceful and intuitive and smart little girl is *my* niece. And that future geek is probably a miniature version of *his* twin cousins, except I don't know if LL has a personality yet.

"Yay!" Then she starts singing. "We moving to Oakland! We moving to Oakland! We get to swim in the swimming pool. We get to go to a nice school where they don't got no guns!" She stops singing. "Do they?"

"No guns."

"I always wanted to live with you, Aunt Marilyn. LL, too."

"Well, there are a lot of things that need to be sorted out first."

"Do I get to pick out the color I want my room? I want pink!"

"You probably can, but if you thought your mama got on your nerves, you haven't seen anything."

"Please don't tell me you do drugs, too, Aunt Marilyn?"

"No, I don't do drugs. But you guys are going to learn to live by a whole new set of rules."

"I already know that."

"And how do you know it?"

" 'Cause you always making us say words right. And now I know why so it won't really get on my nerves no more. I don't want to say things wrong. But ain't nobody but you never told me not to."

This is so fucking unbelievable I just say: "Come here, Tiecey." She walks over to me and I put my arms around her and hug her and she sinks into me and the next thing I know, she's patting me on the back.

"It'll be all right, Aunt Marilyn. Don't worry. I'ma try to do everything you tell me to do. I promise. And I'll make LL promise, too."

"It's been a long time since Aunt Marilyn has had little kids in the house, Tiecey."

"We still be growing, you know."

"I know."

"I like doing homework. I like washing dishes. I don't like to vacuum but if you want me to, I will. LL hates taking out the trash but he'll get used to it. Hide that Nintendo from him and I betcha he'll do it really really fast."

"You guys are the least of my worries right now."

"What about Grandma Lovey? She coming, too, ain't she?"

"Do you think I'd leave her here?"

"No. She been had her suitcases packed. Look under

this bed and look in that closet over there. She been ready to go."

"Well, I have to take her to the doctor tomorrow and see what she says might be the best thing for Lovey."

"That doctor is a lady?"

"Yes, she is, and she's also black."

"I could be a doctor when I grow up if I wanted to."

"I know that. You can be anything you want to be when you grow up."

"Is Mama gonna have a whole funeral?"

"I'm not sure what kind of service it'll be."

"You mean they have more than one kind?"

"Sometimes family members have a small memorial service where you can say good-bye."

"But I don't wanna say good-bye to her when she dead."

"I have to look into it tomorrow."

"When will the memory service be?"

"I don't know yet. Why?"

"Do we *have* to go?"

"I would think so, Tiecey."

"I don't like funerals. And I don't think I'ma like no memory service either."

"How many have you been to?"

"Just one, and I was scart. I don't like 'em. Neither do LL. Mama won't know if we there or not, will she?"

"I think she would. We'll talk about this later, okay?"

"Okay. Well, right now, can I go get some of our Easter candy before LL eat it all up."

"You go on and eat some. In fact, give Lovey a few jelly beans and I'll be out in a minute to eat a few, too. I could use something sweet about now."

She bolts out of the room. I sit on the bed and read every word of this document. This is Lovey's handwriting, for sure. She must have done this when writing wasn't a problem. Under "Health Care Instructions" she wrote: *"First of all, if for some reason I get sick with something they can't cure and the only way to keep me alive is by swallowing handfuls of pills day after day and whatever I got keeps pulling the life out of me, do not get no refills. And if I'm looking like that Scissorhands boy in that movie with tubes coming outta me every which way, unhook them things and let me go. Or if it so happens that my mind starts leaving and I can't seem to make decent decisions for myself, I want my oldest daughter, Marilyn Grimes, to make them for me. Under no circumstances do I want to be a burden to anybody, but especially my daughters, I don't care what they say. I do not want them to fix up a room for me and especially if I have to sleep in a hospital bed. Take me where I can live around my own kind, with other folks who done made it through one side and ready to go on about our business. We all have lived long enough to do as much as we could for ourselves. Here we won't have to struggle. We won't have to pretend. We might be able to reminisce with each other or hell, just in our own mind I don't much care, but ain't no need in my daughters feeling an ounce of guilt for putting me in one of these places. I done read enough about them and even*

*picked out three or four I believe I might enjoy. I wrote
their name and phone numbers on the back of a sky-high
cable bill I got right before Christmas of 2000 and could
not bring myself to pay but thank the Lord they all have
cable and one got satellite though I don't know the difference. I'd like to think of them as Club Med for elders. We
get room service and breakfast in bed I suppose and this
way my daughters can visit me when it's convenient for all
of us. By the way, Joy can have this house and everything in
it. It's all paid for. What else? I can't think of nothing
right now so you can consider this my will and this is the
end of it."* She signed her name.

I fold the papers back and just sit there. So, Joy, you've
known all along what Lovey wanted. But I suppose you
thought if you just took care of her and I didn't have to
find out what her real condition was, then everybody
would be happy. But it got too hard to cover for her and
even harder to lie to yourself. Wasn't that how this happened? You had to start numbing yourself with drugs because watching your mother, our mother, disappear, was
too painful. Is that it? Well, I've been doing the same
thing, really, except I think I used my children, my
home, food—even my husband—to hide mine. I allowed
myself to become unimportant. An imposter. I've been
impersonating myself for so long that even I almost
bought into it. But maybe you haven't lost, Joy. Even
though you're too young to leave this world, maybe
you're better off. Shit, you're free of pain. You don't
have any worries. Don't have to figure out where you're

going to get your next fix or how you're going to feed the kids or wait to see if you're going to get your mother back the way she was. And, Joy, just for the record: kids do count.

Double.

Chapter 28

"R ead this," Tiecey says, shoving a piece of paper into my hands. I barely remember falling asleep on this couch. I spring up to a sitting position. "What time is it? And where's Lovey?"

"It's six-thirty and Lovey still sleep. Snoring loud as always."

"Thank you, Tiecey. What is this and what are you doing up so early and is there any coffee in this house?"

"You sure ask lots of questions at one time. This paper is the same as Grandma Lovey's."

"I already read it."

"But this is Mama's. Her got one, too. She a copy cat. I always get up early to make sure we ain't late for school and if I have to iron something to wear and make sure LL is clean and that Grandma Lovey eat and then hide all the knives and stuff she can hurt herself with. I think I saw a jar of crystal coffee in the cupboard a long time ago. Want me to go look?"

"No, that's okay. Has the phone rung at all? I left quite a few messages for my kids and some other folks but I haven't heard the phone ring."

"Sometime Grandma Lovey act like she calling somebody and forget to put it back on the hook. I'll go check."

And off she goes in the dingiest undershirt and fading floral underpants I've seen in a long time. I can't wait to take these kids to Target.

"Did Joy come ho . . ." I utter and then catch myself. Shit. Sometimes, there's only so much tragic stuff you can register at once and a part of you rejects some of it so you don't have to absorb the pain all at once. Joy is dead and is never coming home and I'm taking Lovey to the neurologist today and I pray to God I hear from my husband or kids or some grown-up.

"Her had it under the covers. Here it is," Tiecey says and hands me the white portable. "It's dead 'cause ain't no sound or lights coming from it. It need to be charged up," and she snatches it back and runs to put it in its cradle. Where's my purse? And my cell phone? I don't see either one of them.

Tiecey comes back and plops down next to me. "What it say?"

"I haven't had a chance to read it yet."

"Well, go on and read it."

"Who are you talking to?"

"You, Aunt Marilyn! You know that." And she smiles. I think she has a loose tooth. The top two are huge and come together like a pyramid. I don't understand why I didn't notice it before. Orthodontist, here we come.

"Did you eat breakfast?"

"Yep."

"What did you have?"

"Instant oatmeal. The same thang I always eat. You want some, Aunt Marilyn? I hid one with peaches. You can have it."

"No thanks, Tiecey."

"Do we gotta go to school today?"

"No. I don't think so. But I have to take Grandma Lovey to the doctor and make arrangements for your mother and please don't ask me what kind of arrangements, Tiecey, because Aunt Marilyn has a lot on her mind right now."

She pats me on the shoulder. "I know how it is. Sometimes I got so many thangs on my mind I can't thank about nothing."

"So what do you do?"

"Color."

"That's good. Have you seen Aunt Marilyn's purse or my cell phone?"

"Yep," she says, bending over me and the arm of the sofa so that her legs fly up and she almost falls off but I grab her ashy legs and pull her back up to safety. In her hands is my black bag. "That was fun! Can I do it again, one more time, please?"

"Okay," I say, as she dives forward this time. She is tinier than I thought after touching her like this. And she is really just a little girl with grown-up concerns. I'm glad there's still time for her and LL to be children.

Now she's lying on my lap like a big red snapper. I kiss

the top of her nappy head and then pat it softly three or four times. "Okay. Up you go, cutie."

She jerks up and looks me in the eye so close I can smell her breath, which smells more like jelly beans than oatmeal. "You really thank I'm cute?"

I look at her like how could you ask me such a ridiculous question, but I follow it with: "Not really. You're cuter than cute, which makes you a very pretty little girl, Tiecey."

"You lying. I ain't pretty."

"Okay, let's get something straight right here. Right now."

"Okay."

"First of all. You don't ever use that tone of voice with me or any adult. Understood?"

"Yes."

"And second of all: I don't lie. So if you don't believe something someone is telling you, then say it in a manner that doesn't make it sound like you're calling them a liar."

"How'm I 'posed to do that? I don't get it."

"Okay. What just happened here. The *polite* thing would have been something like this: 'I don't believe you, Aunt Marilyn, because nobody ever told me I was cute.'"

"That's true," she said. "That's why I said you was lying. But I'm sorry."

"It's okay. Now get your *pretty* little behind up from here and go run some bath water for Grandma Lovey and let me read this to myself, okay?"

"Okay." And off she scampers again. I wonder if this girl knows how to walk. As I unfold Joy's papers, I see now that it's not the same document as Lovey's. It's actually a last will and testament form that was notarized at a Parcel Plus three days after Lovey's health care directive. Joy's handwriting is big and round like a child who's just learned cursive: *"If I die and my kids is still kids, I want my sister, Marilyn Grimes, to raise them the way she raised hers so they will have a chance to grow up right and live their life with somebody who ain't scared to show them what love feel like. I hope she knows how important this is to me. I know I've been a pitiful excuse for a mama but I don't think I was meant to be nobody's mama, really. I can't even take care of myself. I don't want my kids to mess up her life or her plans if her kids is grown and out the house. But please don't let LL and Tiecey go to no foster homes. They good kids. They can be bad, but even good kids is bad sometimes. They smarter than you might think just by listening to them. Teach them how to think and how to solve problems and let them have some fun. Spoil them for a week or two if possible. They don't know what it feel like to do what they want and get what they want. Anyway, I put they trifling-ass daddy's last address on the bottom of this will form but if he ain't locked up he might be dead by now the way he was going and since people don't seem to change when it come to doing drugs, unless he been born again or something, I don't want him near my kids cause he was crazy and mean and it might take at least two or three Gods to straighten his ass out. Anyway, please don't have no damn funeral for me and do not bury me nowhere. I knew a long time ago I wanted to be cremated so won't nobody have to be looking at me and feeling sad, or mad. I ain't got no friends worth calling so please don't have no corny memorial service for me so folks can lie about how wonderful I was. And I don't care what they do with my ashes. I love you, Marilyn, cause you always made me feel like your sister and that's about it. Oh yeah I forgot. If anybody I owe money to come around Lovey's house trying to bribe you, don't fall for that shit. Just tell them they gone have to wait a little longer than I thought to get paid. But don't hold they breath."*

I fold it closed. I'm smiling. And shaking my head.

"Was it funny, Aunt Marilyn? Huh?"

"No, it wasn't funny, Tiecey."

"Then why come you laughing?"

"I'm smiling. When you laugh you make a sound. And before you ask: I'm not going to read it to you because it was meant for me. But I will say this: your mother said that she loves you and LL very much and wants you both to grow up to be happy and smart and make her proud."

"Did she already know she was going to be dying?"

"No, but sometimes when you have something you want to protect—like children—some people write down how they would like them to be raised in case they were to have an accident or something that didn't allow them to be able to raise them."

"Good thang Mama could see into the future, then, huh?"

"Sure is. Now go wake up LL and Lovey."

See how she runs runs runs.

• • •

I have six messages. Sabrina: Mom, I'm sorry to hear about Aunt Joy and wish I could drive down there to be with you and the children but our transmission is shot so we have no wheels. Although this isn't a good time to bring it up but Nevil said this is clearly a case of wrongful death and negligence and he wants to make sure Joy's legacy is preserved and that her children benefit from this tragedy. Oh, we are not moving to London. The short version: I told Nevil he's already got two degrees. I'm not going anywhere until I get mine. He said "fair enough." It's why I love this man. Call me. I'm here. Love you. From Paulette: Girl, just say the word and I'll do whatever you need me to do. You still have two sisters, you know that. From Spencer: Mom, sorry to hear about Aunt Joy. I bet the folk who caused this don't have a scratch on them. This angers me more than you know. Remember how my friend Angelo lost his life? Drunk drivers get away with murder. Maybe I shouldn't have said this now. Sorry, Mom. Anyway, I wish we could make it home for the service, but we've got finals in three weeks. Let me know if you need us there and we'll work it out. Love you. From Simeon: Mom, not happy to hear the news. What exactly went down? Anyway, I'm not in school. I'm in Amsterdam. We got a major gig. But I can't afford to come home until we get paid. I'll be there in spirit. Oh, they're taping some of our sessions, so I'll send a DVD to you and Dad. Love you. Peace out. From Bunny: Paulette just told me what happened and I can drive down there right now and stay as long as you want me to, to help you get things handled. Just buzz me back. If I come, can I bring my cats? And don't forget to breathe. From Arthurine and Prezelle: Baby we feel your loss but know that she's in the Lord's hands and they are the best hands to be in. Where is my son? He better not still be in Puerto Rico or wherever he went. He should be there. Do you have a number for him over there? I got words for him that God might not approve of. Me, too! This is Prezelle. We love you, Marilyn, and let me know if you want us to do anything over at the house. And finally, the voice of an alien who sounds a lot like my husband: Marilyn, I'm sorry to hear all that's happened there and you've been given a lot of misinformation about my stay here, but I won't bother explaining it over the phone and especially under the circumstances. I will say this, however: I'm a new man. And I'll let it go at that. I've been trying to get on a flight since last night and have been at the airport for sixteen hours and just gone on standby. Hello? Because of the time difference, I won't get there until tomorrow night. I know I'm probably not the person you'll be seeking comfort from, but I'm coming to offer it anyway. Will call when I get to SFO."

"Fuck you," I say to the cell phone and turn off the power.

"Auntie Marilyn, did I just hear you say a bad word?"

"No, you did not, Tiecey."

"Yes, I did. I thought you was nice and didn't say those bad words."

"I'm sorry. And I just lied. I did say a bad word, but I promise you will never hear me say another one."

"Do you keep your promises?"

"Yes, I do."

"I'm glad somebody do." She slides down the hallway. I drop the cell into my purse and just sit there on the couch looking at the map of my face between the gold veins on the mirrored wall. I don't want anyone to come down or do anything. I just want to do what I need to do and take my mother and these kids home.

She's had strokes. Probably more than one. They're called ministrokes. They're sneakier. That's what the MRI showed as the main cause of my mother's dementia: it's only going to get worse. The neurologist suggested that I honor Lovey's instructions and consider placing her into an assisted-care facility since technically she is unable to care for herself. But I'm not sure that it needs to be done so soon. She conveyed her concerns to me because she said I was already going to be a caregiver to two youngsters and Lovey would probably require even more supervision and patience than they would, and that I would most likely not have much energy left for myself or my husband. I had forgotten all about Leon, but since he's going to be out of the picture soon anyway, I didn't bother to say anything about him or our situation. Whatever it is. In fact, she said that many adult children of Alzheimer's parents very often end up suffering from depression and guilt because there's not much they can do to help restore their parents back to the healthy beings they once knew, and watching them deteriorate mentally is not only painful, but often so heartbreaking that in the long run the adult children appear to suffer more than the parent. This frightened me. It's what I'd spent the last twenty-two years of my life doing: taking care of everybody and seeing to it that most, if not all, of their needs were met to the point that I ended up not having much left to meet my own. Did I clear the table only to have to set it again?

I'm confused about my devotion. Lovey is my mother. LL and Tiecey may not share my bloodline but they might as well. Hell, they're just babies. And my babies are grown. This time around I have to learn how to nurture Marilyn or I'm going to resent these kids. It has taken me a long time to recognize that I've never put myself first, I'm always on the bottom of my things to do list and I keep getting carried over to the next day/month/year. But not this time. I think I finally get it. You don't have to give up everything to own your life. And you don't have to give everything you own to fuel someone else's. This time I'm not going to pretend I'm the quarterback or the goalie or the last handoff in a relay or the referee. I'm just an older, more experienced member on the team who wants to do her part to make sure we all win. Volunteers welcome.

Chapter 29

ain't staying but a minute," Lovey says when we get to our house in Oakland.

"That's fine," I say, trying to help her get out of the car, but she snatches her arm away.

"I ain't no invalid. I can walk. Whose house is this anyway?" she asks, looking at it as if she's never been here before. Tiecey has gathered up all the McDonald's wrappers and cups from the backseat and has stuffed them into a bag while also dragging her pathetic purple suitcase across the concrete floor of the garage but I'm afraid it's not going to make it.

"This is one ugly monstrosity of a house, don't you think?" Lovey asks, looking at me as if she hopes I'll agree.

I look up. She's right. It has no curb appeal. But neither do I, so what does that make me? "It's a big old house, Lovey, but we might be moving into a new one."

"Hold your horses, little sister. Who said anything

about moving? Why is it because something gets old everybody thank it loses its value? A little paint with some pizzazz would sure help matters. And do something about this yard. It's missing a lot. Grass ain't enough. Don't nobody around here believe in flowers?"

"I used to."

"Used to? You ever dig your fingers in the dirt and it's so cool you just don't want to stop? Don't you have a husband around here somewhere?"

"He's not home."

"Where is he then?"

"He should be here sometime tonight."

"Well, I won't see him. Ain't his name Leroy or LaVerne or something?"

"Leon."

"Oh yeah. I remember now. You married him in college. Didn't you?"

"Yes I did. See your memory is good, Lovey."

"Whoever said it wasn't?"

"Nobody."

"Wait a minute. Didn't you marry one whose name started with a G? He wasn't no Harry Belafonte, but he was a good man. What was his name?"

"Gordon."

"Good guess, Marilyn. You was only married to him for about five or ten minutes, is that about right?"

"I suppose."

"You didn't have no babies by him, though, did you?"

"No."

"What ever happened to him?"

"Well—"

"Oh, never mind, girl, 'cause I really don't care one way or the other. Where is Leonard again?"

"He should be on his way home," I say, just because.

When we finally make it inside, the kids are already reacquainting themselves with the premises by giving themselves a whirlwind tour. Tiecey, of course, is the tour guide. By the time Lovey and I get into the foyer, the two of them are leaning over the railing looking down at us. "Hi, Grandma Lovey!" LL says.

Tiecey pops him upside the head. "You know we don't need to be leaning over this railing now back up before one of us flip over like they do in the movies and this ain't no movie, boy. Hi down there, Aunt Marilyn and Grandma Lovey!" She backs away from the banister and pulls him toward her.

"Do we get to pick which room we want?" Tiecey asks.

"Do this look like a hotel to you, Tiecey?"

"No, Grandma Lovey."

"Everybody stop moving for a minute," I say.

Poor things. They try to freeze like mimes, but of course they can't hold it.

"I just meant to relax. Anyway, do you guys say your prayers at night?"

They both shake their heads no. "We don't know how to pray."

"Well, there are lots of ways to pray but we'll try to find some that you like. We're going to say them every night."

"You, too, Aunt Marilyn?"

"Me, too."

"What about Uncle Leon?"

"I'll ask him the next time I see him."

"Is he still fat?"

I try not to bust out laughing. "I'll let you know the next time I see him. Anyway, Tiecey, you can have Sabrina's old room. It's the one with the walls that look like cantaloupe."

"You mean orange?"

"Okay, then. Orange. And, LL, you can take the room across from that one."

"What color is those walls, Aunt Marilyn?"

"Last time I checked I think they were North Carolina blue."

He lifts his short knee up to his chest and yanks his little Yolo fist down and says, "Yes!"

"Why is everybody so worried about where they sleeping is what I want to know?"

"Well, Lovey, since Joy is gone the kids are probably going to live here."

"You will live to regret it. They will drive you to drink. Do you drink, Marilyn?"

"A little now and then."

"You'll be a alcoholic in a few weeks." And she starts laughing uncontrollably. "You remember that time that fella from Stockton made me some apple wine and I let you drink a glass full 'cause you thought it was apple juice?"

"Sort of."

"You was singing and Lord knows you ain't never

been able to carry a note but you was just carrying on
and doing some kind of jitterbugging until you just
stopped dead in your tracks 'cause you wanted to know
why the living room was going in circles. Poor thang.
You made it to the bathroom and let go all that juice in
the face bowl and then you plopped your little narrow
butt down so hard on the toilet that it went right
through and you was stuck! It took me at least ten minutes to get the hinges off and then I rubbed your little
narrow ass with some Crisco and it slid right off!"

"And I was how old?"

"Nine or ten. Maybe. Do you eat many apples these
days?"

"Can't stand them," I say, and then we both laugh.
And now I know why.

LL and Tiecey reappear and almost tiptoe until they
reach the bottom step, where they sit with what looks to
be a newfound grace. "We like living here already, don't
we, LL?"

He nods his head up and down. "Can I get my Nintendo hooked up pretty soon?"

"No!" Tiecey says. "Aunt Marilyn said you and me
gotta read more books so you ain't going to be pressing
them buttons all day and all night until you can read
something besides SPLAT, KILL, and DIE! Got it?"

"Where's the book at?"

She looks at me. Scrunches her shoulders up, as if to
say: "Help me out here, please."

"You don't have to start reading right this minute, LL,
but the video games can stand to cool off a little while."

"They ain't hot," he says.

Tiecey pops him upside the head again. "We can't say 'ain't' no more, right, Aunt Marilyn? Ain't that what you said?"

"Okay," Lovey says. "This has been a lot of fun up to now but I'm hungry and want to go home so I can eat." And then she turns, heading for the front door, but stops dead in her tracks. "Well, isn't that lovely," she says, and walks over to the lamp I made that once made Prezelle a little jumpy.

"Thank you, Lovey."

"You're welcome. Did you get this at Costco?"

"No. I made it."

"I don't believe you made that lamp with your own hands, Aunt Marilyn," Tiecey says with a huge grin on her face that screams, "How was that?"

"I did. But not the whole thing. Just the shade."

"Stop lying, Marilyn," Lovey says. "And don't worry, I ain't running down to Costco to get one just like it."

"You can have this one, Lovey, if you want it."

She looks at me with a softness I haven't seen in years. These are the eyes I remember. "I'll take it! Tiecey go on over there and unplug it and go put it in the car before she change her mind. Hurry up. And, LL, you go help her. Thank you, Marilyn," she says walking around the room apparently looking for other things that she might fancy. "You ain't got no more nice thangs around here you made that you want me to have? Is that it?" she says, pointing to the entire lamp being tugged toward the garage.

"I've got a room where I make things. I can show you later. You guys, just set it by the door for now." And then I wink at them. Tiecey winks back, like she gets it, and LL is having difficulty winking with one eye, to the point where he stomps his foot and crosses his arms in disgust.

"I won't be here much longer. So show me now," Lovey says.

I thought I just heard the garage door. But Leon didn't drive to the airport. I was trying to beat him home. Especially after I learned I could make all the arrangements for Joy's cremation online. I couldn't believe it when the coroner's office told me this option was available and one that more and more people were using. They're even supposed to send her ashes in a box that was available in a multitude of styles and gave me a choice of using UPS Ground or FedEx. It felt more like I was ordering something from Sharper Image or Amazon.com. Living is definitely hard but apparently dying and being put to rest is a whole lot easier these days. Too easy. I did it because I needed to simplify some part of the entire sequence of events yet to come that would require the long version, not a shortcut.

"Tiecey, where is LL?"

"Him in the garage pushing that button so it go up and down up and down."

"Please go and tell him I said not to do that because he can break it."

"Okay," she says and opens the door that leads out there. I'd forgotten I had turned the chime back on. "What's that sound?"

"That's to let us know that someone is opening a door or a window."

"Don't that get on your nerves?"

"Well, no one really goes in and out of it a lot."

She just looks at the door as if she's looking through it at LL and then she looks back at me. LL sticks his head inside. "LL, Aunt Marilyn said this squeaking noise will drive her nuts if we be running in and out of here so we should think about what we want to do and how long we wanna do it or back to Fresno we be going. You hear what I'm saying?"

"I don't want to go back to Fresno. I'm sorry, Aunt Marilyn."

"Well, I'm ready to go now," Lovey says, after having made a circle walking from the living room through the dining area, the kitchen, and here, the small hall area leading into the family room from the garage.

"But we just got here, Lovey. Aren't you a little tired?" I say.

"I am tired as hell, but didn't nobody ask me if I was tired or not. Ask me if I'm hungry?"

"You just had six McNuggets, small fries, and a whole vanilla milkshake!" LL says.

"Shut up, LL. Are you hungry, Grandma Lovey?" Tiecey asks with a sneer. I think they play this game a lot.

"I might eat you if you don't get outta my way!" And she's smiling! I can't believe it. The thought came too soon because now she's squeezing her lips together when she turns to look at me. "Would it trouble you to make me a peanut butter and jelly sandwich and do you have any cocoa?"

"Mama, I've got—"

"What did you just call me?"

I can't believe I just called her that. "Mama," I said quietly.

"I guess that would make me your mama, then, right?"

"That's right," I say.

"Then what took you so long to say it?"

"You said you wanted me to call you Lovey."

"I must not'a been in my right mind, girl. But let me hear you say it again."

Now I feel silly. "Mama, how would you like to have a delicious nutritious meal for dinner?"

"Yes, Mama Lovey," Tiecey says, now imitating my diction and intonation, "you know what Oprah says about good nutrition, remember?"

"Tiecey, ain't nobody talking to you, child. And what Oprah don't know won't hurt her." She turns to me. "Your mama and Lovey both want a peanut butter and jelly sandwich and some chocolate milk. And do you have a empty bed I can lay my head on until I get it?"

"I do."

"Good, and hurry up. We got a long drive back."

I point to Arthurine's old room and Tiecey leads Lovey into it. And in the blink of an eye, she's back, standing next to me in the kitchen. "I can't lie, Aunt Marilyn, I done been tired of making 'em seem like every day and ain't—I mean isn't—but one way to make a peanut butter and jelly sandwich."

"You know, Tiecey, right now, you keep using all the words you've been using, okay?"

"I thought you said some of them was not right."

"That's true, but you know what I've been thinking about for a long time?"

"No, I do not."

"That maybe over the summer I can teach you and LL right here in this house how to talk so no one will have to correct you, especially when you go back to school in the fall."

"You mean we would be having school right here?"

"Yep. But just for the summer. Not all day. And not every day." I take a deep breath. I have a busy summer ahead, but I'm looking forward to it all: my art and yoga classes, and walking up these hills no matter what. The other school the kids are going to attend is on Sunday mornings, and I'll go more often. Maybe I'll get a social life.

"But what about recess?" Tiecey asks.

"You'll have time to play."

"But me and LL ain't in the same grade."

"I know that."

"What grades you know how to teach?"

"Actually, none."

"Then how we supposed to learn something from you if you don't know how to be no teacher?"

"The school district gives guidelines for summer school."

"Do we got to sit next to each other? LL just learning letters in kindergarten and I already know mine and I don't wanna sit and listen to him saying his a-b-c's and counting to a hundred over and over till it's my turn. Can't you find somebody my age to be in my class? And when do we start?"

"Slow down, Tiecey. First things first. We may have to go back to Fresno for a few weeks until you guys finish this school year."

"We ain't, I mean, we not learning nothing no way."

"We'll just have to take all of this one step at a time."

"My mama was starting to say that. My bad. It was one day at a time. Same difference, though, huh?"

I just nod. LL is now sitting on an ottoman in the family room in front of a cold green TV screen. It's clear that he hasn't been listening to a word we've said. At any moment, I suspect he might start showing signs of withdrawal, but I'm going to let him come down easy. "Just a second, Tiecey. LL? You see those two doors under that TV?"

"Yes, Aunt Marilyn."

"Why don't you try pulling them open and tell me what's inside." He saunters over and does it and when he sees two different types of controllers, he yells: "PlayStation 2! Aunt Marilyn, I didn't know you played video games! You wanna play with me?"

I'm laughing. "Aunt Marilyn can't do two things at once, LL." He looks confused by this.

"Those games are for children who think fast and have quick hands and eyes. I play blackjack."

"What's blackjack?" he asks, suddenly aware of how to turn on the TV and trying to decide which of the two games he's up for.

"They cards that add up to twenty-one, LL, and you too little to play it 'cause you can't add good enough yet. But I'll play with you, Aunt Marilyn. I'm good in math. My teachers said it and wrote it on my report card."

"I believe you, Tiecey. But for now, why don't you take this sandwich to Grandma Lovey for me and I'll be in with her chocolate milk in a few minutes."

I cannot believe that this girl is actually putting one foot in front of the other in slow motion, which to mankind is known as walking! I'm searching the pantry for Nestlé's Quick when Speedelia Gonzales returns with sandwich still in hand. "Her sleep. Her snoring like a truck. But"—she sets the saucer on the counter—"her like it when the bread get a little hard, so please don't put nothing over it."

"Okeydokey, then. So do you guys like pizza or is that a dumb question?"

"It's a dumb question!" LL yells, like he just got the right answer for the "Daily Double" on *Jeopardy!*

I order the kids' pizza but still haven't been able to bring myself to return a single phone call. I just don't feel like talking and explaining and repeating everything. I'm tempted to spell it all out on the machine but what on earth would I say? What I need is a shower. A long hot one.

When the pizza gets here I tell the kids that I'm going upstairs to take a shower and do not answer the phone or open the door for anybody. They nod okay. When I get into my bathroom, which feels foreign for some reason I don't understand, I pick up the scissors lying on the sink and start cutting off these braids in clumps of five, six, ten at a time until I look like Buckwheat. I plaster my head with conditioner and wait five minutes and rake my fingers through my scalp and then pull, causing the hair that's not mine to slip right off.

I towel dry it, then get two boxes of hair dye from my cabinet: "Red Hot Rhythm" (formerly Red Hot Mary) and "Copper Penny" and pour them into a number 40 crème developer. I put a shower cap on. While I'm waiting for the twenty-five minutes to pass, I take off my clothes and look at myself in the mirror. I don't look so bad. But I'm going to look better. Better than I ever have. I wonder if Leon is on his way and if he is, why hasn't he bothered to call?

He should be afraid.

He should be very afraid.

Chapter 30

Leon has not come home. Nor has he bothered to call.
The sun is out already. I look at the clock. It's
after ten. Shit! The kids! Lovey! And my pillow-
case is red! But I remember it's hair dye, not blood. I
roll out of bed and fly downstairs. "Tiecey? Lovey? LL?
Are you guys in here?"

No one responds.

Please, God, don't let anything have happened to them.
I should've known better! Should've known how exhausted I was and not left them downstairs alone. How
could I forget that? When I reach the bottom step I head
for the kitchen. It's empty. But Lovey's sandwich is
gone. The saucer is still there. I turn and head for
Arthurine's old room and open the door. She's not in
here either. A half glass of chocolate milk is on the night-
stand.

I head back upstairs to get dressed and phone whatever number pops up on speed dial. But before I reach

the top step, I see a piece of notepaper on the landing. I must've run right over it because now I see my toe prints. It's been Scotch-taped to the floor. Instead of pulling it up, I crouch down to read the tiny chicken scratch that tells me it's Sabrina's handwriting: "Mom: You must be exhausted, so Nevil and I took the kids and Grandma Lovey for the day so you can get some rest or run any errands you might need. Don't worry about Grandma—Nevil has had firsthand experience dealing with his grandparents and I have a pretty good rapport with her. Will call later. And answer the phone! xoxox Sabrina P.S. I might take the rug rats to Target because it looks as if they could use a trip down quite a few aisles in the children's department. Oh, I've still got your Visa card! P.P.S. I love the new hair and that color is screaming!"

I am so relieved to read this. I try to run my fingers through my hair but it's too knotty and they get stuck. I have so much I could do, or should do, today that I almost don't know where to start. I had actually considered driving back down to Fresno today or tomorrow, depending on how much I got accomplished here—and staying there until the kids get out of school. I need to call Heavenly Creations and let them know that I might need to take a leave of absence—maybe permanently. Trudy can handle it. In fact I'll recommend her one way or the other. She'll be thrilled—she loves telling people what to do. I also need to find out from Child Services just what the process for getting guardianship of the kids entails. And Lovey. It won't hurt to call some of the places she wrote down. After all, she not only had the brochures, but had apparently visited some of them more than once, if the number of brochures she had for each was any indication. Wait a minute. They're all in Fresno. I wonder if I found a really nice one that's close by, would she consider it? I wonder if she really understands. She probably does, knowing Lovey, which is why she did this whole thing in advance and precisely why they're all in Fresno. Who am I kidding? All of her friends—the ones she has left—are still there. And it's home. But how often would I—or we—be able to get down there to see her? It's two hundred miles away.

I can't think about all of this right now. Not all at once. First things first. I do not want to stay married to the man I'm married to. He is not the man I married. He has turned into a sneaky, lying creep, and I don't like sneaky, lying creeps. Even with two kids to raise and being back in school, it's still very clear to me that I'll be better off without him. He was starting to feel like an anchor, which is why I've been sinking instead of floating. Without him I'll be free to do anything I want to. I can date. Or not date. I can go dancing. Or dance with myself at home with the music blasting as loud as I want. The kids like it loud! And I can travel: sometimes solo, sometimes with the rug rats. Our worlds will grow. I can walk across the Golden Gate Bridge in the fog and not hear a complaint about how cold and damp it is. Watch the same movie twice. Leave all the lights on in the house if I want to. And say my prayers out loud. I'll listen to the kids say theirs. And when they're not here or asleep I can swim naked in the pool. Drive down the coast with the windows down and the sunroof open until my foot goes numb. The kids and I can plant flowers and vegetables and trees that bear fruit. And sometimes, I can do absolutely nothing and not feel guilty because he won't know. I might flirt. If I remember how. To see if I still have "It." And I want more friends. Rich in spirit and honest and crazy like Bunny and Paulette and even Trudy and Maureen. Plus, I want some male friends, too. It is possible, Leon. I'm going to get my master's degree because it is important, and because I owe it to myself. I need beauty in my life and I want to be able to share it.

Maureen said she wanted things to be back the way they used to be. She wanted things to be normal again. But we can't go back to relive one day or even a single solitary minute, can we Leon? And if we learn nothing from it, what good has it done either of us? There is, as you always said, tomorrow. But I still want right now. I have found grace in my hands and I want to follow their lead. Plus, I have two new cocoons that I hope to help spin their way into a life they are not afraid to invent. This time though, I will be a spiritual hurricane with no name, a sassy tornado that doesn't rip apart or shred my own needs and dreams.

I will probably feel lonely sometimes, but I'm not going to worry about tomorrow's surprise when it's not here yet.

Chapter 31

I hear voices.

Heated voices. Familiar voices. One of them is clearly Leon's, and the other is unmistakably his mother's.

I can't believe I'm still in bed. I pick up the clock. It claims it's 3:20. I sit up like a mummy and wonder why no one bothered to wake me, and then I slide out and walk softly toward the door and crack it open a little wider so that I can hear better what they're saying.

"But, Mother, I don't understand why . . ."

What did he just say? I lean forward a little more.

"You know good and well . . ."

I open the door very slowly and walk out into the hall-way, grateful it's carpeted and tiptoe down to the land-ing. Prezelle is sitting on the sofa next to the table with no lamp. His legs are crossed. He looks impatient, as if he's waiting for something. I've never seen him look like this.

"May I speak now?" he must be saying to them both because that's when I see Arthurine walk around the coffee table and sit next to Prezelle as if she's protecting him or has decided she wants to be on his team, and then finally, in clear focus, in the middle of the frame, is the man I'm married to.

He does not look familiar.

"You know, Son," Prezelle is saying. "I believe that all the energy you've spent trying to convince your mother and me how difficult it is for you to believe that we are in love has been wasted."

"I didn't . . ."

A finger goes up. "Let me finish. Please."

Leon has lost weight.

"First of all, mister, I've been very patient sitting here listening to you tell us what we're not supposed to be able to feel when we already feel it and don't need you to confirm it for us. And secondly, we got married for the same reasons you did, but apparently you seem to have a memory problem . . ."

"You certainly do!" Arthurine says, tucking her arm through Prezelle's sports coat. "I can tell you right now that Prezelle won't have to catch a plane and go to no jungle to find his soul or whatever you claim you lost. You need Jesus. And that woman upstairs that you have completely forgotten how valuable she is, to you, your kids, to us, and now, to some more kids. Leon, I didn't raise you to be a liar."

"But I haven't lied about anything."

"You said you went down there with your buddy!"

"I did."

"Was he a *she?*"

"There's been a big mix-up, mother."

"Yeah, well all I can say is that a half truth is still a whole lie, ain't it, Prezelle?"

"Indeed it is."

"You went down there with another woman which makes you not just a liar but even worser, an adulterer. Shame on you! Shame shame shame!"

"That's not true, mother. If you would . . ."

"Opportunity knocks once, baby, but temptation leans on the doorbell. Ain't you got no kind of self-control? Is that the problem?"

"No that's not the problem, Mother."

"Then explain it to me, 'cause you should thank God you don't have a drug problem 'cause you'd just have to settle on being a addict for the rest of your life since you can't say no to yourself, since you weak when it comes to the flesh, then, is that what you're telling us?"

"For crying out loud, Mother, absolutely not."

"So you standing here telling me you ain't been cheating on your wife?"

I'm waiting for his answer. But there is total silence down there. It doesn't take this long to tell the truth.

"I will admit that I've had one indiscretion for which I am quite sorry."

"Ain't y'all always? But sorry don't get it," my mother-in-law says better than I could.

"I thought Marilyn was bored and tired of me."

"What's that got to do with the price of beans?" Prezelle says.

"Well, I'm not trying to excuse my behavior, but for a while there Marilyn was so critical of just about everything I did. Nothing seemed to please her."

"That ain't her fault, now is it?" Prezelle says.

"I thought she was going to leave me but I didn't have the heart to ask and I was just lonely and afraid, so I turned to someone else."

"Yeah, and I guess she turned back. So what did it prove?" Arthurine says.

"That I sought consolation and answers from the wrong person."

"So, does this mean you do or do not believe in the sanctity of marriage anymore? Clear it up for us," Prezelle says.

"Of course I do. More so now than ever."

"I beg your pardon," Prezelle says.

"Don't make me get up off this couch and come over there and slap you like you was ten again. I mean it, Leon, you one step away from making me forget I'm a Christian."

"I've tried to be a good husband."

"How? Explain it to God, would you, 'cause He's listening. He could probably use a good laugh. But me and Prezelle, we ain't laughing. We thanking about that girl upstairs who done everything she could ever think about doing to give you a glorious home, raised your children with pride, and from where I sat, looked to me like she loved you better than I've seen on any of the videos me and Prezelle done rented—except maybe for the *Titanic*."

Prezelle is nodding his head up and down in agreement. I want to laugh so badly, I have to bite my bottom lip to stop myself. This is theater at its best. And I want to hear King Arthur speak.

"And the child didn't complain once when I moved in here and tried to take over. No, she did not. Who was it that drove me to Bible study week after week? Not my son. It was my daughter-in-law. I didn't even have to pay for gas. And who bought me the latest designer jogging suits to wear when I walked the mall so I would feel pretty, as old as I am? It was Marilyn. Your very creative wife who could put Martha Stewart out of business if she just wanted to."

"I thank she outta business," Prezelle says. "What happened to that lamp?" he asks, pointing to the empty table.

No one seems to know.

"Prezelle?" Arthurine says.

"Go ahead, talk the talk, Reeney."

She looks back over at Leon, who has yet to sit down. "Do you have any idea how many meals she has cooked for you and those kids and just the two of us since some nights we was the onliest ones here? Do you know how long it takes to prepare some of those fancy dishes?"

Leon looks embarrassed because he has no idea how long it takes.

"I have watched her move around that fancy kitchen

like she on roller skates some nights when I watch *CSI* and *Without a Trace* and she still ain't finished making desserts I can't even pronounce."

"One was called a soufflé," Prezelle says quite proudly.

"And when was the last time you spent time in that laundry room washing and folding sheets and towels and undershirts and your stupid boxers?"

He's shaking his head as in never.

"How many pairs of black socks do you own, Son? Have you ever counted? Have you ever noticed how good your sheets smell? This house? Your wife? Have you?"

He nods no. Then yes.

"You young men make me sick with your lack of respect and appreciation for the people around you that do the most for you. You take so much for granted and it is a very ugly trait and I'm glad most women don't possess it."

"May I ask a question, if I may? And then we need to skedaddle on out of here so we can get to Bible study on time, sugar," Prezelle says.

Arthurine bumps up against him but he doesn't back away. She is almost under Prezelle's armpit.

"First, may I interject something here?" Leon says.

"Please do," Prezelle says, as if he's imitating Leon.

"We all ears," his mother says.

"Everything that you just said is true. I could add more wonderful things Marilyn has done to that list, but you want to know something?"

They just look at him as if to say: you've already got our attention, you nitwit.

"Even though I'm grateful for all the things she's done for me and the kids and you, too, Mother, all these wonderful maternal acts combined didn't help me to see *her*. The clean laundry didn't help me get to know her any better. Her meals never gave me any clues as to what she would rather be doing. I had no idea how unhappy she was and why she gave us more than we needed and not enough for herself."

"It's called love, dummy. I am so glad I was born a woman I don't know what to do. I'm not talking about you, Prezelle."

"No offense taken," he says.

"And you, Leon Grimes, you should learn how to cook and do laundry and a little cleaning wouldn't kill you. And they do sell lawn mowers at the hardware store," Arthurine says. "And flowers that go in the ground if somebody was not afraid to get their hands dirty."

"Back to my original question: why'd you have to go all the way to Costa Rica?"

"Well, Prezelle, because I . . ."

"Spit it out, Son. We are trying not to judge you but you are making it very difficult," he says.

"Because I was lonely and depressed and confused about a number of things going on in my—our life—and I needed to talk about it."

"Did you try talking to your wife? She lives right here in this same house with you. You wouldn'ta had to catch a plane to nowhere that was five thousand miles away. And it woulda saved you a whole lot of money."

"You need Jesus, I'm telling you again," Arthurine says. "Marilyn doesn't understand."

"How in the world can you stand there and say that?"

"Because she doesn't know who I am anymore and I don't know who she is, Mother."

"What in the world are you talking about, Son?" Prezelle says.

"I don't know what to do anymore to make her happy, to make her smile. So I've just been winging it. And guessing. But apparently these methods and strategies aren't so effective."

"Methods? She ain't no building, Leon. Or no golf ball."

"Son, have you ever bothered to ask her what makes her happy?"

"No."

"Has she ever told you?" Prezelle asks.

"Yes."

"And did you do any of those things?"

Silence.

"Did you ever try?"

Silence.

"You got to think about it?"

"Not very often," he says. "Sometimes they were things I just didn't want to do."

"Don't get me started," Arthurine says. "Too late! So you didn't wanna be inconvenienced, huh, Leon? Well let me tell you something, boy. If all women ever did was what we wanted to do, men would be—please forgive me Lord for I am about to sin—shit out of luck."

"But Marilyn's never really asked me either. Not lately."

"Wait a minute, now," Prezelle says. "So you trying to tell us that neither one of you ever does what the other wants?"

"Not exactly. She thinks the things I like to do are boring."

"They are," Arthurine says. "You study earthquakes, Son, now how exciting can that be? And this is what you do all day long. But that don't mean you necessarily boring, Son."

"I think it does," Prezelle says.

"Well, it works both ways, but this is one of the things that was brought to my attention in Costa Rica."

"Let me save you a stack of money for the future, Son, because the one thing you don't seem to understand even after all these years is that a good marriage requires something folks just don't seem to like to do, and that is compromise. Not sacrifice. But compromise. Ain't no other way. And if you want to have a healthy strong thriving marriage, like me and your mother intend to here, then put your wife's needs first whenever you can. If she is willing to do the same, then you two might have a much brighter future."

"You seen a doctor about any of your problems?" Arthurine asks.

"They're not medical in nature," Leon says.

"How do you know that?" she says.

"Because I've recently had a physical and I'm in very good health."

"Did you dye your hair, Son? It wasn't that black when we saw him last time, was it, Prezelle?"

"I don't remember, Reeney, but if he wants to tint his hair, that's his prerogative."

I guess so, Prezelle, because you're a member, too!

"I tried explaining some of what I've been feeling and she just dismisses it."

That's not true! Is it? Is it?

"Like what?" Arthurine says.

"Well, I'll put it this way. I've pretty much reached the top of the ladder at our company and I feel like I have nothing else to prove. I'm bored doing what I do. It doesn't do it for me anymore. And I'd like to try something different."

"Did you tell her that?" Prezelle asks.

"Not in those exact words."

"Then what other words did you use?" Arthurine asks.

"Well, none, at least not in this regard," he says.

"If this is how you get your point across, no wonder she don't understand you," Prezelle says, "because you ain't really said too much of nothing too clearly since we been here. You beat around the bush, Leon, when you need to come on up from around it and just spit it out."

"I'm trying to."

I do not want to hear the rest. I would like to go down those stairs and snuggle up to Prezelle's free side and let Leon have the spotlight at his very first Pity Party. But I'm afraid if I were to appear right now, it would ruin what he's doing, which is talking, for a change, and being honest. Although I still want to know who the woman that was his wife who supposedly doesn't exist is.

"We can see how you're struggling, Son, but we are not the ones who need to hear it. She's upstairs. Sleeping her blues away. Think about what you going to do about her blues and your blues. If you didn't come home with no more clues than what you left with, then you should get your money back from that place and go find yourself a motel 'cause you ain't going to do much good around here," Prezelle says, as he and Arthurine both help push each other to a standing position.

"Jesus will wait. So you better drop down on your knees tonight and repent and beg for forgiveness for fornicating and frolicking and being downright frivolous with the love you promised to give to my daughter-in-law till death do you part. Be the man me and your daddy tried to raise you to be, Son. And keep your promises. As many of them as you can."

"I'm going to try," he says. "And for the record: I have not been fornicating. And what would you two know about that anyway?"

Prezelle looks at Arthurine. And Arthurine looks at him. They then look at Leon and start laughing.

"What's so funny?" Leon asks. "I know you guys don't . . . you couldn't possibly . . ."

"We can and we do," Arthurine says. "Come on, Seattle Slew, let us go and study the Word of God and then how about some KFC tonight?"

"Sounds good to me," he says, and puts his Stetson on

with one hand and slides the other as far as he can around Arthurine's waist.

"Tell Marilyn we stopped by to check on her and lend a hand and we'll call or stop back around here sometime tomorrow just to make sure her and those kids and Lovey are all right."

"They're all going to be taken good care of," Leon says. "Trust me."

"That's what Marilyn wants to be able to do. Don't even worry about us, 'cause you ain't our problem."

Tell it, Arthurine.

You tell him.

Chapter 32

After I hear the front door close, I slide over to the top step and put my elbows on my knees.

"Who is your wife?" I ask.

"You are," he says.

"I divorced you while you were gone."

"I divorced you while I was gone, too."

"On what grounds?" I ask.

"Because we've lost too much ground."

"And why was that, you think?"

"Because I didn't see you."

"This is true."

"And you didn't see me."

"I thought I was, but listening to you tonight, maybe I had you pegged a lot differently."

"How so?"

"You never told me when you first started getting tired of your job or how isolated you were feeling. You never told me any of these things."

"It's hard to explain, especially to your wife, when you know she's getting bored and fed up with you because you've become like a flat tire. That even though you still love her very much, you always thought your life would amount to more than this because you have worked hard to make sure she and the children were comfortable and never wanted for too much. But then emotionally you started missing in action because you realized how long you'd been doing it by the book and you were getting tired of the burden of holding it all together. On some days you fantasized about renting a black convertible—a Carrera—and driving down Pacific Coast Highway at ninety mph even though you had no idea where you were going but you didn't care. But then you reach over and turn off the alarm or spend an hour in traffic and some days you don't even feel like getting out of bed because you know this day is going to be like all the others."

"You weren't the only one feeling like that, you know."

Leon walks up five or six stairs and sits down. There are still at least eight or nine steps between us. I don't want him to come any closer because his honesty might begin to fade again.

"I didn't understand what was behind all these emotions, to be honest with you, and it was daunting because sometimes I felt like I couldn't control them."

"Mine is called perimenopause. And I do believe that the male version is called a midlife crisis."

"I don't care what they call it, but the reason I took a

chance in going to Costa Rica was because I needed some answers and didn't know where else to look."

"Your mother said you should try Jesus."

He just smiles. "I never stopped, but some of this stuff we have to deal with on our own. Don't you think?"

"I suppose we do. Even though all of this feels negative on the surface, I think some good has come out of it."

"I agree."

"I haven't been this honest with myself in centuries, Leon. It's liberating knowing that I still have time to change some things I'm not happy with."

"That puts me on the top of the list, then, huh?"

"Pretty much. But I'm afraid you get the silver and I get the gold."

"But I thought you were bored with me."

"Apparently I've been bored *and* angry with Marilyn much much longer than I cared to admit, and when I got tired of beating myself up or feeling sorry for myself for choices that I made, I made you my next victim."

"I'm not sure what you're saying, Marilyn."

"I was actually relieved when I thought I'd finally caught you cheating because I now had a good excuse to take out all of my anger and frustration on you. It was as if I'd willed it. And you're right, I blamed you for everything I wasn't giving myself. I even made myself believe— and apparently you, too—that you were no longer interesting or worthy of my love, when really my fear was that maybe it was me who'd gotten stale."

"But it's true, I *was* getting pretty close to molding," he says.

"It's amazing how we can make ourselves believe what we want to. As Arthurine would say, 'If you jump to conclusions, you make terrible landings.' "

"I'm sorry for looking for you in someone else. And I can tell you now that I am going to try to better communicate my feelings and fears to you and just deal with the consequences."

"That's what I've been doing and it's expensive sometimes, too."

"But you know, some of your complaints are valid."

"The biggest one, honestly, Leon, is that I've felt unappreciated because what I did for you and the kids was expected of me and I performed it to the best of my ability. But as the kids grew up and needed me less, I thought you would come to realize how much more to me there was to discover. But it didn't seem to be going that way."

"I know," he said.

"I mean, here we were, finally, free to do anything we wanted and we weren't doing anything. That's why I figured you had somebody: you needed a thrill. It just seemed like you forgot that underneath the rubber gloves I was still the same idealistic wild woman you fell in love with. The mistake I made was putting too many things I wanted to do and try on ice. I held you hostage for it, but not the kids."

"It's understandable, because I haven't exactly been a cheerleader for you, Marilyn. I see what you've been doing in your art room, and how you get so much pleasure from it. The things you make are remarkable."

"Remarkable? You've never said anything like this about my work before, Leon."

"I thought I had."

I'm shaking my head.

"Are you sure?"

"Positive."

"Well, quite a few of my friends and colleagues have been bugging me about buying some of it for the longest time."

"You're kidding?"

"No, I'm not. I've taken digitals and brought a few colleagues over to see your work. I do think going to the Academy of Arts to get your master's is a great idea, because you can only get better. We'll figure out how to handle your tuition just like we have for everybody else in this house. And besides, you deserve it."

"Thank you," is about all I can manage to say. I'm still in the ozone here.

"Take a deep breath, Marilyn."

"What?"

"Breathe in hard and blow it out slowly. I learned how to do this in Costa Rica, where I had one wake-up call after another. I mean so many things became obvious to me that it was pretty sad at first, even scary, to see just how much you take for granted and how I stopped participating in our marriage. But it wasn't because of *you*. It was me."

After inhaling and exhaling three or four times, I feel like I've landed back on the ground. I'm glad we don't always get what we wish for. I'm ashamed of myself for all the energy I wasted believing something that wasn't even true. But my husband is right here and he's talking to me and I can't help it when I say, "I don't know, Leon. Sometimes people just come to a dead end. Or there's a fork in the road and they need to go in different directions."

"But where do you want to go?"

"What?"

"Where do you want to go?"

I'm trying to figure out how to respond, since I'm not real sure of the answer, so I just say, "As far as I can."

He looks at me like he knows exactly what I mean. I don't remember him ever looking at me quite this way. But I also don't recall ever describing anything that wasn't in concrete terms.

"I don't want to stop you," he says.

"I'm the only one who can stop me, Leon. I'm the one who's been sitting at the stoplight all these years, waiting for the light to turn green."

"I'm sorry, Marilyn."

"I'm sorry, too, Leon."

"So who is she? Your Costa Rican wife."

He slaps his forehead with his palm. "That receptionist was not the brightest star in the sky. You remember Janice, Howard's wife?"

"You're having an affair with your partner's wife?"

"No. That person was more a confidante than a lover and I've settled it, so it's done. But Janice and Howard have been having serious problems, mostly about her infidelities, and since she knew why Frank and I were going down, she and her sister, who's actually going through a divorce, registered for the same course, but in order to get the double-occupancy rate, we had to pretend to be couples. Frank and I shared a room—and thank God for queen beds, earplugs, and windows because that guy snores like a grizzly and has a bad case of gas at night—but as preposterous as it sounds, this is how it went."

"Why the secrecy?"

"Because I knew you probably wouldn't buy it under the circumstances."

"I know Janice well enough not to think she'd want you."

"Wait a minute, Marilyn. Do you find me that unappealing?"

"I didn't say that, did I?"

"You used to find me attractive."

"Well, you used to be attractive to me."

"I've been working out, can't you tell?"

"I don't mean on the outside, Leon."

"I know. But you look different. I like your hair short and what color is it?"

"Red Hot Rhythm."

"Boy, don't I remember."

"What did you say?"

"Nothing."

We sit here for several long moments. The house is still. And so are we.

"You want me to move out?"

"It might be a good idea for a while, don't you think?"

"Depends on how we do it."

"Tell me what you mean by that, Leon."

"Well, I believe that even though we can't turn back time, there are new things, even old things, about each other that we don't really know."

"And?"

"Unless you want to just call it quits, I wouldn't mind taking you out on a date every now and then to try to get to know you as a person and not as my wife or the mother of my children."

"And eat where?"

"Not dinner."

I think I'm going to fall down these stairs. "Then what other kinds of dates would you have in mind?"

"Well, I don't know. Something we haven't done before."

I feel like I'm about to have a heart attack. But this is my husband talking and these words are indeed coming out of his mouth.

"Haven't you always wanted to walk across the Golden Gate Bridge when it's foggy?"

"Yes, I have, but you always said it was too cold."

"It is, but I'll just wear a warm jacket."

"And you're serious?"

"I know I've been like Elmer Fudd for quite some time, and if my own mother thinks I'm boring . . ."

"Well, I haven't exactly been a thrill a minute, either."

"At least you tried, but I never quite rose to the occasion. And don't you dare say anything. But like I said, I've learned quite a few things and I've also gotten a little assistance."

"So, you've been practicing, have you?"

"I wanted to see if I could test out my new skills on you, first."

"Maybe. But right now I'm just beginning to thaw out. It was you who went to the seminar, not me."

"I wanted you to come with me."

"Then why didn't you ask me?"

"You know why. The whole baby thing and you were so angry at me."

I just nod my head up and down. It feels like it was years ago.

"So, of course I was sorry to hear about your sister and I left at least ten messages but I had to change planes and got bumped and had to wait another twelve hours to get on the next flight which is what took me so long to get here. Where is everybody?"

"The kids and Lovey are with Sabrina and Nevil."

"And you're willing to take on all this responsibility, again?"

"Yes, I am, but it should be a whole lot easier this time because I'm putting something nurturing and healthy for Marilyn on my daily itinerary. It'll balance out."

"Well, I'll help in any way I can. And this time I do not simply mean financial. I'll be available. I just don't want to cramp your style."

"I'm probably going back to Fresno for the next three

or four weeks to get Lovey situated in a nice place and try to sell her house and by then the kids should be out of school."

"So, maybe I'll get a condo by the lake or something."

"Good."

"This place could stand some serious renovating. I never really noticed what bad shape it's in until today."

"You said it, I didn't."

"Some folks would call it a teardown."

"It's too much house. Too much yard. Too much time."

"Well, let me say this. Right after the kids left and you expressed how you wanted to downsize I know I resisted the idea but it was because I wasn't quite ready to accept the fact that they were leaving and I guess I wanted everything to stay just the way it always was in case they came back. But I suppose nothing ever stays the same, does it?"

"Nope. And I'm glad."

"Well, why don't you see if you can find a place you and the kids really love and we'll take it from there."

"What I'd really love is to be rocked."

"I beg your pardon?"

"You heard me."

"Well, how had you planned on spending the rest of your day?"

"Whatever it was it could stand to be interrupted. Why?"

"I was just wondering if maybe you'd like to take a ride with me."

"And go where?"

"I don't know."

"I've been wanting to go there for a long time."

"Then let's go."

"Wait. You don't have a Porsche, Leon."

"Yeah, but I've got a Harley, and I do all my own stunts," he says.

"So do I," I say. "So do I."

Penguin Group (USA)
is proud to present
GREAT READS—GUARANTEED!

**We are so confident that you will love
this book that we are offering a
100% money-back guarantee!**

If you are not 100% satisfied with
this publication, Penguin Group (USA)
will refund your money!
Simply return the book before
October 1, 2006, for a full refund.

**With a guarantee like this one,
you have nothing to lose!**

IT'S OK IF YOU'RE
CLUELESS

AND 23 MORE TIPS
FOR THE COLLEGE BOUND

TERRY
McMILLAN

#1 New York Times Bestselling Author

VIKING

A note on the PREMIUM format

This Premium format paperback is
specially designed for comfortable reading,
featuring remarkable improvements on
the interior design of the traditional
mass market paperback.
The book itself is larger, for easier handling.
The type is also larger. The paper is of
higher quality, more like a hardcover.
There is more white space between the lines
of text, so reading is less of an eye strain.

**So get comfortable and discover this
innovation in paperback books.**

#1 *NEW YORK TIMES* BESTSELLING AUTHOR

TERRY MCMILLAN

HOW STELLA GOT HER GROOVE BACK   (192001)
Stella Payne is a Superwoman who has everything—except a
man to rock her world, something she's convinced she can
well do without. On a spur-of-the-moment Jamaican vacation
she meets Winston, a man half her age, and finds, to her
dismay, that her world is indeed well and truly rocked. Stella
soon realizes that she's come to a cataclysmic juncture in her life,
one that forces new and difficult questions about her passions
and expectations.

WAITING TO EXHALE   (21529X)
"*Waiting to Exhale* is a paean to the sisterhood of all women."
—*Los Angeles Times Book Review*

**Available wherever books are sold or at
penguin.com**